November 1938
From 'Reichskristallnacht' to Genocide

Edited by **Walter H. Pehle**
Translated from the German by **William Templer**

The destruction of synagogues and shops and the persecution of thousands of Jewish citizens during the night of 10 November 1938 represented the culmination of prewar Nazi policies against the Jews. At the same time it signalled the beginning of a new phase of much harsher oppression which would result in the 'Final Solution'. This volume brings together original essays by some of the leading historians in this field with the aim of putting the pogrom of 1938 in its historical context. The authors examine political and economic developments before November 1938, the pogrom itself in the urban centres and in rural areas and how the Jews were affected by the events. Moreover, important aspects of the 'Final Solution' are presented: how it was planned and carried out, and to what extent the German population was aware of this programme. The volume concludes with a brief look at developments in post-war Germany.

Walter H. Pehle, born 1941 in Düsseldorf, Ph.D. in history, Editor for History and Contemporary History, Fischer Verlag, Frankfurt. Collaborator and volume editor for the anthology compiled by Peter Märthesheimer and Ivo Frenzel, *Im Kreuzfeuer, Der Fernsehfilm "Holocaust": Eine Nation ist betroffen* (1979); co-editor of *Der historische Ort des Nationalsozialismus: Annäherungen* (1989).

William Templer is a professional translator and the language editor for the *Tel Aviver Jahrbuch für deutsche Geschichte* of the Institute for German History, Tel Aviv University.

November 1938
From 'Reichskristallnacht' to Genocide

Edited by
Walter H. Pehle

Translated from the German by
William Templer

BERG
New York / Oxford
Distributed exclusively in the U.S. and Canada by
St. Martin's Press, New York

English edition
first published in 1991 by
Berg Publishers, Inc.
Editorial offices:
165 Taber Avenue, Providence, RI 02906, U.S.A.
150 Cowley Road, Oxford OX4 IJJ, UK

English edition © Berg Publishers Limited

Originally published as *Der Judenpogrom 1938:*
Von der 'Reichskristallnacht' zum Völkermord.
Translated from the German by permission of the publishers.
© S. Fischer Verlag GmBH, Frankfurt

Library of Congress Cataloging-in-Publication Data
Judenpogrom 1938. English.
November 1938 : From Reichskristallnacht to Genocide / edited
by Walter H. Pehle.
p. cm.
Translation c: Judenpogrom 1938.
ISBN 0–85496–687–0 (U.S.)
1. Germany—History—Kristallnacht, 1938, 2. Jews—Germany—
History—1933–1945. 3. Holocaust, Jewish (1939–1945)—Germany.
I. Pehle, Walter H.
DS135.09315.18313 1990
942.086—dc20   90–33211
CIP

Printed in Great Britain by
Billing & Sons Ltd, Worcester

Contents

Contents

Editor's Preface

"Back then, we thought that the persecution of Jews had reached its highpoint. In actual truth, it was the final alarm sounding before destruction," wrote a victim a few years after the events whose fiftieth anniversary was commemorated in November 1988. This book deals with that dramatically mistaken assessment of political developments which led to the Reichskristallnacht and on to the Holocaust.

During the night of November 9 to 10, 1938, the synagogues in Germany were set afire by National Socialists, the SA, and the SS. The synagogues were destroyed in a controlled manner, under the very eyes of the public – neighbors, business partners, and associates, one's fellow German citizens; the destruction was condoned by the police and was conducted in full view of the local fire brigades. The burnings were carried out in controlled fashion because nearby property belonging to "Aryans" had to be protected from the flames. The supposedly spontaneous "popular indignation" over the assassination of Ernst vom Rath, third secretary in the German Embassy in Paris, by the seventeen-year-old Herschel Grynszpan, cost nearly one hundred persons their lives that night simply because they were Jews. In that night of destruction, some 7,500 stores and businesses owned by Jews were also demolished, ransacked, and set ablaze – virtually all Jewish-owned shops still in existence at the time.

This pogrom had been painstakingly prepared: with the aid of expertly assembled lists, some thirty thousand wealthy Jews were arrested and shipped off to internment in concentration camps, where many were detained and tormented, sometimes for months, without any legal justification. It is no longer possible to establish conclusively the number of those who never returned.

Nor is it possible today to determine with any certitude the precise origin of the term *Kristallnacht* or *Reichskristallnacht* popularly used to refer to these events. Yet it is clear that the term Crystal Night serves to foster a vicious minimalizing of its memory, a discounting of its grave reality: such cynical appelations function to reinterpret manslaughter and murder, arson, robbery, plunder, and massive property damage, transforming these into a glistening event marked by sparkle and gleam. Of course, such terms reveal one thing in stark clarity – the lack of any sense of involvement or feeling of sympathy on the part of those who had stuck their heads in the sand before that violent night.

With good reason, knowledgeable commentators urge people to renounce the continued use of "Kristallnacht" and "Reichskristallnacht" to refer to these events, even if the expressions have become slick and established usage in our language. The title of this book is in keeping with that suggestion; its choice underscores that the volume deals with barbaric, violent excesses directed against Jewish citizens, excesses which were not merely fortuitous, but rather led quite consistently to a final goal – the annihilation of Jews in Germany and later throughout Europe.

From our present vantage, one cannot view the 1938 pogrom against the Jews in Germany and Austria in isolation. Such a perspective would be blinkered, reflecting a regrettably limited degree of progress in knowledge and insight. The facts and events have been sufficiently known for several decades, thanks to the studies by Hermann Graml[1] and Helmut Heiber[2] of the Munich Institute for Contemporary History. The present volume not only includes events leading up to the pogrom, its causes and pretexts, but also encompasses the immediate and later consequences. It becomes evident that the shots fired in the German Embassy in the Rue de Lille on November 7 were utilized in cold and calculating fashion by a segment of the Nazi leadership to inflict a decisive and well-prepared blow against the Jews. The intention was to strike at the very substance of their existence: the Jews now were to be "removed from the economy" – "raus aus der Wirtschaft," as the slogan went. The approach pursued by the Nazis here urges a comparison with the Reichstag fire of March 1933 – a conflagration that they did not ignite, but one that they exploited to the political hilt.

---

1. Hermann Graml, *Der 9. November 1938: "Reichskristallnacht"* (Bonn, 1956).
2. Helmut Heiber, "Der Fall Grünspan," *Vierteljahrshefte für Zeitgeschichte* 5 (1957): 134–72.

Though many may have cherished the fond hope that the new rulers would not succeed in consolidating their strength and retaining state power over the longer term, notions of this sort proved to be dangerously deadly illusions in November 1938. Nonetheless – or precisely for that reason – many born in a later generation have asked the question, Why was it there were so few who correctly read the signs of the time and then jumped at the first opportunity to leave the country? Two contributors to the present volume (W. Zuelzer and K. Kwiet) explore the serious and knotty problems associated with that question, based on differing personal experience and methodological approaches.

Other essays included here go on to treat the actual and ultimate consequence of National Socialist anti-Semitism, namely, the Final Solution, its procedural/bureaucratic planning and industrial implementation. Also touched on is the question broached by British journalist David Irving, of whether or not there was a specific order by Hitler to implement the mass murder of the Jews (H. Graml). It is no accident that Mr. Irving enjoys considerable popularity in extreme right-wing circles in the Federal Republic as a serviceable lecturer and welcome ideologue.

The answer to Irving's question is important, among other reasons, because it largely determines whether Hitler can be detached, as it were, from the genocide, "delinked," and thus ultimately enter the history books as a positive figure after all – in this way confirming the repeatedly proclaimed thesis that Hitler had "rejected all that," insofar as he had actually been aware of what was happening.

In connection with this is a related question, raised ever more frequently and with an undertone of distrust: What did "average" Germans (no matter how average is understood) actually know about the genocide against the Jews, and what could they have known, had they but had a modicum of interest in the fate of their fellow citizens? Yet perhaps such a question is incorrectly framed; in political terms, after all, the important aspect cannot only be what the average man on the street knew. That is not enough. Rather, what is crucial is to determine the true degree of knowledge of those persons who were employed in the relevant ministries and offices of the bureaucracy, the top levels of management, and elsewhere. In short, the extent of knowledge of those who, in decisive positions, actually had at their disposal a significant degree of leverage and various options to shape, hamper, and prevent decisions, with the objective of insisting on maintaining the simplest rules of human social life for the oppressed victims of the machine.

The volume of essays concludes by addressing a problematic aspect of immediate postwar reality: many Holocaust survivors, instead of finally being liberated from the persecutions of their Nazi tormenters, found themselves after 1945 wandering aimlessly through the devastated streets, only to be rounded up and once again herded together into camps. This time, however, the camps were under British or American military supervision, though on numerous occasions Allied personnel were aided by former Nazi camp guards! Once again they were prisoners, this time marked by the letters DP, and were under strict control and crammed together in barracks behind walls and barbed wire that in many instances had actually been a part of the earlier concentration camps.

Such camps remained in existence down to 1956. Persecution and discrimination do not heed the boundaries of neat and abstractly defined historical breaks, such as that of the so-called zero hour. Rather, history consists of both caesurae and continuity, as illustrated by the example of Holocaust survivors penned up in camps for Displaced Persons.

I would like to express my gratitude to Ms. Ursula Büttner for her kind assistance in providing the contributions by Avraham Barkai and Hermann Graml, originally published in the festschrift for Werner Jochmann edited by her.[3] I owe an especial debt of gratitude to my friend Wolfgang Benz, who provided the suggestion for this volume and gave useful assistance and advice in aiding its realization. Finally, I wish to thank my colleague, Ms. Cornelia Wagner, for her untiring efforts in seeing the original German manuscript through to publication and William Templer for his sensitive and painstaking rendition of the German text into English. For the English edition the chapter by Abraham J. Peck was translated by the author himself.

---

3. Ursula Büttner, ed., *Das Unrechtsregime: Internationale Forschung über den Nationalsozialismus*, Band 2, *Verfolgung, Exil, belasteter Neubeginn* (Hamburg, 1986).

The Relapse into Barbarism

Wolfgang Benz

On Friday the Jews were rounded up, on Saturday they were burned. There were an estimated two thousand of them. Those willing to be baptized were spared their lives. Many young children were taken out of the fire against the will of their fathers and mothers and were then baptized. What was owed to the Jews was now cancelled, and all the promissory notes and pledges which they had were returned. The cash in their possession was seized by the town council, which apportioned it up among the artisans. This was also the poison that killed the Jews.[1]

This report, recorded in the *Straßburger Deutsche Chronik*, describes the destruction of the Jewish congregation in Strasbourg in February 1349. This was one pogrom, one among many during the plague year 1348–49 which befell Jewish congregations in France, Switzerland, and Germany. In more than three hundred congregations, Jews were "beaten to death, drowned, burned, put to the wheel, hanged, exterminated, strangled to death, buried alive, and tortured with all manner of killing for the sanctification of the divine name."[2]

The external occasion for this wave of persecution was the charge that the Jews had poisoned the wells and thus brought the scourge of the Black Death upon the populace. In actual fact, however, economic and social tensions were provided with an outlet in these pogroms, as illustrated by the example of Nuremberg. In December 1349, members of the guild there murdered the Jewish residents of the town, although Nuremberg had been spared from the ravages of the plague. Religious zeal, fused with the traditional hatred for Jews (nourished by the charge of Jewish usury) among the rural small gentry and urban artisans, erupted repeatedly in outbreaks of a mass hysteria that sought

1. Quoted in Alex Bein, *Die Judenfrage: Biographie eines Weltproblems* (Stuttgart, 1980), vol. 1, p. 104.
2. *Nürnberger Memorbuch*, quoted in Hermann Grieve, *Die Juden: Grundzüge ihrer Geschichte im mittelalterlichen und neuzeitlichen Europa* (Darmstadt, 1980), p. 105.

its victims in the Jewish congregations. A series of pogroms, triggered by the call to the First Crusade issued by Pope Urban II in November of the year 1095, began in Metz and Rouen and then spread to Speyer, Worms, Mainz, Trier, Cologne, Xanten, Prague, and other cities. The unchecked aggression of large crowds was discharged in the form of these pogroms.

This was repeated in the medieval period, not only in Germany, and the riots were always based on new reasons and pretexts. In 1235, for example, the accusation was raised in Germany for the first time that Jews were committing ritual murders (this charge had been made much earlier in England, and the upshot had been bloody persecution of Jewish communities there). At the end of the thirteenth century, the charge arose that Jews were desecrating the host. Such a desecration supposedly committed in Röttingen in Franconia served a Franconian nobleman named Rindfleisch as a pretext for leading a marauding band of killers through southern Germany and Austria. In this private war by Rindfleisch and his cohorts, 140 Jewish congregations met with destruction, and some twenty thousand Jews lost their lives. There were pogroms again and again during the Middle Ages. For the Jews, these were barbaric times in which they were faced with ever new and different accusations, each equally absurd, but all equally suited to implementing the veiled anti-Jewish intentions and designs which motivated such charges. When it was not their property and possessions that were at stake, then they had to serve as scapegoats and objects upon which to vent popular anger in times of social and economic crisis, discontent, and political frustration.

The Age of Enlightenment had brought Jews in Germany emancipation and civil equality, and the times of barbarism were long since a thing of the distant past. Only the continued presence of anti-Semitism, also cultivated by many in Germany, served as a reminder of those darker times. Yet murder was something even the wildest anti-Semites in the nineteenth century only *dreamed* of: a pogrom, and especially one organized for and by the state, seemed inconceivable in the civilized German Reich of the twentieth century. Even after the Boycott Day against the Jews on April 1, 1933, and the anti-Semitic excesses that occurred in connection with the Nazi takeover, the notion of an imminent murderous pogrom, planned in cold blood, would have appeared abstruse fantasy to most individuals.

The Staging of the Pogrom and Directing of Public Opinion

An editorial accompanying the report on the assassination attempt against Ernst vom Rath published in the November 8 edition of the *Völkischer Beobachter*, the main party paper of the NSDAP, contained threats leaving little doubt that the advent of a new era in National Socialist policy toward the Jews was imminent:

> It is clear what conclusions the German people will draw from this latest event. We shall no longer tolerate a situation where hundreds of thousands of Jews within our territory control entire streets of shops, throng places of public entertainment, and pocket the wealth of German leaseholders as "foreign" landlords while their racial brothers abroad incite war against Germany and shoot down German officials. . . . The shots fired in the German Embassy in Paris will not only mark the beginning of a new German attitude in the Jewish Question, but will hopefully also provide a signal for those foreigners who up to now have not grasped that ultimately there is only one thing standing in the way of international understanding between nations – international Jewry.[3]

The fact that this newspaper, as the veritable flagship of the National Socialist press, had expressed such views at this juncture was the product of careful and conscious stage direction. The scenario for the staging of popular indignation in November 1938 has been preserved, and the stage directing of public opinion at the time can be readily reconstructed. The channeling, orientation, and *Gleichschaltung* (coordination) of the German press took place on a regular, daily basis in the press conferences of the Ministry for Popular Enlightenment and Propaganda; it was here that journalistic instruments were tuned prior to performance and given the proper pitch.

On November 7, all editorial staffs were provided with a circular from the officious DNB, with the following instructions regarding the form and content of reports on the event in Paris:

> All German newspapers must carry large-scale reportage on the assassination attempt against the life of the third secretary in the German Embassy in Paris. The news must completely dominate

3. *Völkischer Beobachter*, November 8, 1938.

page 1. News reports on the grave condition of Mr. vom Rath will be issued by the DNB. His condition is extremely serious. It should be pointed out in several editorials that this assassination attempt perpetrated by a Jew must have the most serious consequences for Jews in Germany, even for the foreign Jews in Germany. In expressions in keeping with the indignation felt by the German people, it can be pointed out that the same Jewish clique of emigrés that placed a revolver in Frankfurter's hand also bears responsibility for this crime. The question should be raised whether it might be the intention of this Jewish clique to provoke difficulties between Germany and France by sending a murderer into the German Embassy and thus onto the soil of the Reich, after the Jewish poison has dominated the German broadcasts of French radio for so long.[4]

Important in this press instruction was the suggestion that a connection should be inferred with the murder in Davos of Wilhelm Gustloff, head of the National Socialist organization of Germans resident in Switzerland. Gustloff had been shot in 1936 in his home by David Frankfurter, a Jewish student with Yugoslav citizenship. Also important in this connection was the conspirational reference: the public should be led to believe that the shooting in Paris was part of an organized conspiracy by some sort of allegedly existing "world Jewry" and by German-Jewish emigrés resident in France. As a result of the fact that the Olympic Games were put on in Germany in 1936 as an international event functioning to stabilize the regime, as well as the fact that the time was apparently not yet ripe for public actions against the Jews, the propaganda machine had not been able to seize on the assassination of the Nazi functionary in Davos and turn it into a major media event. The intention now was to make up for that by utilizing the shooting in the Paris embassy.

On November 8, it was announced at the press conference that "the vom Rath case must be written about once again." The responsible official in Goebbels's ministry, Helmut Diewerge, had discovered that the assassin was a Jew (this had been pointed out in reports the day before as well, but was now reiterated for added emphasis), and in fact a Jew

who had apparently been intentionally selected for the task. He is still in his youth and, as in the Gustloff case, not a citizen of the

4. Records, Press Conference, Propaganda Ministry, by Fritz Sänger, BA, ZSg. 102/13 (Sammlung Sänger), November 7, 1938.

4

country where the deed was perpetrated. . . . The same circles were behind the assassination attempt as in the Gustloff case. Collections had been made for weeks for a Jewish struggle fund. Jewry made no distinction between so-called wild party fanatics, as had been stated in the Gustloff case, and quiet officials. Moreover, they had even dared to enter the premises of the embassy, a place normally respected by the enemy even in time of war.[5]

Another suggestion made was to mention, in enumerating individuals responsible, the especially hated writer Emil Ludwig. On this occasion, the question could also be raised as to whether the German writers living in exile in Paris were still deserving of being referred to as writers. This instruction was carried out, as was the "orientation" of November 9 stating that "the latest communiqué on the physical condition of Third Secretary vom Rath is to be featured prominently on page 1." Aside from the fact that only fanatic Nazis believed that emigré writers and intellectuals had had anything to do with the attempt on the life of the twenty-nine-year-old government official, who himself was only nominally a National Socialist, there were many who thought that, due to the pitch and intensity of the propaganda storm surrounding it, this shooting had been staged by the regime – just as a good many opponents of the regime were convinced the Nazis themselves had set fire to the Reichstag in 1933 in order to create a pretext for persecuting communists.

A young Berlin journalist who was not on the side of the regime and had many Jewish friends noted in her diary for November 9:

In the bus, on the street, in shops and cafes, the Grünspan case is being discussed, vociferously and in a quiet voice. Nowhere can I see any anti-Semitic indignation, though one senses a feeling of oppressiveness, as if before the outbreak of a thunderstorm. On the Kurfürstendamm, Tauntzienstraße, and Leipziger Straße, the shops forced to mark themselves as Jewish, spelled out in large white letters according to an official order, remain strikingly empty of clientele.

The journalist then asked a former colleague from her paper –

5. Ibid., November 8, 1938.

long since dismissed because he was a "non-Aryan" and now awaiting the catastrophe, wiling away his days by writing letters – whether Herr vom Rath might die, and if he should, what would happen then. Dr. Heinrich Mühsam answered:

> Naturally he's going to die. Otherwise what would be the use of all this? In order to avenge him, you first have to cry for him. And the greater the sadness, the more fanatic the hatred. Didn't you know that political incidents only tend to happen when people are prepared for them, from top to toe, down to the last button on one's spats? After all the ordinances have been issued, all preparations made, all measures discussed and agreed upon? There can be no doubt about it: the Jewish War is imminent. As for myself, well, I intend to remain a pacifist. Even a Jew can't do more than die.[6]

It was also reported on November 9 that Hitler had promoted the third secretary (who had only held this foreign service ranking since September 1938) "to the rank of legation counsellor [*Gesandtschaftsrat 1. Klasse*] in recognition of his bravery. Newspapers should feature this report prominently. His condition is so grave that he is not expected to survive." This was followed shortly later by the DNB communiqué: "Since Herr vom Rath has just died, newspapers are requested to refrain from publishing the news of his promotion. In mentioning his official rank, naturally it should be that of legation counsellor."[7]

Already on November 7 and 8, the tension generated by the official mechanism of press guidance was discharged in isolated incidents of violence against Jews and Jewish institutions. This occurred in a number of localities in Hesse, for example, in the city of Kassel. The local paper there carried the following report:

> The murderous deed in Paris has triggered spontaneous demonstrations by the population against Jewish businesses and institutions in Kassel and numerous localities in northern Hesse (Kurhesse). In so doing, the populace of northern Hesse expressed its sense of outrage, an indignation coming from the depths of its heart. The smashed windowpanes and damaged interiors of synagogues and other Jewish institutions are the spontaneous price to be paid by

6. Ruth Andreas-Friedrich, *Der Schattenmann: Tagebuchaufzeichnungen, 1938–1945* (Berlin, 1947), p. 28.
7. Press Conference, Propaganda Ministry, see n. 4 above.

world Jewry, a price this people of agitators and swindlers owes to its own actions.

When the news of the murderous deed perpetrated in Paris became known in Kassel during the course of the afternoon, hundreds of persons from all parts of the city were initially drawn to that most visible expression of Jewish hunger for power, the Kassel synagogue at the corner of Untere Königstraße and Bremer Straße. Angry shouts were heard, and the crowd could no longer be contained and stopped from passing on a warning to the Jewish institutions in response to the bloody deed in Paris. The crowd gave visible expression to its anger by further demonstrations in front of Jewish businesses, such as a quite well-known Jewish cafe on Moltkestraße. In the course of these demonstrations, hundreds also gathered before the Jewish community building located on Große Rosenstraße, in a spontaneous protest against world Jewry. The fact that here too windows were broken and similar acts of destruction occurred can be explained, as can the demonstration as such, by the profound impression which the shots fired in Paris have engendered.[8]

Pogroms initiated by local group leaders of the NSDAP (who were often at the same time the mayors of their localities) were reported for an entire series of small towns and villages. What is noteworthy about these actions was that, though instigated by overzealous local party functionaries who believed they were acting in harmony with higher party offices, they surged beyond the control of these local officials because the population took active part in the rioting and violence. Thus, for example, the mayor of Wachenbuchen near Hanau, after ordering that the Jewish school be demolished and the teacher be given a "solid thrashing," found it necessary to request aid from the subdistrict party head (*Kreisleiter*) and the district superintendent (*Landrat*), because the entire matter was threatening to get out of hand. He even tried to deny he had been one of the leaders, but claimed he was in bed when the trouble started.[9]

These were still isolated actions, local in character, in which old accounts were settled and social envy and other feelings discharged. However, the picture altered significantly during the course of November 9. At this point, Nazi activists, who were not from the local area, appeared on the scene here and

8. *Kurhessische Landeszeitung*, November 8, 1938.
9. District Court, Hanau, verdict of March 17, 1937, Archives IfZ, Gh 04.06.

there and proceeded to provoke violent incidents against the Jews. The hour of militant anti-Semitism had come. Under its influence, old feelings of animosity toward the Jews were translated into action, without such action having been specifically ordered from above. However, this was only the prelude to the general pogrom whose mise-en-scène was to be handled personally by the Reich minister for popular enlightenment and propaganda on the evening of November 9, 1938.

November 9 was a sensitive and historic date for the NSDAP: there was an annual commemoration, in a ritual mystique unique to the party, of the abortive 1923 putsch, marked in Munich by a march to the Feldherrnhalle. The core event of the celebration was the evening of camaraderie, at which the old "party stalwarts" gathered around Hitler. There could have been no more favorable occasion for spurring on the party leadership to action in a manner that was at the same time informal and yet promised future success. Around 9 P.M., a messenger arrived with the news that vom Rath had succumbed to his wounds. After an exchange of words with Goebbels, who was sitting next to the Führer in the Town Hall, Hitler left the gathering, and Goebbels went to work. At about 10 P.M., the propaganda minister announced the diplomat's death and gave a spiteful anti-Semitic speech, which climaxed in a call for revenge and reprisal. Those leaders of the party and the SA who were present received the impression it was now their turn to take corresponding action. This was exactly what had been intended, though no express order had been issued.

It was also a part of the tactical calculations that Hitler had left before Goebbels proceeded to incite primitive anti-Semitic instincts and passions in such a way that the party leaders believed they had in fact been ordered to unleash a wave of hatred against the Jewish population. After all, Hitler was also the head of state and had to keep open a possible path of retreat, both vis-à-vis foreign countries as well as potential critics within his own party. And indeed, there in fact were several such critics, including Göring as well as Himmler and Heydrich. (Of course, the disapproval of Goebbels voiced by his colleagues was, as became abundantly clear several days later, not due to any philanthropic sentiments they harbored toward the Jews, but rather was a product of tactical considerations as well as rivalry.)

The soil had been prepared by the press campaign on November 8 and 9. The speech by Goebbels was the signal to launch the attack and at the same time constituted an instruction on what action to take. The Supreme Party Tribunal of the NSDAP, which later investigated the events of November 9–10, in February 1939 presented Göring with a report detailing Goebbels's role and effect (in the Munich gathering acting in his official party capacity as Reich propaganda chief of the NSDAP, not as minister of propaganda). With Hitler's knowledge and approval, he had ignited the fuse:

> On the evening of November 9, 1938, the Reich propaganda minister, party comrade Dr. Goebbels, informed the party leaders who had gathered for an evening of comradeship in the Old Town Hall in Munich that there had been anti-Jewish demonstrations in the districts of Kurhesse and Magdeburg-Anhalt; several synagogues had been set ablaze and Jewish businesses destroyed. At his [Goebbels's] suggestion, the Führer had decided that such demonstrations were neither to be prepared nor organized by the party, but insofar as they were spontaneous in origin, they should likewise not be quelled. The orally presented instructions of the Reich propaganda chief were understood by all party leaders in attendance to mean that the party should not appear from the outside to be the initiator of the demonstrations, but that in reality it should organize and implement them. These instructions, with this understanding, were passed on immediately – and thus a good deal of time before transmission of the first teletype message – by a large number of party members in attendance at the party headquarters of their respective party districts [*Gaue*] over the telephone.[10]

There was a smooth and rapid transmission of instructions to the district-level propaganda offices and from there to the sub-district (*Kreis*) and local heads of the NSDAP and to the SA staffs throughout the entire Reich. And everywhere party members sprang from their beds to heed the call for a pogrom. The terror continued from midnight into the morning hours, a terror such as Central Europe had not seen for centuries, a terror no longer conceivable from the time of the Enlightenment – a relapse into barbarism.

The execution of the pogrom order by local protagonists of

10. Report, Supreme Party Tribunal, to Göring, February 13, 1939, Nuremberg Document PS 3063, published in *Der Prozeß gegen die Hauptkriegsverbrecher vor dem Internationalen Militärgerichtshof* (Nuremberg, 1948), vol. 32, pp. 20–29.

National Socialism occupied a goodly number of courts during the early years of the Federal Republic. The incidents of the Reichskristallnacht were reconstructed using the instruments of justice. There is no other event in the history of the Nazi state that is so minutely documented as is the November 1938 pogrom. A judgment handed down in proceedings before the Wiesbaden District Court describes how the destruction of the synagogue in Rüdesheim was initiated during the night of November 9–10:

> The accused G, leader of the SA standard Niederwald situated in Wiesbaden, was waiting on the night of November 9, 1938, in the waiting room of the main train station in Wiesbaden for the return of the regimental flag from the November celebrations in Munich. He was accompanied there by the defendant A, SA regimental driver, and the defendant M, secretary of the unit with the rank of an SA *Obertruppführer* [technical sergeant].
>
> At approx. 2 A.M., the defendant G received the order by telephone from General Kraft in Mainz to destroy the synagogues located in the area of his company. This order, Kraft explained, had been issued by the highest echelon of the SA leadership in response to the murder of the embassy third secretary vom Rath. The action should be carried out in civilian dress. The police and fire department would act to prevent any flames from spreading to nearby dwellings. Completion of the task was to be reported to brigade that same day by 6 A.M. G informed the defendants M and A who were waiting together with him, as well as Sturmbannführer [Major] S. . . . After learning from them that there was a synagogue in Rüdesheim, he ordered them to go home, change into civilian clothes, proceed to regimental headquarters, and then travel with him to Rüdesheim. Shortly thereafter, all four met at company headquarters and then went in the service car driven by A to Rüdesheim. During the trip, G spoke with the other men once again about the order they had been given and how he thought it should be implemented.
>
> In Rüdesheim, A drove the car past the apartment of the janitor Dries located near the synagogue, where the lights were already on, and parked about two hundred meters away from there on Schiffergasse, a small side street, around 4 A.M. At this point the four men got out of the car and proceeded on foot to the synagogue. G caught sight of the janitor Dries at the window of an apartment where the lights were burning. He called to him to come downstairs and told him that what he – Dries – would now hear and see was none of his business. Everything was okay, and Dries should keep his mouth shut about the matter.

Then the four men continued on toward the synagogue. There they pushed in its heavy oak door by force. G, M, A, and S then entered the synagogue, going first into an anteroom separated by a curtain from the main prayer hall. The room contained a number of prayer books and other papers. G, though he had no such orders, told S and M to take all these books and papers to the car. They needed to make two or three trips back and forth to carry all the material to the vehicle. During this time, A remained in the immediate vicinity of the defendant G, who was in the anteroom of the synagogue.

In the meantime, a five-liter can full of gasoline, which had been brought along in the car, had been poured out inside the synagogue, though it could not be determined by whom. After having unsuccessfully tried to light a match, G ignited a piece of paper in order to throw it into the gasoline. At this point there was a powerful explosion, a large flame shot up, and G suffered burns and was hurled against the frame of the entrance door. He was stuck in the door, which slammed shut [after A was blown through it]. The coat of the defendant A, who was standing several feet away, had been caught by the flames and singed. As a result of the force of the explosion, A had been thrown outside through the open door. After G had freed himself from the door where he was caught, he proceeded together with A and the defendants M and S, who had returned in the meantime from the car to the scene of the crime, back to the parked vehicle. Because of his injuries, G – who thought he had some broken bones – wanted to be driven to a doctor. . . .

By this time, several residents of Rüdesheim, including the witnesses B, R, B, and T, awakened by the noise of the explosion, had rushed to the synagogue. There they saw that the building was filled with smoke; the chairs were smoldering; and a curtain, as well as several Torah scrolls lying on the floor, were charred. In the synagogue, they found an empty gasoline can and a piece of paper on which was written, "SA High Command Munich." The witness B then immediately doused the still-smoldering chairs, using a Minimax hand extinguisher that had been rushed to the scene. All this occurred within the span of a few minutes. The building of the synagogue itself, aside from a window that had apparently burst due to the force of the explosion, had not suffered any damage. . . . Soon after the fire in the synagogue – and in any event prior to the additional acts of destruction that began later that afternoon – the local police headquarters in Rüdesheim had received the order by radio from its superior authority to condone the violence against Jewish religious institutions.

Nonetheless, the following morning the police filed a complaint with the district attorney's office in Wiesbaden charging arson,

11

suspects unknown. The police did not receive a formal response to this, but merely a brief note from the district attorney's office stating their displeasure that Rüdesheim had been the only community to file a complaint on the burning of the synagogue.[11]

Yet the matter did not rest with this foolish attempt to set the synagogue ablaze. The following day, the Rüdesheim synagogue was indeed destroyed, and as elsewhere, there was looting and maltreatment of Jewish residents.

According to the report of Rabbi Max Eschelbacher, the following is what happened in Düsseldorf. The couple returned around midnight from a visit at the home of friends:

> I had just arrived, when the telephone rang, and a terrified voice on the other end cried out: "Doctor, they're ransacking the community center and smashing everything to bits. They're hitting people, we can hear their screaming all the way over here." It was Mrs. Blumenthal who lived next door. I thought I would go over to the community center, though I couldn't be of any help. However, at about the same moment, the doorbell rang loud and long.

> I turned out the lights and looked outside. The square in front of the house was thick with SA men. In an instant they had arrived upstairs and smashed in the hall door. All I could see was that the stairway was full of them, those of lower ranks and all sorts of superior officers, you could recognize them from their caps and military insignia. They forced their way into the apartment shouting the chorus: "Vengeance for Paris! Down with the Jews!" Then they pulled wooden hammers out of the bags they were carrying. The next second you could hear the crack of smashed furniture, the crash of broken glass from the cabinets and windows. These ruffians lunged at me with closed fists, one grabbed hold of me and shouted, saying that I should come downstairs. I was certain they were going to kill me. I went into the bedroom, put down my watch, wallet and keys, and said good-bye to Berta. All she said was: "*Chazak!* [Be strong!]"

> I don't know how I got downstairs. In such moments, you luckily feel so confused and dazed that you hardly notice what's happening around you. This is the source of the lack of fear that you appear to have in such moments. If you were more conscious of things, then you'd be more afraid. Downstairs the street was full of SA men. All together, with those in the house, there were between fifty and sixty

11. Verdict, District Court, Wiesbaden, July 18–19, 1949, Archives IfZ, Gw 05.03–12.

of them. I was received with the shout: "Okay, now give us a sermon!" I started to speak about the death of vom Rath, that his murder was a greater misfortune for us than for the German people, and that we were innocent when it came to his murder. . . . Around the corner, on Stromstraße, I could see that the street was covered with books that had been tossed out my window, along with papers, files, letters. My typewriter lay smashed in the street.

While all this was happening, the SA men had forced their way into the Wertheimer apartment one floor below us. They had destroyed many things there and had dragged Mr. Wertheimer and his wife from bed and had brought them downstairs. I myself was grabbed by an SA man and hurled across the street against the wall of a house. A neighbor who was an eyewitness told me afterward that this had happened repeatedly. Then I was thrown into the entranceway and shoved in between the elevator and the wall. After this the party *Kreisleiter* came and said, "I'm taking you into protective custody."

That's when the march to police headquarters began. A unit of SA men preceded us. I followed behind, escorted by two men. Then came a group of SA men and behind them Mr. Wertheimer, with a similar escort. Behind them, separated from us by another group of SA, was Mrs. Wertheimer in pajamas. The tail end of the column was another group of SA men. The entire time we were marching, they chanted: "Vengeance for Paris! Down with the Jews!" One of them said to me, "Now you can celebrate the Feast of the Tabernacles." Passersby who encountered us also joined the chorus: "Vengeance for Paris! Down with the Jews!"

The rabbi was in custody for twelve days and was released on November 22. Only then did he learn in detail what had occurred.

Many persons had been killed. What had happened that night was indeed a pogrom. Paul Marcus, the proprietor of Cafe Karema, fled after his restaurant had been completely destroyed. He was shot during the night and was found lying dead in front of the home of Dr. Max Loewenberg on Martin-Luther-Platz. Mrs. Isidor Willner and her son Ernst were stabbed to death in Hilden. In addition, Carl Herz and Nathan Mayer were either stabbed or shot. Dr. Sommer in Hilden, age sixty-eight, a man who had married a non-Jew and had never been concerned about anything Jewish, went down into the garden together with his wife and their old domestic servant, who was also Aryan, after his house had been ransacked and he himself had been badly roughed up. The three then took poison there.

The bodies of Marcus, Herz, and Mayer, as well as those of Mrs. Willner and her son Ernst, were initially seized by the authorities. Berta did everything she could to arrange that the Gestapo release the bodies for burial. The release was finally approved. The bodies came from the police in sealed coffins. Sally Rosenbusch said the prayers since I was in jail. Otherwise, no other Jew was allowed to be present late on that evening of November 15, almost eight days after their murder. However, a number of Gestapo officials were at the scene.

No investigation of the possibility of murder was begun. The night of November 10 cost two others their lives, Stefan Goldschmidt and Lewkowitz, both of them in their seventies. I was unable to find out whether they had been murdered or whether they had suffered heart attacks from all the commotion. . . .

The first thing I did was to go to the synagogue. It was surrounded by a high fence of wooden boards, the windows had been smashed, the dome was still on the roof but had been burned out, the rafters were jutting toward the sky. During the night of the pogrom, a band of men had shown up there; it was rumored that some were doctors from the municipal hospitals, along with several officials from the district court. Large quantities of gasoline had been brought over from the Flora drugstore at Schadowplatz, while tar had been obtained from elsewhere. The scrolls of the Torah were removed from the Aron Hakodesh (Torah shrine) and set afire in the yard. The murdering arsonists danced in a a circle around the burning scrolls, some of them wearing the robes of the rabbis and *chazanim* (cantors). Then everything made of wood, especially the roof truss and the benches, was covered with gasoline and tar and set on fire. Soon the roof truss was burning brightly. That is how our synagogue was burned down. Other synagogues were blown up. The mortuary at our old cemetery was destroyed.

Rabbi Eschelbacher was convinced that the pogrom had been the product of minute and careful planning. "The plundering, arson, murder, arrests, and mistreatment took place according to a precisely prearranged plan. The gangs of murdering arsonists had been decided on and planned in detail beforehand. Mr. vom Rath succumbed to his wounds in the late afternoon of November 9. The murdering and destruction began around midnight. The instructions for the pogrom were relayed by radio after careful preparation."[12]

12. Max Eschelbacher, "Der Pogrom vom 10. November 1938 in Düsseldorf," manuscript July 1939, Wiener Library, coll. P II d, No. 151, Archives IfZ,

The stage directions for reporting on the day following the terrible night of November 9 were also quite detailed. The official version was propagated by a bulletin of the DNB. It read as follows: "DNB Berlin. 10 November. After it became known that the German diplomat, party comrade vom Rath, shot down by the cowardly hand of a Jewish murderer, had died, spontaneous anti-Jewish demonstrations broke out throughout the Reich. The German people gave vent to their most profound indignation in a number of forceful actions directed against Jews." In its press conference of November 10, the Propaganda Ministry provided directives and language usage guidelines (*Sprachregelung*) for placement and prominence of the news bulletin for November 11:

Local reports can be included along with the DNB bulletin released this morning. Windows have been smashed here and there, synagogues caught fire themselves or went up in flames somehow or other. The reports should not be presented in too prominent a manner, no headlines on the first page. For the time being, there should be no photographs. Survey reports on the Reich should not be assembled, but it can be mentioned that similar actions were carried out elsewhere in the Reich. Descriptions of specific incidents in this connection should be avoided. All this should appear only on page 2 or 3. If editorial commentary is deemed necessary, it should be brief and state, for example, that the great and understandable popular anger provided a spontaneous answer to the murder of the third secretary.[13]

These directives were faithfully adhered to throughout the length and breadth of the land. Thus, the *Trierer Nationalblatt* reported:

When news of the death of Embassy Counsellor vom Rath at the hands of a murderous Jew became known in Trier, anger among the populace, at a high pitch even prior to this, was intensified. One could see groups of people standing together everywhere, milling around and moving through the streets on that Wednesday night. Greatly agitated, they were not only discussing the tragedy of the

---

MZS 1/1, extracts also in H. Weidenhaupt and F. Wiesemann, eds., *Juden in Düsseldorf* (Münster, 1982).

13. Press conference, Propaganda Ministry, BA, Zsg. 102/13, November 10, 1938.

death of a young German. Based on their genuine and natural folk instincts, they did not think that only the murderer alone was responsible for the deed: rather, they saw in the racial affiliation of an individual the true cause for this assassination. . . . And so it was that in Trier and everywhere in the surrounding countryside, spontaneous demonstrations against Jews broke out in the course of Wednesday night and during the early hours of yesterday morning. In some instances, these demonstrations of anger resulted in the destruction of Jewish property. In Trier itself, the display windows of Jewish businesses were smashed, their contents hurled into the street, and interior furnishings were considerably damaged in certain cases.[14]

Events in Nuremberg and nearby Fürth, which were in keeping with the pervading spirit of the time for the city selected as the regular venue of the NSDAP party conventions and as the residence of the notorious chief anti-Semite of the party and *Gauleiter* of Franconia, Julius Streicher, had resulted in the deaths of at least twenty-six persons, and the SA had engaged in an exceptional wave of pillage and plunder there. The *Fränkischer Kurier* reported the following:

News of the death of the German legation third secretary vom Rath, victim of bullets fired by a Jewish criminal, triggered great agitation among all the residents of Nuremberg and Fürth, as it did throughout the entire Reich. This anger intensified during the course of the evening and night, leading to actions against the Jews in Nuremberg and Fürth. The synagogues on Essenweinstraße in Nuremberg and in Fürth were set on fire during the night of Wednesday to Thursday. Both synagogues were completely gutted by fire. The fire department, which was on the scene immediately, prevented the flames from spreading. The Jewish stores and businesses were demolished, windows were smashed, and the inventory of shops was tossed about. There was no looting anywhere. The goods are still lying strewn about in the Jewish shops.[15]

The *Göttinger Tageblatt* carried a report marked by a greater degree of energy and élan:

---

14. *Nationalblatt Trier*, quoted in Jacques Jacobs, *Existenz und Untergang der alten Judengemeinde der Stadt Trier* (Trier, 1984), pp. 85f.
15. Quoted in *Schicksal jüdischer Bürger in Nürnberg, 1850–1945*, Ausstellungskatalog mit Dokumentation (Nuremberg, 1965), pp. 60f.

The blow struck at us by international Jewry was too powerful for our reaction to be only verbal. A fury against Judaism pent up for generations was unleashed. For that the Jews can thank their racial fellow member Grünspan, his spiritual or actual mentors, and themselves. . . .

Yet the Jews themselves were treated quite well in the course of what happened. This has indeed been a vivid demonstration of the degree to which the anger of the German people has reached, without Jews suffering any physical harm as a result. . . . We do not have to hush up the events that transpired in Göttingen in the early hours of November 10. Whoever finds himself unable to understand this is incapable of comprehending the voice of the people. We could see the yellow temple of the vengeful Jewish god on Obere Maschstraße going up in flames and noted that the display windows of several stores still in Jewish hands were no longer in existence yesterday morning. The security authorities made sure that things did not go beyond such demonstrations of popular anger.[16]

The editor of the paper *Hohenzollerische Blätter*, who reported on events in Hechingen in central Württemberg, also gave a spirited account:

The announcement of the death of the German diplomat, party comrade vom Rath, cut down by the hand of a cowardly and murderous Jew, triggered the deep sense of indignation and just wrath of the people in our city too, as it did throughout the entire Reich. During the night of Wednesday to Thursday, indignant *Volksgenossen* gathered on Goldschmiedestraße in front of the synagogue. In completely understandable and justifiable anger, they had seized on this Jewish place of worship to vent their will for vengeance. Within a short period of time, the doors had been broken in and the entire interior furnishings and fixtures had been destroyed. In their inordinate anger, the *Volksgenossen* went about their work so thoroughly that it will be impossible to restore the interior furnishings to their previous purpose.

The building, constructed in 1775, which had served the Jews since its inception as a place of religious gatherings, is a total ruin inside. All the windows and doors were also smashed. Already in the early hours of Thursday morning, inhabitants streamed in large numbers into Goldschmiedestraße and agitatedly discussed the heinous

16. *Göttinger Tageblatt*, November 11, 1938, quoted in Peter Wilhelm, *Die Synagogengemeinde Göttingen, Rosdorf und Geismar, 1850–1942* (Göttingen, 1978), p. 55.

assassination of a young German full of hopes for the future. In an open and frank manner, they expressed their satisfaction with the painful vengeance taken in response to this insidious and vile deed. Everyone is speaking with disgust about the Jewish rabble that now, here in Hechingen too, has come to feel the force of the clenched fist of the people.

May this serve as an example to show Jewry that Germany can no longer be trifled with and knows how to strike its enemies where it hurts them the most. It is superfluous to note that nowhere was there any sign of violent excesses or acts of looting. Rather, whoever witnessed these anti-Jewish actions had to be impressed by the degree of discipline maintained by the large crowds despite their indignation over the murderous Jewish act.[17]

The *Münchner Beobachter,* the local supplement to the *Völkischer Beobachter,* carried a report on the "enormous indignation against Jews in Munich" on page 13:

> November 10 in Munich and throughout the entire Reich has given a clear sign! A gutted synagogue on Herzog-Rudolf-Straße, smashed storefront windows in many Jewish shops on Neuhauserstraße, Weinstrasse, and Theatinerstraße, on im Tal, Rosenthal, am Stachus, and Lenbachplatz (to name but a few streets and squares), as well as a large number of Jews taken into protective custody – these constitute an initial and but limited warning, by which the only too admirable forbearance of the German people has given vent to its anger.[18]

The North German edition of the *Völkischer Beobachter* carried the official version of events in the capital, Berlin:

> All over the west side of Berlin, as in other parts of the capital where Jews still swagger and strut, not a single storefront window of a Jewish business has remained intact. The anger and fury of the citizens of Berlin, who maintained the greatest discipline despite everything, was kept within definite limits, so that excesses were avoided and not a single hair was touched on a Jewish head. The goods on display in the store windows, some of which were decorated in a quite magnificent manner, remained untouched. At the

---

17. *Hohenzollerische Blätter,* November 12, 1938, quoted in Paul Sauer, *Dokumente über die Verfolgung jüdischer Bürger in Baden-Württemberg durch das nationalsozialistische Regime, 1933–1935,* 2 vols. (Stuttgart, 1966), vol. 2, pp. 21f.
18. *Völkischer Beobachter* (Munich edition), November 11, 1938.

most, a few objects here and there may have been damaged as the result of a stone being hurled into a window or a fragment of glass falling. . . .

The three Berlin synagogues were set ablaze. . . . In all of Berlin's streets, in the towns of Mark Brandenburg, everywhere where Jews live and "work," passersby are greeted by the same vista – a gaping void in the emptied display cases and store windows and not a Jew to be seen anywhere. Occasionally one can spy a son of Israel busy clearing away the debris behind the entrances, some of which are bolted shut and protected by iron grilles. The populace today is completely quiet, each person busy with his own pursuits; people only acknowledge the demolished display windows in passing, although not without a quite understandable sense of delight and satisfaction at the sight.[19]

Further examples of this officially ordained cynicism in the press could be readily recounted. In contrast with the protestations and assurances about how spontaneous the popular anger had been, how disciplined the indignant masses had behaved, and how there had been no looting, that indeed hardly a hair had been touched on a Jewish head, is the more factual account – the balance sheet tallied up by the exponents of the regime under Göring's chairmanship at a meeting on November 12, 1938. The meeting, attended by representatives from all Reich ministries and other government and party offices and called also to discuss the further course of measures against the Jewish populace, heard Gestapo chief Heydrich recite the following figures: 7,500 destroyed stores and shops, with a total amount of damage to stock, goods, and premises preliminarily estimated at several hundred million reichsmarks. An insurance expert then reported on damage incurred as a result of looting and theft. He illustrated the facts by citing the example of the jeweler Margraf on Unter den Linden in Berlin. His store had been totally ransacked, and he had submitted a claim to the insurance firm for losses amounting to 1.7 million reichsmarks. Göring ordered large-scale raids to locate the stolen jewels. Kurt Daluege, SS general and chief of police, said that an order for this had already been issued and that 150 suspects had been arrested. Heydrich, head of the political police and the criminal investigative police, added that there had been some eight hundred

19. *Völkischer Beobachter* (North German edition), November 11, 1938.

cases of looting in the entire Reich, but that several hundred looters had already been apprehended. In light of the magnitude of the material damage, Göring dropped a remark that he would have preferred that two hundred Jews had been killed instead of such valuable assets having been destroyed. Heydrich commented that there had been a total of thirty-five Jews killed in connection with the actions; yet that figure was indeed only a small fraction of the actual number of victims killed as a result of the pogrom, to which the suicides and those who died later as a result of maltreatment must also be added.

However, Göring was only upset about the economic consequences of this "popular anger" kindled and fanned by Goebbels because the damage inflicted with such great destructive glee had been felt in part by persons who were not Jews. Thus the smashed windows in Jewish stores and shops, estimated at between six and ten million reichsmarks in value, had to be replaced by the insurance companies in response to claims filed by the owners of the property, who were in the main not Jewish. The insurance expert Hilgard explained this to the gentlemen in attendance, and in response to the stupid remark by Goebbels that the Jew would have to pay the damages, Göring became furious, saying that this did not make any sense because Germany had no raw materials and was obliged to buy the glass from abroad, using its foreign currency reserves. Plate glass for shop windows was manufactured exclusively in Belgium, and the heroes of the pogrom night had smashed the equivalent of half of the annual production output of the entire Belgian glass industry within the course of a few short hours.[20]

In contrast to official pronouncements, the champions of the German popular anger had robbed and looted, pilfering Jewish property in grand style. But even in small things they had unabashedly helped themselves to large servings. Erna Philipp, a social worker and secretary in the employ of the Jewish community in Bochum, described how fifteen men forced their way into her apartment in the dead of night on November 10:

> Between the hours of 2 and 3 A.M. during the night of November 9–10, 1938, fifteen men forcibly entered my apartment. They broke

20. Stenographic transcript of the discussion of the Jewish question with Göring on November 12, 1938, Nuremberg Document PS 1816, published, among other places, in *IMT*, vol. 28, pp. 499–540.

open the front door (my Christian landlord's) and threatened the latter with pointed revolvers, while two men stood "protecting" me with their guns. After enough had been stolen and smashed (ten people and their leader took care of that), they then took their leave of me, bowing politely, assuring me they had been there to make sure I was not harmed. It was the organization of the theft that was striking. Cash, a typewriter, a Leica camera, jewelry, silver tableware, and art objects were crammed into my briefcases and suitcases. Valuable pictures and drawings were carefully cut from their frames. Nothing fragile in the apartment was left intact.[21]

The formal end to the officially staged demonstration of the "people's rage" against the Jews had already been declared by Goebbels on November 10 in an announcement on the first page of the daily *Völkischer Beobachter*: "A strict order is now issued to the entire population to desist at once from any further demonstrations or action of any kind against the Jews. The final word on the Jewish assassination in Paris will be communicated to the Jews in the form of legislation and decree."[22] Yet just as little as the pogrom was a "spontaneous" action on the part of the population, just as hard did it now prove to put a swift end to it. Goebbels was unable to rid himself so quickly of the spirits he had summoned. The claims that the German people had "heeded the call of the government willingly and in a disciplined manner," and that "within hours demonstrations and other action had been terminated"[23] were patent lies. Violent excesses continued in some communities until November 13.

Not only was the organizer of the pogrom heavily criticized by Göring; in February 1939, the Supreme Party Tribunal of the NSDAP expressed its criticism of the way Goebbels had stage directed the events. Its task in dealing with the events of November 1938 was bound up less with meting out punishment for the excesses; the main focus of the tribunal's concern was to remove those acts of murder, looting, and rape committed by NSDAP members from the sphere of public prosecution. The party tribunal recommended to Hitler that proceedings before regular courts should, in most instances, be dismissed on the grounds that these cases involved "killings under orders,

21. Erna Philipp, "Ereignisse in der Pogrom-Nacht, 9.–10. November 1938," Wiener Library, P II d, No. 98, Archives IfZ, MZS 1/1.
22. *Völkischer Beobachter*, November 10, 1938.
23. *Völkischer Beobachter*, November 12, 1938.

killings on the basis of unclear or presumed order, unordered killings resulting from hatred of Jews and from a view that the death of party comrade vom Rath should, in accordance with the will of the party leadership, be avenged; or killings stemming from decisions made suddenly on the spot and actions taken in the excitement of the moment." For this reason, the NSDAP tribunal had dealt in thorough fashion with the problem of general responsibility for the excesses and had come to the conclusion that Goebbels's veiled issuance of orders had been untimely:

> Another question is whether an order left intentionally unclear and issued in expectation that the recipient of the order will recognize the intention of the giver of the order and act in due accordance should not, in the interest of discipline, be relegated to the practices of the past. During the "period of struggle" in the early years of the party, such an order may have been necessary in individual instances so as to bring about a political success, yet without affording to the state the possibility of demonstrating that the party was the author of the act. Today such a perspective is no longer relevant. The public, down to the very last person, is likewise well aware that political actions such as those which occurred on November 9 were organized and carried out by the party, whether or not that is admitted. If all synagogues burn down within a single night, that must somehow have been organized and can only have been organized by the party.[24]

The Perpetrators

Thus, as everyone knew and activists after 1945 repeatedly asserted in court, the pogrom had been ordered. Yet the dedication and alacrity with which that order was everywhere implemented gave the event its actual scope and character. Goebbels had appealed to base instincts and had unleashed a wave of aggression, vandalism, lustful destructiveness, and desire to kill, a wave which temporarily transformed upstanding citizens and innocuous average people into raging beasts. Two children in Cologne watched the destruction of a small Jewish shop for secondhand goods:

24. Report, Party Supreme Tribunal to Göring, February 13, 1939, Nuremberg Document PS 3063.

SA men had posted themselves in a half circle in front of the shop of the parents of my schoolfriend and were taking turns hurling a huge iron ball into the shop windows while chanting the refrain, "Jews get out!" They demolished the storefront and destroyed its displays. We children stood there as if frozen and glanced over at the parents of my schoolfriend, who also stood looking on in silence as their property was destroyed. I didn't understand why these people didn't resist this frenzy of destruction, and it was also incomprehensible to me why so many people just stood there and didn't make the slightest effort to intervene.[25]

In the town of Esslingen near Stuttgart, the Jewish orphans' home was the target of the roused Nazis:

On November 10, between noon and 1 o'clock, civilians and SA men armed with axes and heavy hammers appeared in the dining room of the orphanage and forced us, shouting "Get out of here!" to leave the building and gather at the compost heap in back. Some of the children ran away, the rest were guarded together with us by the SA. Personally I did not know any of the people, but I have a special recollection of someone with red hair and a man with a hump. While some men did nothing, remaining in the halls and outside, the others proceeded to destroy everything within reach. Books were tossed from the rooms of the teachers and from our apartment; prayer books, Torah scrolls, and memorial plaques were thrown from the prayer hall, and all this was placed on a bonfire. One of these ruffians threatened that the children who were crying would also be tossed on that pile and burned. . . .

Then the order was issued to remove the children before nightfall. After long negotiations, my husband was permitted to call acquaintances in Stuttgart to request that they help pick up the children in their cars. We were obliged to put our signatures to a statement that my husband and I would be the last persons to leave the building by 7.30 A.M. the next day, or that we would be taken into protective custody. Taxi drivers and private persons who offered to transport the children were forbidden to have any connection with us. Former pupils at the orphanage came in roundabout ways from Stuttgart during the night to assist us. We left the building carrying rucksacks. . . . A number of children had set out on foot toward Stuttgart and were given assistance underway by passersby.[26]

25. Quoted in Horst Matzerath, ed., " . . . *vergessen kann man die Zeit nicht, das ist nicht möglich . . .*": *Kölner erinnern sich an die Jahre 1929–1945* (Cologne, 1985), p. 173.

26. Ina Rothschild, "Bericht über die Kristallnacht im israelitischen Waisenhaus

The fate of a doctor's family from Nuremberg is reflected in condensed form in the testimony given by a witness in one of the restitution proceedings held in 1954:

> The night after the "crystalline Thursday" of November 9–10, 1938, I immediately looked up several friends in order to help them in so far as one could do anything at the time. I went directly to Nuremberg to the family of Dr. Albert Weinstock, and the spectacle that met my eyes will remain with me the rest of my days.
>
> I didn't think it was possible that there were people who could cause such devastation. They must have been animals, beasts who, in their hatred, no longer knew any limits. The Weinstock apartment was a picture of horror. The pieces of broken glass and china lay so thick in the living room that you could hardly walk. The living room furniture, massive and heavy, had been completely demolished. The doors of the sideboard cabinet, for example, had been smashed open with a hatchet and all the china and glasses had been thrown to the floor. The piano had been so demolished that it is hard to imagine its condition. Maliciously, the individual keys had been broken and knocked out using a hatchet! Whatever marble could be found had been smashed to pieces. The dining room furniture had been destroyed; many books had been tossed out the window. Tables made of precious woods had been so badly smashed that they could no longer be repaired. In the bedroom, the dressing table, with its mirror and glass top, had been smashed, the clothes cabinet had been broken open and linens strewn about in order to find the money and jewelry hidden underneath the linen inside. . . .
>
> So much then for the material side of it, where compensation can be made. I would also like to say something about the human aspect, since it had far greater consequences and cannot be recompensated – such heinous deeds cannot be measured in terms of money. The people I encountered when I entered the apartment, namely, Dr. Albert Weinstock, his wife Dora, and their two sons aged about twelve and fourteen, were a picture of misery. And psychologically, it was at the time very trying for me as well to give these poor people a bit of encouragement. The young teenage boys were totally distraught. The SA ruffians had forced the boys, who were still children, to stand with their faces to the wall and had threatened them with their pistols. They were led through the entire apartment, with the repeated threat they would be shot, and were forced to look

---

'Wilhelmspflege' in Esslingen," in Paul Sauer, *Die Schicksale der jüdischen Bürger Baden-Württembergs während der nationalsozialistischen Verfolgungszeit, 1933–1945* (Stuttgart, 1969), p. 420.

on while the family valuables and momentos were destroyed. Mrs. Weinstock was also threatened with a pistol and ordered to hand over her jewelry (some of it had been in the family for many years) and money. Under such circumstances, she found it impossible to refuse. I don't need to mention that Dr. Weinstock himself was not treated with velvet gloves. Despite this, he was the quickest to regain composure, at least outwardly, because he was concerned about his family.

The upshot: Dr. Weinstock was unable to get over the fact that a person like himself, who enjoyed such great respect personally and as a physician in Nuremberg, should be treated as a common criminal solely because of his origin. He committed suicide! Kurt Weinstock, the older son, who had a rather weak constitution, was never able to overcome the consequences of the shock he suffered and died at the young age of thirty, leaving behind a mother broken in sorrow. Mrs. Weinstock herself was never able to forget this horrible night, and likewise failed to ever recover from the shock and horror of it.[27]

In another case, where the victim was an elderly man and the perpetrator a young unskilled laborer aged seventeen, the only identifiable motive for the severe maltreatment was a vague and inchoate sense of aggression as a result of incitement. The scene of the crime was the small town of Assenheim in Hesse (1933 population: 1216 inhabitants, including 21 Jews); this crime was then brought to trial in the autumn of 1946. The accused was sentenced to two years in prison due to aggravated breach of the peace coupled with dangerous bodily injury. However, it proved impossible to bring the ring leaders and instigators to justice. The accused was repentant and confessed his deeds. He had gone to elementary school in Assenheim, then had broken off an apprenticeship as a mason, and had been employed since 1937 in the construction of the Western Wall [of defense]. On November 8–9, 1938, he had been given leave to return home:

He had returned to Assenheim on the day of the action at about 1 P.M. Since he didn't find any of his family at home, he took his bicycle and went to the village to look for them there. When he was near the drugstore, he saw a large crowd of people gathered in front of the Liebmann house, for the most part young men. Moving closer, he could already hear the voice of Hergert, the local chief of the

27. Statement by Paul O. Schlick, January 14, 1954, quoted in *Schicksal jüdischer Bürger in Nürnberg*, pp. 64f.

Wolfgang Benz

NSDAP, calling on those present to go into the house and drag Liebmann out.

The accused then parked his bicycle nearby, mingled with the crowd, and soon thereafter went on into the courtyard of the Liebmann residence. From there he went together with a few others into the house. First of all, he went upstairs, where he claims he found the furniture lying about, already destroyed. He took a clock and tossed it out the window. He kicked a window in, climbed out onto the balcony and then through an already broken window back into the room. Then he went down to the ground floor. As he descended the stairs, he noticed several men unknown to him punching the bleeding Liebmann, who had been shoved into a corner. Liebmann was trying to defend himself with a cane. The accused, who wished to move past this group, felt he had been struck by Liebmann. In defense, he grabbed the cane and took it away from Liebmann. He then started to hit Liebmann. However, he no longer remembers the object he was holding in his hand, nor what part of Liebmann's body he struck. He insists though that he didn't have a hatchet.

Liebmann, who was in dire straits, now tried to get away. His attackers followed him, at their head the defendant, who caught up with Liebmann. With kicks and blows, he pushed Liebmann along in front of him. This pursuit went on for about one hundred meters. Then the defendant swung out at the leg of the man he was pursuing with the cane in his hand, causing the latter to fall. He hurled himself down upon the man lying there defenseless in order to continue to batter him. At this point, the defendant K intervened, pulling the accused away from his victim. Liebmann, who visited his son, the witness Liebmann, arrested during the meantime, a bit later in detention, told his son that shortly after the crowd had forced its way into the house, he had received a blow from a hatchet across his forehead just above the bridge of his nose and had lost his sight as a result.[28]

The events of November 10, 1938, in the small Hessian town of Büdingen were no different from the excesses elsewhere in the German Reich when it came to the degree of crudeness marking the actions and participation of the population:

First of all, numerous Jewish residents of Büdingen were dragged from their homes by persons no longer identifiable and brought to

28. Verdict, District Court, Gießen, September 17, 1946, in Klaus Moritz and Ernst Noam, *NS-Verbrechen vor Gericht, 1945–1955: Dokumente aus hessischen Justizakten* (Wiesbaden, 1978), pp. 132–33.

the district court jail. In the early afternoon a large crowd formed, which then moved through the streets of town, perpetrating violence. While numerous curious onlookers lined the street, groups generally consisting of teenagers and schoolchildren forced their way into Jewish homes, smashed the furniture and other objects, broke windows and dishes, slit open mattresses, and threw pieces of furniture, linen, and other objects out into the street. These activities, which died down at times, only to be rekindled anew, continued on into the late evening hours.[29]

The First Penal Chamber of the District Court in Gießen reconstructed these facts – classifiable in legal terms as creating a nuisance, breach of the peace, wrongful deprivation of personal liberty, and coercion – in proceedings in early 1949. One of the accused, the apprentice butcher L, was eighteen at the time of the incident. He was neither a member of the HJ nor the NSDAP and was regarded as industrious and capable. He married in 1939, was drafted first into the National Labor Service and after that into the Wehrmacht. In 1945, after having returned from British captivity, his old boss hired him once again because he was so hardworking and experienced, orderly and pleasing to work with. In the meantime, he had become the father of two children, and the appeals board had granted him special amnesty because of his youth. The following facts were confirmed not only by several credible witnesses, but by the defendant himself:

On November 10, 1938, L left the slaughterhouse in the afternoon after finishing his work. He brought his equipment back home and then proceeded to the Schloßgasse, since on the way he had observed a lot of people running in that direction. He joined them and came to the Hirschmann house, where the work of destruction had almost been completed. However, groups of youths and several adults as well were still busy in the house. For that reason, L also went inside. When Mrs. Hirschmann, nearly sixty years of age, who had been sitting with her paralyzed husband in the kitchen, was pushed down the stairs by two young men, L followed them, grabbed hold of Mrs. Hirschmann suddenly on the street, and pulled her through the crowd for a distance of about three hundred meters along Schloßgasse. He was holding her by her clothes, while beating and kicking her with his butcher's boots. When several young people

29. Verdict, District Court, Gießen, January 6, 1949, Archives IfZ, Gg. 01.08.

held out their legs and tripped the old woman a number of times so that she fell to the ground, he pulled her up again onto her feet, pushed her on ahead of him, and shouted that he wanted to throw her into the water.[30]

It is unnecessary to note that the victim had never done any harm whatsoever to her tormenter, who was sentenced to one year in prison. As disgusting and incomprehensible as were the excesses perpetrated by young people without any recognizable ties to National Socialism, the crimes committed by anti-Semites and followers of Hitler were no less despicable. After the fact, party members also showed themselves to be less "brave" than they had during the pogrom.

The classic example was offered by a Mannheim pharmacist, known in town as a fanatic Nazi and virulent anti-Semite. This pharmacist had secretly joined the NSDAP even before 1933, though he tried to deny this later in court. During World War I, which the man, born in 1881, was unable to take active part in due to his poor health, he had been a member of the extreme right-wing, chauvinistic Vaterlandspartei. On November 10, 1938, he participated as the ringleader of a group of uniformed SA men, goading them on to destroy and ransack the homes of Jewish citizens. In June 1948, the District Court in Mannheim found him guilty of breach of the peace. The local association of pharmacists solemnly disassociated itself from the matter in a resolution unanimously adopted in March 1946: they condemned "with a sense of disgust, the behavior, beneath human dignity and professionally abhorrent," of their colleague during the Nazi period, declaring "they could no longer tolerate that he be considered one of them." If his fellow professionals expressed themselves in such drastic terms later on, he must indeed have been particularly extreme.

In court, this pharmacist denied any involvement in the pogrom; in contradiction of the credible testimony of a large number of witnesses, he claimed that, since he had known nothing about developments on November 8 and 9, he had traveled during the early morning hours of November 10 to Heidelberg and had returned to Munich only later that afternoon; by the time he got back, the violence was already over.

30. Ibid.

This audacious cowardice of a rabble-rouser after the fact of his crimes was an additional factor in setting the judges against him. They sentenced him to two years in prison, giving the following justification for the decision:

It is true that the accused is a first-time offender. However, this fact alone was not sufficient to secure for him an acknowledgment of mitigating circumstances. He is a university graduate and thus had a level of education that necessarily should have made him aware, more than anyone else, of the injustice and monstrosity of the crime. Yet far from concluding on the basis of this awareness that he should attempt to prevent other, less educated and less intelligent persons from perpetrating such outrageous acts, which contradict the normal feelings of any cultured individual, he misused his authority to provide others with the worst example and this to a degree and extent impossible to surpass in such a short span of time.

The fact that, as he himself mentioned, he received financial support from Jewish circles in earlier years, was not considered exonerating. Rather, it incriminated him all the more, since he had recompensed this previous assistance in such a despicable manner. In his actions, he gave no special consideration to those who were sick and dying, to earlier acquaintances and women living alone. He was driven solely by a desire to destroy. He is lacking in any insight whatsoever into his deeds. He now takes cover, entrenching himself behind the claim he was unaware and not present at the scene, in unreconstructed arrogance; and in addition, he now cowardly repudiates the ideas and actions which he once propagated as exemplary behavior.

Given these facts, there was no place for granting mitigating circumstances in this case. Only the full severity of the law will perhaps be able to impress upon him an awareness of the injustice of his actions. Such a degree of shameful and ignominious action can only – and indeed must – be punished by a prison sentence. A sentence of two years behind bars appeared to be appropriate. Given the baseness of mind and attitude manifested by the behavior of the defendant, it was also necessary to strip him of his civil rights for a period of two years. Since the defendant was himself responsible for the protracted length of investigative custody due to his persistent denials, it did not seem appropriate to count this time toward his total penalty.[31]

---

31. Verdict, District Court, Mannheim, June 24, 1948, Archives IfZ, Gm 02.05.

Wolfgang Benz

The Victims

At the time of the Nazi takeover, there were some 830 Jews living in the city of Erfurt. The night of the pogrom, all men between the ages of eighteen and eighty were taken into custody. Among them was the attorney and notary public Dr. Harry Stern, president of the local lodge of B'nai B'rith. Dr. Stern was taken past the burning synagogue to a hall for athletics:

> There was an awful din in the place, due in part to a number of quite obviously intoxicated members of the police, SS and SA, in part to persons dressed in civilian clothes. . . . My identification was checked at a table, and then I was grabbed by two men and led to a washroom. In the washroom, there were two SA men with truncheons, who apparently were supposed to give us a beating. One of them raised his club and touched me with it. The other said, "Scream as loud as you can," which I did. They evidently wanted to circumvent the order they had been given to beat us. Then I was shoved out of the washroom and grabbed by other SA men and made to stand with my face to the wall.
>
> There were already a large number of other Jews standing there. They forced us to walk with bended knees, the worst torture I have endured. . . . Some of the Nazis singled out Jews they knew personally in order to vent their anger on them. The lawyer Flesch, who was a baptized Christian, was tormented and insulted especially by an SA man whose wife he had represented in court in a divorce case. A number of Jews – irrespective of age and physical constitution – were forced to climb up the ladders mounted in the gym. Nazis stood at their bases, wielding riding whips, and struck out at their victims on the ladders as long as they remained in reach. . . . We had to stand in formation and march around to the tune of the "Horst Wessel Song." Then the command was given to shout "Juda verrecke!" [Judah perish!], which we were *compelled* to do. After that we were loaded onto busses and transported to Buchenwald, where we arrived at dawn.[32]

The true impact of what internment in one of the three camps – Dachau, Buchenwald, Sachsenhausen – meant after this night of terror is difficult to depict, despite the fact that there are numerous descriptions. The bald facts were that some thirty

32. Interview with Dr. Harry Stern, October 31, 1954, Wiener Library P II d, No. 2, Archives IfZ, MZS 1/1.

thousand men had been arrested throughout the German Reich, that the action was limited to a few weeks' duration, and that the intimidation and harassment served to animate victims to emigrate and was not (yet) aimed at their extermination. Yet these facts are of far lesser import than the impact of the catastrophe of confinement in such a concentration camp on the victims' consciousness and what it signified for their bourgeois existence, the destruction of their previous way of life: "How enormous was the disgrace which, in the concept of the concentration camp, subjugated and threatened daily existence like a scourge."

Erich Guttman, son of a rabbi, was transported during the night of the pogrom to the Sachsenhausen concentration camp, where thousands, after enduring all the beatings and torments upon their arrival, waited for what was to come:

> The hours slip by and the chilly, damp air of a night in November joins the soul's ordeal. It rains off and on, but we hardly notice. We have been standing here for eight hours already, our eyes constantly to the wall. Bareheaded and without overcoats. At intervals, groups of some one hundred persons are forced to move off into the darkness, and when they come back, they are marching in strict formation, silently, dressed in convicts' uniforms, as it appears, or in old, ragged army coats. Their heads have been shorn, their beards removed. They became unrecognizable, initially hard to distinguish one from the next save for a number stamped on their coat and trousers, along with a star of David in harsh red and yellow colors.

Most were at liberty again several weeks later.

> Once healthy persons, they often departed this godforsaken place old and broken men. Frequently, their freedom after these terrible hardships was more difficult than one might imagine. Psychologically, it was a hard task to reintegrate these men who had been so tormented into the daily round of life, to direct them toward a life leading out of this bondage and on to countries wishing to give us a new home.

Erich Guttman, who changed his German name after emigrating and wrote this report in 1941, was among the last to be released from this arrest action. In the early spring of 1939, he was transferred from the concentration camp to the police jail in

31

his hometown. His application for an emigration visa, for which his parents had submitted the papers, was not immediately successful, and four weeks later he was interned a second time in the Sachsenhausen camp. It was on this second occasion that he made the frightening observation of just how the concentration camp was changing the psychology of its inmates, transforming respectable citizens into obtuse prisoners:

> I once again joined my former fellows, to the extent that they were still in the camp. And those I saw once more had certainly not altered for the better. Those four weeks that I had been away and the burden of my own worries had often made me forget the memory of their faces. But now I was shaken. They had changed, externally and psychologically – or perhaps I should say, they had changed morally. With gaunt faces in which their grief, or surrender to their fate, had etched its inevitable traces, they endured their burdensome lot. To a frightening degree, they had become acclimated to the tenor and routine of camp existence. Their own egos had long since crumbled away, and their bodies contained nothing now that might hint at the existence of a personality. They had turned crude and disconsiderate, their voices shrill, often coarse. They received me with a roughness which was profoundly repulsive to me.[33]

One of the six thousand Hamburg Jews arrested in November 1938 and brought to the Sachsenhausen camp described the events between November 10 and 21, between his own arrest and his release immediately thereafter. In comparison with other fellow sufferers, his experience was nothing exceptional, and he was even reckoned among those who were considered to have "gotten off easy":

> First we were brought to the Fuhlsbüttel prison and taken to a dark room. Our numbers were about five times the capacity of that room. We remained there without food for the entire day and were then transported in an open boxcar at night to Sachsenhausen, arriving there at 2 A.M. On the way, a young man aged seventeen from Bremen had suffered a nervous breakdown because he had been forced to witness how SS men had shot his mother after she had begun to shout in her distress at seeing him being taken away and then had left her lying there.

33. Eric Goodman [Erich Guttmann], "Die Tage nach dem 9. November: Ein Bericht" (London, Spring 1941), Wiener Library, P II d, No. 528, Archives IfZ, MZS 1/1.

We were met by a large contingent of SS men upon our arrival in Sachsenhausen. They immediately started to mistreat us so badly by kicking and beating us with rifle butts and truncheons that the police guard which had accompanied us stood aside aghast and then quickly departed. The degree of physical exertion and the incessant pounding and pushing by the SS was such that two from our group perished during the fifteen minute march.

Then began the most awful thing, something that in its impact, especially on me, made all the physical punishment we had been subjected to seem minor: we were forced to stand in the camp for nineteen hours (in some cases, this period was even up to twenty-five hours). During this time, if someone collapsed, he was greeted by a hail of kicks and blows from the butts of rifles. The first thing we heard was a shout for the rabbi in the group, who was dragged by his beard and roughed up. He was then presented with a sign reading, "I am a traitor and share responsibility for vom Rath's death." He was forced to carry this sign at arm's length for a period of twelve hours. The SS men, hardly any of whom was over the age of twenty-one, had it in especially for elderly, fat, Jewish-looking men who appeared socially better-off, such as rabbis, teachers, and lawyers, and treated athletic-looking younger Jews with greater lenience. Thus a former high-placed senior Jewish official, who gave his title when reporting his name, was manhandled in a particularly severe manner, and the proprietor of a large restaurant was subjected to similar treatment. I could not get rid of the impression that an undertone of homosexuality was an element affecting the behavior of the SS.

Then our beards and heads were shaven, and we were forced to stand out in the pouring rain for six hours without food, drink, or head covering. So we had already gone two days and nights without sleep or food and were compelled to stand for a long period of time. . . . The work we were marched to at double-time pace was performed in the clinker factory (Hermann Göring Werke) and consisted of transporting sand and sacks of cement. To carry the sand, we inmates had to take off our jackets and then put them back on backward. Then the back of the jacket was lifted up to serve as a container and filled with a heavy load of sand that we had to drag with outstretched arms, double-time, for some five minutes and empty it into a dump truck. Then we went back again, running double-time. Sacks of cement weighing a hundred kilos were lifted without distinction onto the backs of men sixty and sixty-five years old, and they were then forced to drag this heavy burden the same distance at a similar quick pace, drop it down, and run back. Occasionally the sand was carried on so-called stretchers. But that was even worse, since the wood would cut into your flesh so deeply that, in the case of my own hands, the skin was broken open all the way down to the bone. . . .

During the return march from work, we trotted in rows of five. Those who collapsed along the way were beaten and then carried on stretchers inside the rows of five men. This was to ensure that persons whom we had to pass on the street would not see any stretchers being carried outside the rows of marching men. Whoever did not perform exercises in a sufficiently energetic manner was compelled to "roll around," that is, he had to roll and spin in the sand until he fainted. These unfortunate souls frequently threw themselves onto the electric fence and were electrocuted or shot by a guard who saw them trying to get across the barrier.

Finally, on November 21, the news came of our release, and we were transported back in groups of seventy. When we reported to the camp commander for release, several higher SS officers were discussing whether it wouldn't be a good idea to slaughter or burn one or another especially heavyset Jew. This conversation, conceived as a joke, had a horrible impact on the men, whose nerves by then were shattered. Yet the path of suffering was still not at an end.

That morning, after our release was announced, we were compelled to stand in the pouring rain from 6 A.M. to 6 P.M. without any head covering and again the next day from 11 A.M. to 3 P.M., without food and without being given permission to go to the toilets. Finally it was announced that the Jews were not being given any tickets; the announcement was accompanied by the remark, "You can go on foot all the way to Stargard for all I care." Then we paid for those among us who had no money and were forced to wait at the station for twelve hours before we could leave. Our clothes were completely ruined. Since all Jews are "full of lice," the garments had been fumigated.[34]

There is a quite unusual story concerning a release from the Dachau concentration camp, which came about as the result of the courage of a young girl. Ruth was from Allenstein in East Prussia and lived with a married sister in Berlin. She must have also been very attractive at twenty-five and had met her future husband shortly before the November pogrom. He was the co-owner of a large furniture store on Alexanderplatz, which had been destroyed during the pogrom.

34. Anonymous report, November 26, 1938, Wiener Library, P II d, No. 658, Archives IfZ, MZS 1/1.

The morning after Kristallnacht, he phoned me and asked whether I couldn't perhaps help him get out alive from his store. It lay in ruins, and I found him hiding behind a pillar and led him by the hand through the wildly shouting crowd. He then phoned his parents in Frankenthal (Palatinate) from a post office. His mother was desperate, his father had already been transported to Dachau. She asked him to come to Mannheim, from where she was planning to flee abroad.

He traveled to Mannheim and then called for Ruth's assistance immediately because he was unable to cope with his distraught mother and the entire situation:

> My parents, who accidentally overheard the conversation, were against my going, because they thought it was immoral to allow me, as a young girl, to travel alone to meet a man. However, my sister was able to convince my parents that in such abnormal times the normal moral principles no longer held and that now the main thing was that one person should help the next. So I went to Mannheim. . . . With great difficulty, I was able to locate Mrs. Abraham, who had found shelter together with about twenty other women and young girls in a relative's apartment. All the men were already in Dachau.
>
> After I had taken stock of the situation, I plucked up courage and told myself that I would only be able to accomplish something in one way and be able to do something for my future father-in-law by risking going to Dachau myself and trying my luck there. When I told those present about my plan, they thought I was insane, for what rational person would voluntarily put himself or herself into such a situation? I wanted to assist, nothing else mattered, and I had the feeling and faith in God that my trip to Dachau would result in Mr. Abraham's release. I myself didn't know at the time how that would come about. Nonetheless, I traveled that very same night to Munich. I had two photos of Mr. Abraham in my handbag, since I didn't know him, and one of his son.
>
> After arrival the next morning in Munich, I saw some buses at the train station, one of which was to Dachau. Deciding quickly without asking anyone, I got on as the first passenger. The bus rapidly filled up with men wearing SS uniforms, and I felt very strange: no one asked me where I wanted to go or told me to buy a ticket. The weather was like my mood, overcast and oppressive, and the bus was soon approaching the gates of the camp. On the way, I saw the barbed wire surrounding the camp. When we continued on into the camp, I caught sight, with my own eyes, of Jews of all ages, with

shaven heads and careworn faces, dressed in inmate uniforms, standing in formation for the morning roll call. I shuddered, but now there was no going back.

When the bus emptied, I got off too and stood there lost, not knowing what to do. An SS man came up to me and asked what I wanted there, to which I replied, in a determined voice, "Please take me to the camp commander." His reply was that I would have to wait until I could see the commander. Apparently they thought I was a girl from the BDM, which was probably the reason why the SS man didn't ask further questions. After a while, I was called in to see the commander, and he asked me why I'd come. I told him, "I've come from East Prussia, a long journey, to ask you to release an old man from captivity." He asked for the man's personal data and promised that he would give me an answer after three days. He gave me his telephone number, and I was free to go.

Outside it was raining heavily, and I set out to leave the camp. After a few minutes, I was completely soaked. Suddenly I heard a car driving up slowly behind me. The driver spoke to me and asked me to drive with him to Munich, without paying any attention to my resistance. I told him: "If you're looking for an adventure, you've got the wrong girl; I'm Jewish and don't wish to endanger you or myself. Please continue on driving." He insisted that I get in, and at this point it was all the same to me and I no longer cared about anything related to my person. I was no longer afraid and decided to take a chance and drive on with him. "You don't have to tell me anything, I know everything, I listened to your talk with the commander from the next room, I want to help you," he said. "Don't ask me what my job is here in the camp; I'll never be able to wash myself clean. But I have sympathy for your situation. Trust me. A good friend of mine is a lawyer for the party. You should contact him after I've spoken to him."

Once we arrived in Munich, he took me over to the notorious Brown House. He was a well-known jeweler in Munich, and his name was Joseph Müller. At this point in time, Jews were no longer allowed to stay at hotels; the only place they were permitted to spend the night was in a Jewish home. Mr. Müller offered me a place to sleep in his office behind his shop, but asked me to leave very early the next morning so that none of the personnel would see me. I accepted his offer. In the meantime, Müller located a Jewish bed-and-breakfast hotel. I went there and the owners were very reserved toward me; they didn't believe I was Jewish and suspected me of being a spy. I told them about what had occurred in Dachau and the meeting with Joseph Müller. When I asked them whether they happened to be familiar with the name, they said he was a well-known jeweler in Munich. For that reason, they didn't believe what I had told them about him, and said I must be phantasizing. However, when Mr. Müller phoned me at their place and then picked me up with his car, the owners of the hotel didn't believe their own eyes. Yet from that point on they believed everything I had told them.

Meanwhile, I had contacted the party attorney; he had already spoken with the camp commander and was able to give me the hope that my request for the man's release would be granted on the third day. I was very depressed the entire time and very much on edge. Neither Joseph Müller nor all the others with whom I came into contact in Munich believed I was Jewish. This was a circumstance that helped to open a lot of doors for me back then. In order to help take my mind off these matters a bit, Mr. Müller invited me to have 5 o'clock tea with him in the Hotel Vierjahreszeiten. The place was packed with people from the SS and SA; I felt very uncomfortable but didn't let it show.

On the third day, I phoned Dachau myself, as the commander had ordered. To my enormous joy, he told me that I could pick up my father-in-law that evening at the Munich train station. I had let the commander mistakenly think that Mr. A was already my father-in-law and thanked him. When the train from Dachau rolled in, I saw emerge, among the other passengers, a tired, broken old man. Although I had never seen Mr. A before, I knew it couldn't be anyone else but him. His shaven head and anxious demeanor were the external signs marking an inmate. I went up to him, took him by the hand, told him who I was. To verify this, I showed him the two photos his wife had given me. He was very dazed and put up no resistance. I brought him across to the other platform, from which the trains left for Mannheim. While we were waiting for the train, I telephoned Mr. Müller and gave him the good news, thanking him for his assistance, which had facilitated matters so greatly. He himself regretted this brief good-bye over the phone, assuring me he was always ready to help me should I be in need.

It was very uncomfortable in the train to Mannheim. Most of the passengers were air force officers; they looked at Mr. A with contempt, made disparaging remarks about him, and would have preferred to throw him from the moving train. They asked me what business I had as a "German woman" being with this Jew, and I gave them no reply.[35]

35. Ruth Abraham, "Meine Erlebnisse während der nationalsozialistischen Zeit," manuscript, Leo Baeck Institute, New York.

Bureaucratic Postludes

For official reasons, many persons were obliged in the Third Reich to report to superior authorities about the November 1938 events: police officers, mayors, district heads (*Landräte*), local governors (*Regierungspräsidenten*) from the civil service sector, as well as functionaries of the NSDAP and its associated organizations. Of course, critical remarks could not have been expected from the latter; nonetheless, indirectly it was noted that the pogrom had not enjoyed the enthusiastic support of the entire population. A report from the district of Traunstein in Upper Bavaria stated:

> The mood, in view of the peaceful annexation of the Sudetenland into the Reich, is good. Basically then, it was impossible to darken that mood as a result of the action against the Jews. The farmers and middle class, especially the "black" conservatives, including even a party member, denounced the use of violence against the "chosen people." Such acts no longer had anything in common with culture, decency, and propriety. Yet there was likewise no lack of those who jumped to the defense of such actions. They criticized these self-appointed critics, proving to them that the burning synagogues and smashed windows, on the one hand, are only a modest vengeance compared with the damage inflicted by the Jews on the Germans (war, revolution, inflation, tyranny, and civil war) – yes, on the peoples of Europe. And that, on the other hand, here too, as in the Roman Catholic church, the end justifies the means, namely, that as a result of this, the hope is that Jews would lose any desire to stay on within the Reich.[36]

In contrast, the subdistrict propaganda office of the NSDAP in Eichstätt claimed that, in the "action against the Jews," "the people had been totally in the hands of the party" and that the population had unanimously approved of the "attack." However, the mood of the people was described as mixed in the monthly reports of the rural police stations in the district of Ebermannstadt in Upper Franconia. The destruction of Jewish businesses and synagogues, it was noted, had been welcomed

36. Monthly Political Report (Politischer Monatsbericht), NS Lehrerbund Kreis Traunstein, November 19, 1938, published in Martin Broszat, Elke Fröhlich, and Falk Wiesemann, eds., *Bayern in der NS-Zeit: Soziale Lage und politisches Verhalten der Bevölkerung im Spiegel vertraulicher Berichte* (Munich, 1977), pp. 470f.

by a portion of the populace, namely, "party stalwarts and younger people who had come up through the ranks of the Hitler Youth. In contrast, the majority of the population rejected the idea that it is permissible to destroy someone else's property without giving it a second thought."[37] Another rural police station reported:

In respect to the most recent action against the Jews, the populace has divided views. One segment of the people is of the opinion that the conscious actions and associated arrests and destruction were far too mild. The other segment of the population, by far larger, feels that all this destruction was uncalled for. In this connection, it appears worth noting that the question was repeatedly raised among the population as to whether those who took part in the action should be punished or not.[38]

Many such observations are included in the report of the administrative District Office in Ebermannstadt. The writer described the material damage in his district and mentioned special forms of enrichment, along the following lines: "Debtors forced their Jewish creditors, by threat of physical bodily harm, to sign prepared receipts for supposed payment of the debt. Yes, even the ownership of plots of land with buildings was transferred in this fashion, without payment." This correspondent also did not hesitate to report to his superiors – in this case, the *Regierungspräsident* of Upper and Central Franconia – that the conception of law among the population had been undermined and shaken by the pogrom. He opened the report in a businesslike manner with the sentence: "The most important topics of conversation were, and remain today, the reprisal measures against the Jews and the shortage of pork." He later went on to note:

From the standpoint of the police officers, I can add the following: the people can only permit the authorized organs of the state to carry out measures of reprisal against individual *Volksgenossen* who transgress against the people. Such organs are the authorities for criminal prosecution and the courts. The individual *Volksgenosse*, alone or

37. Monthly Report, Gendarmerie-Station Waischenfeld, November 25, 1938, ibid., p. 123.
38. Monthly Report, Gendarmerie-Station Muggendorf, November 26, 1938, ibid.

acting in unison with other *Volksgenossen*, is not so authorized. This is the reason for the strict regulations regarding punishment for the crime of aggravated breach of the peace. The authority of the police must necessarily suffer a heavy blow if it allows such a crime to occur without making an objection. Such a procedure is either judged to be partisan in nature or is viewed as an inability to ensure the maintenance of public tranquillity, order, and security. Justitia fundamentum regnorum![39]

On the level of the local administrative governors, reports were, at least in tone and style, in conformity with the expectations of the higher authorities. Thus, a report of the chief administrative office in Upper and Central Franconia noted the following:

The impudent provocation of world Jewry through the cowardly murder perpetrated in Paris provided an occasion for numerous teachers in the administrative district to terminate instruction in classes on religion as a result of their National Socialist views on the Jewish Question. During the course of the protest action in Wunsiedel, two Protestant ministers and four Catholic clergymen, who were regarded as Jewish stooges [*Judenknechte*], were brought through the angry crowds to the police post and held there in temporary custody. A number of windows were shattered in their parsonages.[40]

The administrative governor of Swabia also made use of the language and phraseology of the *Völkischer Beobachter* in his report:

The cowardly assassination of Legation Counsellor vom Rath awakened angry indignation in all quarters. Clear to all eyes, this murder underscored the world-historical importance of the Jewish Question and the necessity for an uncompromising solution, which had been emphasized repeatedly in the speeches of leading personalities, the propaganda work of the party, and other opinion-shaping media, such as the press and radio.

After such a vivid lesson, there was general understanding of the reactions of the people, in the form of demonstrations and actions against Jews and Jewish property, in particular synagogues, and the reactions of the national government in the form of new legislation,

39. Monthly Report, District Office Ebermannstadt, December 2, 1938, ibid., p. 124.
40. Monthly Report, December 8, 1938, ibid., p. 473.

in particular the ordinance on the atonement fine to be paid by German and stateless Jews and the move to exclude Jews from economic life. Moreover, the measures in economic policy came to enjoy the basic approval of ever more *Volksgenossen*, especially since the Jews were still permitted full development of their own cultural life.[41]

In other reports, the official phraseology was flexibly applied, but then attention was called to the fact that many citizens disapproved of the pogrom:

The Jewish murder of the German third secretary in the Paris Legation triggered angry indignation in all sections of the population. It was generally expected that the national government would take some action. For this reason, there was full appreciation of the legal measures instituted against the Jews. Yet the greater portion of the populace had far less understanding and sympathy for the manner in which the spontaneous action against the Jews had been implemented. Rather, that was censured by many, including numerous party members. The demolishing of display windows, of store contents, and of furniture in homes was viewed as unnecessary destruction of valuable property which, in the final analysis, constituted a loss for the wealth of the German nation [*das deutsche Volksvermögen*]. This destruction was in flagrant contradiction of the goals of the Four-Year Plan and in particular the just completed collection of used goods. The fear was also expressed that this could reawaken destructive impulses in the masses. Moreover, these events prompted an unneeded sense of sympathy for the Jews in towns and rural areas.[42]

A mild protest was even reported from Lower Franconia, in the form of a refusal to make contributions to the winter relief program of the NSV, which were solicited in connection with the so-called stew Sundays. This refusal by the rural population was prompted less by any sense of sympathy with the Jews than by a disapproval of the wanton vandalism against property and groceries:

The indignation over the cowardly Jewish murder of Secretary vom Rath led to anti-Jewish demonstrations throughout the entire

41. Monthly Report, Regierungspräsident, Swabia, December 7, 1938, ibid., p. 472.
42. Monthly Report, Regierungspräsident, Lower Bavaria and Upper Palatinate, December 8, 1938, ibid. p. 473.

administrative district during the night of November 9 to 10. Synagogues everywhere, as well as a number of Jewish shops and private apartments, fell victim to these demonstrations. There is general approval for the atonement measures introduced, especially the levying of a fine. A large segment of the population, particularly in rural areas, regrets that valuable goods were destroyed in these actions. In view of the situation regarding raw materials in the country, such material wealth could have been more effectively utilized for the good of the society as a whole.

A further criticism is that the action was continued even after the decree by the minister of propaganda ordering an immediate halt to it and that foodstuffs in particular were wantonly destroyed. Thus, for example, 350 kilos of flour were thrown onto a pile of manure and a box of eggs scattered in the street in Oberelsbach, in the Bad Neustadt (Saale) district. According to the report of the district administrative office, during the following Sunday stew collection, numerous citizens stated that after so much property had been uselessly destroyed, they found themselves unable to make a donation to the collection. Other administrative offices have also voiced apprehension regarding the willingness of the populace to contribute to the winter relief campaign.[43]

Although official reports are not the appropriate place for the expression of feelings, the degree of callousness with which Jewish victims killed as a result of the pogrom are mentioned is indeed striking. The regret over destroyed valuable property and goods was in all instances greater, and the opinion was frequently voiced that one could have resorted to less violent means in order to dispossess Jewish citizens, strip them of their civil rights, drive them out, and chase them abroad. In other respects, the attitude remained cool and composed, as reflected in the words of the mayor of Ingolstadt, who reported: "The action against the Jews was concluded swiftly and without any particular friction. Pursuant to this measure, a Jewish couple drowned themselves in the Danube."[44] Was that cynicism or savagery?

Whether it was a lack of political courage, cowardice, or pressure to conform, the fruit of propaganda or an agreement with National Socialist anti-Semitism, general disapproval of the

43. Monthly Report, Regierungspräsident, Lower Franconia, December 9, 1938, ibid.

44. Monthly Report, Mayor of Ingolstadt (Upper Bavaria), December 1, 1938, ibid., p. 471.

pogrom went hand in hand with looking the other way when personally confronted with Jewish misfortune. One final example can serve to illuminate this. Four weeks after the pogrom, a sixty-seven-year-old woman named Klara Dapper committed suicide by poison in Bayerisch Gmain near Bad Reichenhall in the Berchtesgadener Land of southeastern Bavaria. A widow since 1924, she had lived in seclusion in her house. During the night of December 10, unknown persons had affixed a note to her front door reading: "All Jews should leave, get out once and for all!" Mrs. Dapper, who had been living for some time in fear, committed suicide by taking an overdose of sleeping tablets. The police report commented laconically, "The town of Bayerisch Gmain is now clean of Jews [*judenfrei*]."[45]

This report had been a bit retouched: though the date of death, December 13, was correct, the cause of death was dated falsely. This was to hide the fact that Mrs. Dapper had lain in a coma fighting death for three days. The housemaid had found her unconscious on the morning of December 10 and had notified several doctors in nearby Bad Reichenhall, yet these physicians had refused to treat her. There was no legal regulation forbidding "Aryan doctors" from offering assistance in such a case, and they had all sworn the Hippocratic oath, which obligated them to assist. By the time a Jewish doctor was located, it was too late.

45. Monthly Report, Gendarmerie-Station Reichenhall, District Berchtesgaden (Upper Bavaria), December 29, 1938, ibid., p. 476.

The Background for Kristallnacht
The Expulsion of Polish Jews

Trude Maurer

My dearest ones!

You've probably already heard from Cilli about my fate. On October 27, Thursday evening at 9 P.M., two detectives came and demanded my passport. They then asked me to sign a deportation document and ordered me to go with them immediately. Cilli and Bernd were already in bed. I'd just finished my work and had sat down to have a meal, but I had to get dressed right away and then leave with them. I was so agitated I could hardly say anything. I'll never forget that moment as long as I live. Then they locked me up immediately in a cell in the castle prison – just like a common criminal.

That was a terrible night for me. Early Friday morning at 4 A.M. we were escorted under heavy SS and police guard to the main train station. Each of us was given a loaf of bread and some margarine, and we were loaded onto the train. It was a cruel spectacle to behold. Women and children sobbing, heartbreaking scenes. Then we were transported in sealed cars and under strictest police guard to the border.

After arriving at 5 A.M. Saturday at the border, we were deported across it. A new cruel spectacle met the eye here. We were compelled to spend three days crowded together on the station platform and in the halls, eight thousand people. Women and children fainted, went insane; people died, faces turned yellow like wax. A veritable cemetery of corpses.

I was also one of those who fainted. Nothing to eat but the dry prison bread and nothing to drink. Going without any sleep, two nights on the platform, one in the station hall, where I collapsed. There was no room left to stand. The air was foul, pestilential. Women and children half dead. The fourth day, relief finally arrived. Doctors, nurses with medical supplies, bread and butter from the Jewish Committee in Warsaw. Then we were brought to barracks (military cattle pens), that had been covered with straw we could lie down on. Finally a warm mouthful of tea, the joy of that.

The old man Fränkel, who had a furniture business, lay down in his grief on the tracks (dead), and there were four [other] cases of death. Finally, after eight days, portable goulash kitchens arrived from the Red Cross (hot food). I'm glad that Cilli isn't here with the kids, like families from some other towns, and can thank the Lord for that. Because you have to have nerves of steel to endure these hardships.[1]

This man, surprised by the police at a late evening hour in his home, had *personally* not given any cause to the authorities for arresting him. Otto Buchholz was one of approximately seventeen thousand Jews of Polish nationality who were rounded up in the German Reich for deportation on October 27 and 28, 1938. The objective was to transfer them, literally at the last minute, back across the border into the country whose citizenship they still possessed. Yet that was a country which was not a home for them and was attempting for its part to exclude them permanently. There had been repeated deportations of Polish Jews from Germany in the previous two decades, and Poland had frequently declined to accept these persons. Yet such deportations had always involved *individual cases* (even if their total numbers reached into the thousands), and each case had to be justified. In this instance, both sides were attempting to rid themselves of an entire *group* within the population in one fell swoop.

The Dilemma of Polish Jews in Weimar Germany

Jews from Eastern Europe had begun to emigrate to Germany as early as the seventeenth century, but a mass exodus did not start until after the pogroms in the Russian Empire in 1881, and its main destination remained the United States. Germany was principally a country of transit for the emigrants, yet a small portion of them – not only from Russia, but also from Austria-Hungary – stayed on and settled there. In 1910, they numbered

1. Letter from Otto Buchholz to his relatives, Zbąszyń, December 19, 1938, printed in Hans-Joachim Fliedner, *Die Judenverfolgung in Mannheim, 1933–1945*, vol. 2, *Dokumente*, Veröffentlichungen des Stadtarchivs Mannheim, vol. 2 (Mannheim, 1971), pp. 72–74, here 72f. For the correspondence of another family from Zbąszyń, see Jerzy Tomaszewski, "Letters from Zbaszyn," *Yad Vashem Studies* 19 (1988): 289–315.

Trude Maurer

some seventy thousand. Although the Kaiserreich had tried up until then to reduce the number of Eastern European Jews and deter further would-be immigrants by means of administrative measures[2] – particularly limitations on taking up permanent residence and mass deportations – in World War I it recruited workers in Poland, including Polish Jews, or even brought such workers by force to Germany. Some thirty thousand additional Eastern European Jews entered the Reich in this way. In April 1918, however, the border was closed to Eastern Jewish workers, the reason given being the danger that they might bring in typhoid fever; but a ban prohibiting entry only for Jews from the affected areas lacked any scientific foundation, even in terms of medical knowledge of the time.[3]

After the Revolution, a general entry ban was enforced along the eastern frontier, and it was only possible to enter the Reich on the basis of a special, limited visa obtainable after an investigation of the reasons for the requested entry. Despite this restriction, thousands more Jews came to Germany, especially in 1919 and 1920; they were fleeing from pogroms in the newly established Republic of Poland and the Ukraine and often lacked the necessary papers. Initially, because of the dangers faced by these refugees in their homeland, the German Reich tolerated them as long as they committed no offenses and Jewish organizations provided for their support. However, minor transgressions, the lack of a place to live or a job, often were sufficient reason for deportation.

Beginning in 1923 though, a basic regulation was instituted stating that no foreigners who had entered the country before 1914 should be deported from Prussia. This, as a rule, also applied to those foreigners who had lived continuously in the Reich for a period of at least four years and who had a secure income. Thus, after the initial first few years in which new immigrants had felt extremely threatened by the possibility of being deported, now even those who had violated regulations regarding entry and registration with the police could look

2. For further details see Jack L. Wertheimer, *Unwelcome Strangers: East European Jews in Imperial Germany* (New York and Oxford, 1987).
3. See Trude Maurer, "Medizinalpolizei und Antisemitismus: Die deutsche Politik der Grenzsperre gegen Ostjuden im Ersten Weltkrieg," *Jahrbücher für Geschichte Osteuropas* 33 (1985): 205–30.

forward to a relatively secure existence in Germany when it came to their status under the law.

In contrast, they could hardly count on any protection from Poland. After the collapse of the Austro-Hungarian and Russian Empires, the home areas of most Eastern European Jews had come under the control of the new Republic of Poland (in 1925, 50, 993 of the 107,747 Jewish foreigners in the Reich held Polish citizenship, some 47.3 percent). Yet in numerous cases, the Polish authorities refused to recognize the right to citizenship of those Jews affected. Poland often denied them a passport or engaged in a kind of blackmail when they applied for it: they were asked in return to purchase Polish state bonds or serve in the military.

Yet a foreigner in Germany who was not in possession of a valid passport violated German law. Often enough, the application for a passport was also utilized by the Polish consulates to begin formalities leading to a revocation of the applicant's citizenship. At most, Poland was prepared to represent the interests of Polish Jews vis-à-vis Germany in order to have additional argumentative ammunition in the German-Polish dispute in order to be able to make countercharges against Germany when German accusations were brought against Poland (for example, regarding the treatment accorded the German minority within its borders). Or, and this was especially the case when it came to deportations, Poland supported the notion that these Jews be allowed to remain in Germany, since they did not wish to see them return to Poland. For example, when Bavaria issued deportation orders against a large group of Eastern European Jews in October 1923, Poland in turn countered with the deportation of German citizens. Such a procedure was permissible under prevailing international law and was in general practice.[4]

The Jewish Experience in Interwar Poland

The state of Poland resurrected after World War I was obligated

---

4. On the Weimar period, see: Trude Maurer, *Ostjuden in Deutschland, 1918–1933*, Hamburger Beiträge zur Geschichte der deutschen Juden, vol. 12 (Hamburg 1986). For an English summary see Trude Maurer, "Between Expulsion and Integration: The Dilemma of East European Jews in Weimar Germany," *Tel Aviver Jahrbuch für deutsche Geschichte* 17 (1988): 193–207.

by the treaties on protection of minorities concluded at the Paris
Peace Conference to guarantee its national minorities equal civil
rights; in addition, such minorities had to be allowed to establish their own schools as well as religious, social, and charitable
institutions. The Jews, who in 1931 numbered 3.1 million and
constituted 9.8 percent of the population, suffered from social
and economic discrimination. For example, they were almost
totally barred from entering government service and from 1937
had also been excluded from various professional associations.
There was no formal legal quota for Jews at the universities, but
in actual practice such a quota was in effect, and Jewish students
had to sit on special chairs and benches. Jewish merchants and
businessmen were discriminated against in favor of Christian
bidders in the awarding of government contracts, and the Sunday closure laws aggravated their economic difficulties since
independent businessmen were thus compelled to close two
days a week. Moreover, firms with mixed Jewish and Christian
personnel no longer had any special reason to hire Jews.

Boycott initiatives and the creation of cooperatives were
aimed at rendering Jewish middlemen superfluous and forging
an ethnically Polish middle class. Although recent research has
served to refute the previously held notions about Jewish poverty and even suggests that the Jewish majority was better off
economically than most non-Jewish Poles, a salient fact remains:
the official policy of the government as well as the attitude of the
preponderant majority in Polish society was anti-Jewish in
orientation.

From 1936 on, the Polish government pursued the plan of
encouraging a mass emigration by Jews, a notion welcomed by
the majority of the populace. For this reason, the Polish government not only endorsed and supported Zionist efforts in Palestine, but also demanded mandates from the League of Nations
for colonies as well, in order to settle Polish Jews there. And in
1937 they even suggested Madagascar as a locale for Jewish
resettlement – as the Nazis were to do later on.[5] Yet an important point should not be overlooked: Poland also allowed the

5. On Jews in Poland in the interwar period, see Celia S[topnicka] Heller, *On
the Edge of Destruction: Jews of Poland between the Two World Wars* (New York,
1977); Joseph Marcus, *Social and Political History of the Jews in Poland, 1919–1939*,
New Babylon: Studies in Social Sciences, Vol. 37 (Berlin, New York, and
Amsterdam, 1983), with revision of thesis on pauperization.

Jewish minority in its borders ample freedom for cultural and political activity. "The experience of Polish Jews between the wars was a combination of suffering, some of which was caused by antisemitism, and of achievement made possible by Polish freedom, pluralism, and tolerance."[6]

The Treatment of Jewish Foreigners in Nazi Germany

The census of June 16, 1933, four-and-a-half months after the Nazis came to power, indicated there were still 98,747 Jews with foreign citizenship resident in the German Reich. Of these, 56,480 (57.2 percent) were Polish citizens. However, by this point in time, several thousand Eastern European Jews had already returned to their native countries in eastern and southeastern Europe.[7]

Government treatment of Eastern European Jews continued to be based on the various regulations laid down in legislation pertaining to aliens. These were generally stiffened and supplemented by special administrative instructions regarding Eastern European Jews. In accordance with an ordinance on foreign workers issued immediately *prior* to the Nazi takeover, the employer required a special permit to hire a foreign worker, while the worker himself was obliged to procure a work permit; that permit was valid only for the specific job in question. Foreigners who had already been working for a period of ten years could obtain a special permit (*Befreiungsschein*) valid for the

6. In Ezra Mendelsohn's enlightening examination of the different interpretational approaches, "Interwar Poland: Good for the Jews or Bad for the Jews?" in Chimen Abramsky, Maciej Jachimczyk, and Antony Polonsky, eds., *The Jews in Poland* (Oxford, 1986), pp. 130–39, quoted on pp. 138f. See also his more detailed exposition, Ezra Mendelsohn, *The Jews of East Central Europe between the World Wars* (Bloomington, 1983), pp. 11–81.

7. Exact statistics are not available. The Central Bureau for Jewish Migrant Relief (Hauptstelle für jüdische Wanderfürsorge), which provided aid for returning migrants, lists this activity area separately only from 1937 on. The total number of returning migrants is estimated at twenty-nine thousand for the period 1933–39, but peaked in 1933. See S[halom] Adler-Rudel, *Jüdische Selbsthilfe unter dem Nazi-Regime, 1933–1939, im Spiegel der Berichte der Reichsvertretung der Juden in Deutschland*, Schriftenreihe wissenschaftlicher Abhandlungen des Leo Baeck Instituts 29 (Tübingen, 1974), p. 216, see also pp. 95–97. According to *Der Morgen* 9 (1933–34): 332, some twelve to thirteen thousand Jews migrated from Germany back to eastern and southeastern European countries between February 1 and October 1, 1933.

entire territory of the Reich. Already in 1934, the director of the Reich Office for Job Procurement and Unemployment Insurance issued an instruction enjoining the granting of such special permits to foreign nationals who were Jewish. Traders required a permit or license as itinerant tradesmen. While in the case of German citizens, such a permit was valid for the entire Reich, its validity was restricted in the case of foreign nationals to the district in which it had been issued.

Although even according to the administration of justice in the Third Reich, the fact of being categorized as an alien or non-Aryan was insufficient grounds for an assumption of "unreliability" by the special commercial police, a court dealing with Eastern European Jews could proceed on the practical assumption of unreliability; in such cases, the court was permitted to demand proof of reliability from Eastern Jewish defendants, thus turning the judicial tables and placing the burden of establishing their innocence on them. Moreover, there is evidence that already, starting in the spring of 1933, some Jewish aliens were denied licenses to trade at fairs and open-air markets. In this way, they were stripped of their source of livelihood and were made dependent on welfare for survival. However, any alien who became permanently dependent on public welfare assistance was subject to being ordered to leave the country and, if he or she failed to comply, could then be forcibly deported. Beginning in 1933, a new practice was introduced: Eastern European Jews who had previously been in the possession of an unlimited residence visa were summoned by the police and were given new permits limiting their further stay to a period of from three to six months. In subsequent years, regulations were issued in various German states stipulating that foreign Jews seeking to relocate and take up residence there should in general not be granted a residence visa.

Legal regulations were tightened by a ruling that the deportation orders pertained to the Reich as a whole and not only to the constituent state where the foreigner resided, as before. In addition, protective options were reduced. Thus, for example, the 1932 regulation in the Prussian Police Code stipulating that aliens residing in the Reich for ten years or more should not be deported was revoked. In the case of Jews, even minor misdemeanors were a sufficient reason to order expulsion. In part, such deportations had the character of an organized campaign.

On the other hand, it was possible to note that leniency was occasionally applied in the execution of deportation orders. It is conceivable that implementation of these exportation orders was dependent on the state of foreign relations at the particular time and that thus the practice varied. On the one hand, the Jews' legal status as aliens subjected them to restrictions greater than those operative for German citizens; on the other hand, however, that status also opened the door to an option for greater protection. Foreign missions frequently intervened on behalf of their citizens – as evidenced inter alia by the diplomatic actions of the Polish mission after violent excesses against Polish Jews in March 1933 and again in 1935 – in order to obtain greater leniency in the use of the Foreign (i.e., visitors') Police.

Although the National Socialist government was in principle striving for the application of a similar approach to both German and foreign Jews, foreign-policy considerations played an important, mitigating role for a number of years. Thus, foreign Jews were exempted from the April 1933 boycott and were not required to pay the *Sühneleistung* ("atonement fine") for the damages resulting from the November 1938 pogrom; finally, they were even exempted from the decree on the forcible closing of Jewish retail shops issued on December 31, 1938. Anti-Jewish legislation was not extended in its entirety to foreign Jews until 1942–43.

Stateless persons were worse off than foreign nationals. All rules and regulations pertaining to aliens also applied to them; however, in their case, the principle of reciprocity was not applicable, that is, that Germany granted a foreigner those benefits that a German citizen was entitled to in the foreigner's country, such as social security insurance or school fees. Above all else, though, their situation was aggravated by the basic fact that they had no government to intervene on behalf of their interests. Thus stateless Jews were subject to the same legislation as German Jews.

In July 1933, one of the first laws of the National Socialist regime directed against the Jewish population raised the possibility of revoking all naturalizations that had been carried out during the Weimar Republic. The ordinance on implementation made specific mention of the Eastern European Jews as the principal target group for the law. That law almost exclusively affected those persons who had been resident for several decades in

Germany because they were the only foreigners who had had the legal opportunity to qualify and become naturalized citizens. Since as a rule they were unable to regain their former citizenship, they were made stateless by revocation of their German citizenship. Such stateless persons were unable to return to their homeland, and the emigration options open to them were severely restricted since most countries only allowed in those foreigners whom, if necessity arose, they could deport back to their countries of origin. Ironically enough, by the immediate realization of the oft-repeated demand by the Nazis during the Weimar Republic that naturalized foreigners should be stripped of their German citizenship, the National Socialists themselves created a major obstacle to the policy of encouraging Jewish emigration, at least for the stateless: this, after all, was one of the main objectives of anti-Jewish policy in the initial years of Nazi rule.[8]

Poland's Expatriation Plan and Germany's Response

The prospect that Germany would suddenly have to accommodate an additional and even larger group of stateless Jews arose as a consequence of the Polish law dated March 31, 1938, on "revocation of citizenship." According to this law, a person living abroad could be stripped of his/her Polish citizenship if that person (a) had acted to the detriment of the Polish state there, or (b) had lost all ties to Poland as a result of an uninterrupted stay abroad of five or more years, or (c) had not returned to Poland by the stipulated deadline after having been summoned to do so by a Polish government office. The expatriation order was executed by the Interior Ministry at the request of the foreign minister, did not need any justification, and could be implemented immediately.[9]

The occasion for passage of this law, which cleared both chambers of Parliament, the Sejm and the Senate, within a few

8. See Trude Maurer, "Ausländische Juden in Deutschland, 1933–1939," in: Arnold Paucker et al., eds., *Die Juden im Nationalsozialistischen Deutschland, 1933–1943,* Schriftenreihe wissenschaftlicher Abhandlungen des Leo Baeck Instituts 45 (Tübingen, 1986), pp. 189–210.

9. Text in *Dziennik Ustaw Rzeczypospolitej Polskiej* [Legal Gazette of the Polish Republic], 1938, I, No. 22, Poz. 191, p. 340. Shortened, paraphrased German version (therefore incorrect in Art. 5) published in *Jüdisches Gemeindeblatt Leipzig*

days, was the Anschluß of Austria by the German Reich. Poland now feared that the approximately twenty thousand Polish citizens living in Austria would return to Poland in order to escape German anti-Jewish measures. This attitude was communicated later on by the deputy foreign minister Szembek to the French ambassador. Moreover, it had already been evident in the remarks made by the official reporter in the Polish Parliament.[10] Up until passage of the law, only five hundred Jews were granted entry visas from Austria to Poland, in accordance with instructions by Prime Minister Sławoj-Składkowski.[11]

During a conference of various institutions held at Gestapo headquarters on April 21, 1938, there was clear recognition of the problems posed by this legislation for the German Reich. The argument can be summarized as follows: if Polish Jews are made stateless, it will be difficult to force them to emigrate because no country will accept them when even Poland refuses to do so. However, if they are compelled now by the German authorities to return to Poland immediately, then Poland might, as a reciprocal move, deport German citizens resident there. Thus, the only option would be to obtain assurances from the Polish government that it would also accept expatriated Polish Jews if Germany should so demand. But the Polish deputy foreign minister did not wish to agree to such a formal obliga-

---

14 (1938), no. 17, April 29, 1938, p. 2, reprinted in Adolf Diamant, *Chronik der Juden in Dresden: Von den ersten Juden bis zur Blüte der Gemeinde und deren Ausrottung* (Darmstadt, 1973), p. 355.

10. Eliahu Ben Elissar, *La diplomatie du IIIe Reich et les Juifs* ([Paris], 1969), p. 303. Ben Elissar presents the fundamental analysis (pp. 301–21) of German and Polish measures and conflicts in respect to the deportation of Polish Jews from Germany.

11. Emanuel Melzer, "Relations between Poland and Germany and Their Impact on the Jewish Problem in Poland (1935–1938)," *Yad Vashem Studies* 12 (1977): 193–229, here 217. Melzer's presentation is an important supplement to that by Ben Elissar, especially in respect to Polish behavior toward the deportees. The deportation action is also described in: H[ans] G[ünther] Adler, *Der verwaltete Mensch: Studien zur Deportation der Juden aus Deutschland* (Tübingen, 1974), pp. 91–105. A short survey is presented by [Helmut] Heiber, "Die Ausweisung von Juden polnischer Staatsangehörigkeit im Oktober 1938," *Gutachten des Instituts für Zeitgeschichte* 1 (Munich, 1958): 90–93. For sources on German agencies, foreign diplomatic legations, Jewish relief organizations, and personal testimony by persons affected, with commentary and informative introduction, see Sybil Milton, "Menschen zwischen Grenzen: Die Polenausweisung 1938," *Menora: Jahrbuch für deutsch-jüdische Geschichte* (1990): 184–206; idem, "The Expulsion of Polish Jews from Germany October 1938 to July 1939: A Documentation," *YLBI* 29 (1984): 169–199.

tion, despite all efforts to allay the fears of the German ambassador in Warsaw, von Moltke, who made representations in this matter on May 24.

The official note came one month later. At the same time, von Moltke learned from a confidential source that Polish officials who had requisitioned the passports of Polish Jews living in Poland had no intention of returning those passports to their holders. Already in May of that year, the Reich Interior Ministry had issued instructions not to extend the residence permits of Polish Jews.[12] In August, the interior minister announced new comprehensive regulations dealing with foreigners. Now residence was to be granted only to those foreigners "who, in terms of character and the purpose of their visit to the Reich, could guarantee that they were deserving of the hospitality granted to them." It was possible to forbid residence to a foreign national who did not fulfill these requirements. A confidential service directive stipulated that Jews should be regarded as "undeserving" in the sense of the ordinance. Another new regulation was that the residence permit would expire if the foreigner changed or lost his citizenship, an obvious reaction to the Polish law on expatriation. According to this new ordinance, implementation of deportation was no longer dependent on the willingness of a foreign country to accept the person deported.[13] In a further conference at Gestapo headquarters on September 20, it was decided that Polish Jews could be deported even for the most minor infractions, such as a traffic violation. In addition, through a step-up in persecution measures, Polish Jews should now be brought to the point where they would "voluntarily" leave the German Reich.[14]

On October 6, 1938, the Polish interior minister announced a new ordinance for a onetime check of all passports issued by Polish legations abroad. It was to go into effect on October 30, two weeks after official publication on October 15. All passports had to be presented to the authorities and would receive a special stamp. That stamp could be denied if there were doubts

12. According to Ben Elissar, *La diplomatie du IIIe Reich*, pp. 304f.
13. RGBl, 1938 I, pp. 1053–56, quotation on p. 1053. The reference to the secret service directive is found in Peter Hanke, *Zur Geschichte der Juden in München zwischen 1933 und 1945*, Schriftenreihe des Stadtarchivs München, Heft 3 (Munich, 1967) pp. 209f. Reference to the connection with Polish law can already be found in Adler, *Der verwaltete Mensch*, p. 93.
14. Ben Elissar, *La diplomatie du IIIe Reich*, p. 305.

as to the genuineness or validity of the passport or if there were circumstances justifying a revocation of citizenship. Passports lacking this special stamp would not be valid for "crossing the border of the Polish state," that is, for entry into Poland.[15]

As the American Embassy in Warsaw learned from an official of the Polish Foreign Ministry, this ordinance was principally aimed at preventing a general deportation of Polish Jews from Germany.[16] The German side was also quite clear about this after receiving the report about the ordinance on October 18. On October 26, the head of the legal section of the Foreign Office telephoned an order to the German Embassy in Warsaw. Among other things, that order stated: "Jews with Polish citizenship in Germany are therefore, as a precautionary measure, to be expelled from Germany at very short notice. The German government would only refrain from carrying out these instructions if the Polish side were for its part to refrain from implementing its ordinance of October 6, 1938, in the territory of the Reich," or if "it gave a binding declaration that Poland obligated itself to accept holders of Polish passports without the new official stamp."[17]

On October 27, the Polish Foreign Ministry replied that all that was involved was "the checking of passports held exclusively by persons who, on their own initiative, apply to the authorities for the purpose of entry into the country across the border of the Republic of Poland." The ministry did not expect that "such applications, and the related checking of passports, would acquire a mass character." The ministry then referred to earlier interventions by Polish legations abroad in order to protect Polish citizens "from the consequences of legislation of the German Reich, which is legally binding for German citizens of Jewish extraction." But such efforts had not proved successful. "Without concealing that the Polish government does not wish for large numbers of persons to return to Poland who have lost their property as a result of the orders of the German government and have been rendered destitute," the Polish Foreign Ministry expressed its readiness to engage in talks aimed at "clarifying the material situation" of these individuals

---

15. Text in: *Dziennik Ustaw*, 1938, II, No. 80, Poz. 543, p. 1231.

16. Report of the American Ambassador, November 5, 1938, published in Milton, "The Expulsion of Polish Jews," pp. 183–86, here 184.

17. *ADAP*, D 5, no. 84, p. 93.

and "resolving the problem as a whole."[18]

In fact, the German government had not expected the Poles to be accommodating, and the Reichsführer SS and Chief of German Police Himmler had already instructed subordinate authorities in two successive teletype communications on October 26, "after coordination with the Foreign Office,"[19] to act as follows:

> Using the full force of the Security Police and Regular Police and setting aside other tasks, all Polish Jews in the possession of valid passports are to be taken into custody immediately for the purpose of deportation, while announcing formal prohibition on residence for these persons anywhere in the territory of the Reich. They are to be taken in a group transport and deported without delay over the Polish border. The collective transports are to be carried out in such a way that their transfer across the Polish border can be completed on or before October 29, 1938. As large a number as possible of Polish Jews, especially adult males, must be successfully transferred across the frontier to Poland before the deadline mentioned.[20]

Deportation and Life in the Internment Camps

The Buchholz letter quoted at the beginning of this paper provides an excellent description of what then occurred. That letter, like almost all reports made by those persons immediately affected, indicates that this action, whose prehistory we have just reconstructed, caught Polish Jews in Germany unawares and unprepared. The move was a total surprise for them. Certainly, "after the announcement of the new Ordinance on Foreign Police, . . . foreign Jews living in the Reich had to consider" how long they might still be counted in the group of

18. *ADAP*, D 5, no. 88, p. 97.

19. Express Letter, Reichsführer SS, October 26, 1938, in Kommission zur Erforschung der Geschichte der Frankfurter Juden, ed., *Dokumente zur Geschichte der Frankfurter Juden, 1933–1945* (Frankfurt, 1963), p. 422.

20. [Second] Express Letter, Reichsführer SS, October 26, 1938, in *Dokumente zur Geschichte der Frankfurter Juden*, pp. 422f. For examples of deportation orders, see Paul Sauer, comp., *Dokumente über die Verfolgung jüdischer Bürger in Baden-Württemberg durch das nationalsozialistische Regime, 1933–1945* (Stuttgart, 1966), vol. 2, pp. 11f. (Esslingen); Regina Bruss, *Die Bremer Juden unter dem Nationalsozialismus*, Veröffentlichungen aus dem Staatsarchiv der Freien Hansestadt Bremen 49 (Bremen, 1983), p. 220.

those "deserving of" German hospitality.[21] Yet even when they learned about the specifics of this ordinance, for example, from Jewish newspapers,[22] the question remained: Should they, after having lived for decades in Germany, now reckon with sudden deportation? Almost 40 percent of Jewish foreign nationals in Germany in 1933 had been born in the Reich.

Yet even if they had recognized the imminent danger, what could they possibly have done in those few weeks up until the deportation action? Should they have abandoned their jobs or businesses and have fled to Poland, where they were only second-class citizens and where most of them hardly had any remaining ties? Moreover, had not emigration to a third country become difficult even for German Jews, who constituted the immediate object of anti-Jewish legislation, as demonstrated by the recent International Conference on the Refugee Question held in Evian in June 1938? At Evian, representatives of the thirty-two participating countries asserted their sympathy for the victims of persecution, though at the same time making clear that the difficult economic and social situation in their country did not permit any increase in quotas for immigration.

In Berlin some persons, especially those active in the Association of Polish Jews (Verband der polnischen Juden), saw developments differently and with greater clarity. Spokespersons at the Interior and Foreign Ministries had initially assured one of the leaders of the association, who was repeatedly in Warsaw on business and had contacts there with government officials via Jewish representatives in the Sejm and Senate, that the new regulations were not directed against Jews; rather, they were aimed at Communists, especially those of Ukrainian nationality from East Galicia. Nonetheless, the Polish consul in Berlin openly admitted in private conversations that his government did not desire any "immigration" by Jews.[23] Yet even in Berlin, when rumors about a possible deportation of Polish Jews began

---

21. Helmut Heiber, "Der Fall Grünspan," *VfZ* 5 (1957): 134–72, here p. 137.
22. See, for example, *Jüdische Rundschau* 43, no. 70 (September 2, 1938): 4.
23. Report, Zigmund Glicksohn, Tel Aviv, September 1944, YVA, 01/7, p. 1. The Association of Eastern European Jews (Verband der Ostjuden), founded in 1919 and renamed Verband der polnischen Juden in the Third Reich, was required at the insistence of the Polish Consulate to exclude stateless members, see Maurer, *Ostjuden in Deutschland*, pp. 681–708 and Maurer, "Ausländische Juden," pp. 207–10.

to spread in September 1938, they were initially given no credence.[24]

The deportation action did not begin everywhere at the same time: in many cities, it commenced the evening of October 27; in others, the roundup did not get underway until the morning hours of October 28. The upshot was, for example, that Jews in Leipzig were forewarned by Jews in Halle, so that only some 50 percent of the Polish Jews in Leipzig were deported, while the figure in Dresden approached 90 percent and reached 78 percent in Chemnitz.[25] In Berlin, Rabbi Freier had learned of the impending action during the night of October 27–28 and was able to warn several persons who lived nearby. In some cases, those who had been affected informed their friends. Due to later developments, "whoever happened not to be seized on that specific day . . . remained unmolested."[26] Himmler had ordered deportation "especially [of] adult males." Such an approach promised the chance of achieving the greatest effect, given the limit on available time until the anticipated closing of the Polish border: one could assume that the father of a family would be followed, in one way or another, by his wife and children, if only for reasons of material distress.[27]

The deportation was handled differently depending on locale: in Württemberg, entire families were deported; in Baden, as a rule, only males were taken; in Saxony, women and children (who in some instances even made up the majority) were generally deported too, and this was also true in Hamburg, Frankfurt, and Munich.[28] While Otto Buchholz was happy that his wife

---

24. Report, Anni Nieder, Tel Aviv, August 1944, YVA 01/15, p. 1.

25. Saxon Interior Minister to Reichsführer SS, November 1, 1938, in Diamant, *Chronik der Juden*, pp. 367f. Cf. also the documents on the dispute between the Gestapo and police headquarters in Leipzig regarding responsibility for the late start of the action, in Diamant, pp. 369f., 372, 375f.

26. Report, Nieder, YVA 01/15, p. 1, quote on p. 2. See also Rabbi N. Wahrmann, as rabbi in Oels from 1929 to 1939, April 4, 1960, YVA 01/270, p. 2. Wahrmann taught at the Jewish Theological Seminary in Breslau and was there that day. By the time he returned to Oels, the action was already over.

27. Ben Elissar, *La diplomatie du IIIe Reich*, p. 307.

28. For Baden and Württemberg, see Paul Sauer, *Die Schicksale der jüdischen Bürger Baden-Württembergs während der nationalsozialistischen Verfolgungszeit, 1933–1945* (Stuttgart, 1969), p. 251. For Saxony, see Diamant, pp. 357, 359, 362, 366 (majority). For Hamburg, see Report by the Couple Rosa Friedfertig and Koppel Friedfertig, Tel Aviv, November 1944, YVA 01/35, pp. 1f. For Frankfurt, see Report, Dr. Hans Pomeranz, Tel Aviv, January 11, 1960, YVA 01/275, p. 10. On Munich, see Hanke, *Juden in München*, p. 210.

and children had been spared this cruel action, others thought its special harshness was perhaps precisely the fact that it had brought about the separation of families. In some cases, that separation was a product of events, where family members were taken from different localities in Germany to different border crossings and thus were subsequently interned in different camps.[29]

The actual arrest proceeded in quite a different manner, depending on the behavior of the individual police officers and possibly also on the fact that they came from different police units. Thus, one of those seized reported that he was told by Gestapo officials that he was being sent to Palestine,[30] a form of ridicule thoroughly in keeping with National Socialist propaganda, which even utilized such means as deceptively genuine-looking tickets marked "Jerusalem, oneway." In another instance, officers took their time, allowing the person "to get dressed without a rush and say prayers and then coming back ten minutes later"; they also decided to leave without taking along the man's wife, even though they could have demanded that she go with them.[31] In Bochum, one of the guards offered an automobile to the persons sent by the Jewish community to assist in order that they could transport the steaming pot of hot food they had brought.[32] At stations where the train stopped during the transport to the Polish border, a number of police officers got water for the deportees, who were in sealed trains, while first-aid attendants accompanying the transport refused to assist. According to a young reporter, officers of the Regular Police in particular behaved in a very decent manner; in contrast, the SS men seemed to him to be simply criminals.[33]

During the waiting period at the assembly points, those taken into custody received very little to eat from the police in some instances. However, their rations were later described for propaganda purposes with such verve and detail (as in the case of Hanover) that they conveyed the "impression that people

---

29. Milton, "The Expulsion of Polish Jews," p. 170.
30. Letter, Julius Rosenzweig to His Sister, August 19, 1939, ibid., pp. 175–81, here 176.
31. Report by Friedfertig, YVA 01/35, p. 1.
32. Report by Ottilie Schönewald, in Rita Thalmann and Emmanuel Feinermann, *Die Reichskristallnacht* (Frankfurt, 1987), pp. 32–37, here 33.
33. Letter by Rosenzweig, Milton, "The Expulsion of Polish Jews," pp. 177f.

had gone on a quite happy vacation trip."[34] They generally had been asked to take along enough food for two days. In addition, they were allowed the amount of ten reichsmarks, the maximum legal limit at that time for the export of German currency.[35] In reality, it was the Jewish *Gemeinden* which furnished provisions for those deported at the assembly points – in jails or large dance halls – and at the intermediate stops all the way to the border. Thus, it was probably not unusual that "the entire community" literally "competed" in order to furnish these unfortunate souls with articles that could make the trip easier;[36] in some places, especially prudent Jews had also arranged for power-of-attorney papers in order that relatives, friends, or the Jewish *Gemeinde* could take care of business matters for those deported.[37]

Solidarity in a time of need becomes especially clear when viewed from the perspective of a convinced Zionist since the Zionists, though with little justification, had always accused the majority of the German Jews of having disassociated themselves from the Eastern European Jews in their midst: "On that day, all contrasts and social differences vanished completely. . . . Even the assimilated circles, at that time especially associated with the Reich League of Jewish Combat Veterans (Reichsbund jüdischer Frontsoldaten), understood that this was a dress rehearsal for scenes to come."[38]

The platforms from which the special trains departed were cordoned off, though it is not clear whether this was universally the case. Other passengers and railroad workers were kept at a distance. Nonetheless, there were spectators who mocked those

---

34. Heiber, *Fall Grünspan*, p. 138. In contrast, cf. the statement by Sendel Grynszpan on the situation in Hanover in 1961 in "Eichmann-Prozeß in Jerusalem," in Thalmann and Feinermann, *Reichskristallnacht*, pp. 43–45. On the minimal catering by police, see Diamant, *Chronik der Juden*, pp. 362, 400 and the letter by Buchholz, Fliedner, *Judenverfolgung in Mannheim*, pp. 72–74.

35. Milton, "The Expulsion of Polish Jews," p. 170; Hanke, *Juden in München*, p. 210.

36. Recollections, Head of Munich Community, quoted in Hanke, *Juden in München*, p. 210.

37. Cf. the reports by Schönewald, in Thalmann and Feinermann, *Reichskristallnacht*, p. 34: "The trust in the effectiveness of German conceptions of law and business practices was still very great." On the assistance provided by Jewish *Gemeinden*, see Heiber, "Fall Grünspan," p. 137 (Hanover); Letter by Rosenzweig, Milton, "The Expulsion of Polish Jews," p. 178 (Beuthen), 180 (Kattowitz); Report by Friedfertig, YVA 01/35, p. 1 (Hamburg).

38. Witness Report by Pomeranz, YVA 01/275, p. 10.

to be shipped away.[39] Only after they were on the train and moving were many of the deportees presented with the deportation ruling, though this had been the actual legal basis for their arrest.[40] The transports were initially accompanied by local or regional police; at a later point, for example in Upper Silesia, the local police took over from them. The strength of the accompanying force is given in one case as 59 police officers and 16 medical attendants for a total of 482 deportees; in another case, 61 police officers are reported for a group of 724 deportees. However, in some instances there were only 16 to 17 guards for a total of some 400 persons in custody.[41] The chief of police in Leipzig reported to the interior minister: "Basically, the transport went off quite smoothly without any special incidents, aside from one death (female), some cases of fainting, and several nervous breakdowns."[42] On the most important deportation route (Berlin-Posen), the last seven kilometers to the border station Zbąszyń had to be traversed on foot. If someone was unable to carry his baggage or straggled on behind, the baggage was taken away and disposed of. "Whoever didn't keep up with the rest was beaten."[43]

At the Polish border crossings, the first transports that arrived were allowed through into Poland, but then entry was denied. A shocking report describes how deportees were herded by the SS down into the river forming the border at that point and then were pursued by Polish border guards. After the Jews wandered about for hours, a dispute finally erupted between the Polish guards and the SS about the question of where these people should go.[44] The following account describes another transport:

On the Polish side, there was a single guard armed with a rusty rifle. He refused to let anyone through. Yet the Germans pushed us from behind, saying, "You're not going to let just one man stop you, are

39. Report, Reichsbahn Station Hanover (closure) and Report of Schönewald (derision), both in Thalmann and Feinermann, *Reichskristallnacht*, pp. 36, 38; Letter by Rosenberg (closure), Milton, "The Expulsion of Polish Jews," p. 177. Cf. also Grynszpan's 1961 statement: "The streets of Hanover were full of people shouting 'Palestine!'" Thalmann and Feinermann, p. 44.
40. Report, Dresden Chief of Police, Dresden, to Saxon Interior Minister, facsimile in Diamant, *Chronik der Juden*, pp. 363f.
41. Examples in Diamant, *Chronik der Juden*, pp. 362, 363, 373.
42. Extract in ibid., p. 365.
43. Report by Friedfertig, YVA 01/35, p. 2.
44. Letter by Rosenzweig, Milton, "The Expulsion of Polish Jews," p. 179.

you!" Finally, a few younger men formed a chain, went underneath the barrier, and called to the Poles [!], "Hey, start shooting at us." On the Polish side a few shots were fired into the air, but since the crowd was pushing and the barrier had already been lifted, the entire train finally entered into Polish territory.[45]

According to documents from the Foreign Office, the Poles even mounted machine guns and laid down barbed-wire barriers. Even threats to open fire on those camping in the no-man's-land between the two frontiers are mentioned.[46]

While the first arrivals were allowed to travel on into Poland, later deportees who reached the frontier were interned in settlements at the border. The best known of these was Zbąszyń; others were Chojnice and Drawski Mlyn, the latter of which was exclusively for male internees.[47] If they had money, that is, if they had brought some cash along in violation of regulations and had not been caught during the body searches, the detained deportees were allowed to rent rooms in Zbąszyń.[48] But of course, a barrier prevented them from leaving Zbąszyń. The others were housed in military barracks and former horse stables. Initially, all basic prerequisites for providing for the needs of the deportees were lacking. The state of hygiene was catastrophic. Yet within a short period of time, a functioning "town" came into being, with workshops, stores, a welfare office, arbitration court, cleaning services, its own police force, language courses, and a library. All this was created through the common efforts of a Jewish Relief Committee established in Warsaw during the first few days of the deportation action and the internees. Five hundred internees were thus given employment. At various times, there were between five and eight thousand persons living in the Zbąszyń camp, which was not dissolved until July 1939.[49] The problems created by crowded

45. Report by Friedfertig, YVA 01/35, p. 2.

46. Notes of Amtsrat Gerste, September 11, 1938, ADAP, D 5 No. 98, pp. 103f; other notes on the threat of fire summarized in p. 104, n. 1.

47. On Drawski Mlyn, see the Report by Israel Bleyberg, January 1957, YVA 01/169.

48. Report by Friedfertig, YVA 01/35, p. 1.

49. See Milton, "The Expulsion of Polish Jews," p. 171; Ben Elissar, *La diplomatie du III*e *Reich*, p. 320; Melzer, "Relations between Poland and Germany," p. 224 and the letter by the historian Emmanuel Ringelblum, known especially for his Warsaw diary and ghetto archives, to Raphael Mahler, Decem-

conditions can be easily imagined.[50]

The relief work was carried out almost exclusively by the local Jewish population, but was financially heavily dependent on foreign Jewish organizations, especially the American Joint Distribution Committee (JDC). Its Warsaw representative, Isaac Gitermann, also reported, with some surprise, that the expellees were able to move freely around the town of Kattowitz, which he considered to be very anti-Semitic, without being accosted and that they were even given presents by a few Christian Poles. The Voivode of Silesia had done much to arrange transportation out of the border area, and even in Zbąszyń, the local population had followed the fate of the deportees with great sympathetic interest.[51] In contrast, the Polish government had not granted any assistance, and Gitermann suspected that it wanted to use this occasion to push for Jewish emigration from Poland.[52] In actual fact, its diplomatic representatives in Washington, London, and The Hague lodged formal complaints, stating that this matter would have to be resolved before the general question of Jewish refugees from Germany could be dealt with. If the Polish-Jewish problem could not be resolved immediately, it was likely there would be pogroms in Poland.[53] However, on December 2, 1938, the Intergovernmental Committee set up in Evian rejected a request that the Polish government be allowed to present and transfer this deportation matter to the committee.[54]

---

ber 6, 1938, printed in Milton, "The Expulsion of Polish Jews," pp. 190f. (Ringelblum worked in Zbąszyń for five weeks).

50. See also numerous reports on this, especially those from the English press sent by special correspondents at the camp, in the press clippings section of the Wiener Library, Tel Aviv, PC 4/30d and PC 4/33d.

51. See extracts from his report in Milton, "The Expulsion of Polish Jews," pp. 192–95.

52. Letter by Ringelblum, Milton, "The Expulsion of Polish Jews," p. 191; Gitermann, according to Melzer, "Relations between Poland and Germany," p. 225.

53. Notes on a conversation between Karl-Heinz Abshagen and the head of the Europe section at the State Department, Robert Pell, printed in Milton, "Expulsion of Polish Jews," pp. 189f. Cf. also Ben Elissar, *La diplomatie du IIIe Reich*, pp. 315f.

54. Ben Elissar, *La diplomatie du IIIe Reich*, p. 317.

Polish-German Negotiations and Settlement of the Repatriation Question

In the meantime, the deportation action had been halted. On the afternoon of October 29, Poland had ordered the deportation of German citizens from Posen and the voivodship of Pomerania. But after the German declaration that the deportation of Aryan citizens of the Reich would only aggravate the conflict, Poland restricted its actions to bringing German Jews to the border. The German precondition for negotiations, namely, an extension of the deadline for checking of passports to November 15, had already been accepted by Poland the day before, on October 28.[55] However, the Polish ambassador instructed the Polish consular authorities in Germany to the effect that only in rare cases should they issue an official stamp to Jewish passport holders after checking their documents and that, after November 15, they should take energetic steps to arrange for expatriation.[56]

The deportation action was subsequently terminated on October 29 after even the Gestapo had declared conditions at the border to be "intolerable," and Poland and Germany had agreed to refrain from any further deportation of their respective citizens and to embark upon negotiations the following week. Those deportees already on Polish territory remained initially where they were, while the others, still at the frontier, were permitted to return to Germany. The suggestion by a lower-level Gestapo representative that these persons should be placed in concentration camps was flatly rejected by both the Gestapo and the Foreign Office.[57]

When negotiations opened on November 2, 1938, Germany renewed its demand that all Polish Jews be sent back to Poland.[58] In an effort to relieve the tense situation, Undersecretary von Weizsäcker assured Polish Ambassador Lipski the following day

---

55. Ibid., pp. 308–10; Adler, *Der verwaltete Mensch*, p. 95.

56. Lipski, Polish ambassador in Berlin to Polish Foreign Minister Beck, November 12, 1938, in: Wcław Jędrzejewicz, ed., *Diplomat in Berlin, 1933–1939: Papers and Memoirs of Józef Lipski, Ambassador of Poland* (New York and London, 1968), pp. 462–65, here 464.

57. On this summary, cf. Reichsführer SS to Chief, Reich Chancellery, October 29, 1938, and the remark of the head of the Political Section, Foreign Office, October 29, 1938, both in *ADAP*, D 5, nos. 91–92, pp. 98f., 100f.

58. Ben Elissar, *La diplomatie du IIIe Reich*, p. 311.

that it would have been possible to avoid this entire action by means of a dialogue between them had Lipski not happened to have been absent from Berlin the end of October. However, von Weizsäcker continued to insist that Germany could not accept "that by way of expatriation, we were being saddled with a mass of 40,000–50,000 [!] stateless former Polish Jews." He was unable to understand how the "taking over of Polish property," which these Jews in fact were, could constitute a sacrifice for Poland.[59] On November 8, the Reichsführer SS prohibited "the deportation of Jews to Poland until further notice, due to the technical difficulties involved."[60]

An agreement in the German-Polish negotiations began to take shape. According to this compromise, Poland had to retain those deportees already on its territory and allow them to be joined by their wives and children. Germany, in turn, declared it was ready to permit deportees to reenter the country for a brief period to put their personal affairs in order. Yet while the Foreign Office was ready to put its signature on the agreement even though not all of the objectives desired by Germany had been achieved, the Gestapo representatives refused to sign without Hitler's express consent. Hitler had been upset about the halt of the deportation action and had an even more critical view of the agreement with Poland.[61] The negotiations were then suspended on November 10 after the assassination of a German diplomat in Paris by a young Polish Jew and were not resumed until December 17.[62] The added time was also a useful respite for Germany since there was still no list of Polish Jews resident in the Reich nor was their total number known. When that was finally established to be only thirteen thousand, the gap between the German and Polish positions narrowed.

59. Notes by von Weizsäcker, November 3, 1938, and November 8, 1938 (quote), facsimile in John Mendelsohn ed., *The Holocaust*, vol. 3: *The Crystal Night Pogrom* (New York and London, 1982), pp. 13, 14f. The second also in *ADAP*, D 5, no. 95, p. 102.

60. Reichsführer SS to HSSPF (Higher Police and SS Leaders), November 8, 1938, YVA 05/111.

61. Ben Elissar, *La diplomatie du IIIe Reich*, pp. 312f. Compare also following documents: Record of a telephone call to Spitz, November 11, 1938, *ADAP*, D 5, no. 97, p. 103. Discussion of the Jewish Question chaired by Field Marshal Göring, November 12, 1938, in *IMT*, vol. 28, pp. 499–540, here 522f.

62. On the reasons for Poland's "sudden patience," see Ben Elissar, *La diplomatie du IIIe Reich*, p. 315.

Finally, on January 24, 1939, an agreement was reached. The German government permitted the temporary return of deportees, but no more than one thousand were to be allowed to be within the German borders at any one time. All had to return to Poland by the final deadline of July 31, 1939. The deportees were authorized to send their furniture, personal effects, and professional equipment back to Poland. Their capital and assets from liquidation had to be paid into a special account with the German Foreign Exchange Bank. Initially, further modalities remained open. Permission to export capital would have constituted a precedent which the countries of immigration and the Evian committee could have utilized to their benefit.

Poland accepted the obligation to permit the wives and children of deportees to enter without any time restriction.[63] In the implementation regulations for the police, it was stated that all wives and children who had remained behind in Germany were to be registered immediately using special personal data sheets and that the residence prohibition pertaining to the husband/father should be extended to them as well, insofar as this had not already been done. Temporary police seizure of their property and homes should now be canceled. It was stated that the sealing of their apartments had had only one purpose, namely, to prevent entry by unauthorized persons. On the other hand, confiscation actions by court bailiffs should not be interfered with.[64]

For months complaints had been lodged with the authorities, especially by landlords who had received no rent but could not rerent their apartments, and by other creditors. The Saxon interior minister had already stated at the end of December that he refused to be responsible for the situation and had informed Himmler that he planned to lift all restrictions on "resolving questions arising from the deportation action" on January 10, 1939. "In so doing, I will assume that only the interests of the affected German *Volksgenossen* are to be given consideration and that, in particular, damage claims by the deportees or the Polish government are to be ignored."[65] However, when the deportees

63. Ibid., pp. 314, 317–19. The text of the agreement is found in Adler, *Der verwaltete Mensch*, pp. 98–100.

64. Express letter from the Reichsführer SS, January 26, 1939, printed in *Dokumente zur Geschichte der Frankfurter Juden*, pp. 424f.

65. Printed in Diamant, *Chronik der Juden in Dresden*, p. 385. Examples of corresponding complaints are found in ibid., pp. 382f., 384, 387; for cancellation of the temporary securing of a dwelling, see p. 393.

were given the opportunity to order their own affairs, he retained police seizure of their property until it was clear who among those deportees wished to return.[66]

Among other organizations, the Palestine Office in Berlin and the Association of Polish Jews provided aid for those wishing to return. In individual cases, such as that of a wife who had undergone an operation and was to go to Poland with her husband, the period of stay was even extended by a few days.[67] Many who attempted to make arrangements from a distance and put their affairs in order by writing from Poland had to absorb heavy losses. So-called liquidators rushed to get rid of inventories and stock as soon as possible.[68]

Further Efforts toward Deporting the Remaining Jews

However, since no assurances could be obtained from Poland to the effect that those who had remained in Germany would not be expatriated, it was argued that an attempt should be made "to force as many of these Polish Jews as possible to leave the territory of the Reich, utilizing measures provided by the legislation on aliens."[69] On May 8, 1939, Heydrich ordered the Foreign Police to report all women and children to the post at the border crossing point so that it would be certain they would depart by the deadline of July 31 (up until then, the necessary personal data sheets for only 1,500 persons had been submitted). In addition, Heydrich issued the following order: all Polish Jews not in possession of a valid passport allowing them to return, along with those persons whose citizenship had been revoked by Poland, were prohibited from staying on in Germany. If they did not leave voluntarily, they should be deported. However, that should not be done by mass transports similar to those in October 1938, but should be carried out unobtrusively across the open frontier. By July 31, all such persons had to leave the Reich

66. Saxon Interior Minister to Reichsführer SS, February 14, 1939, printed in ibid., p. 394.
67. Communications by Dr. Fritz Berger, June 7, 1958, YVA 01/272, p. 5 (Palestine Office); report by Nieder, YVA 01/15, p. 2 (Association of Polish Jews); report by Bleyberg, YVA 01/169, p. 2 (extension).
68. Bruss, *Die Bremer Juden*, p. 222.
69. Reichsführer SS to Chief, Reich Chancellery, February 3, 1939, *ADAP*, D 5, no. 127, p. 141.

or should at least be interned in concentration camps "in order to put them in detention prior to deportation."[70]

Yet due to the heightened level of Polish border controls, no large-scale deportations could be carried out across the open frontier in July. At most, one or two persons could occasionally be deported in this manner. For that reason, certain categories of persons (the aged and infirm; children whose transfer to a place abroad was not possible by the specified deadline; persons who were planning to emigrate within the next six months, and others) were now even exempted from detention prior to deportation.[71] In the summer of 1939, many of these Jews also tried to get across the border to Poland illegally by bribing Polish officials or even with the assistance of the German police; the latter were extremely helpful in these cases, going so far as to help persons carry their luggage during the illegal crossing![72]

The Desperate Act of a Jewish Youngster: The Pretext for Kristallnacht

The deportation action of October 1938 had a broader impact on the persecution of Jews in Germany, extending far beyond the circumscribed circle of those immediately affected. The seventeen-year-old Herschel Grynszpan from Hanover, who was living with an uncle in Paris and had himself already been presented with a deportation order to leave France, received a postcard on November 3 from his parents and family interned in Zbąszyń. This news and the descriptions in the press, such as that in the November 4 edition of the Paris Yiddish newspaper *Haynt*, ultimately drove him to commit his desperate act, which in turn provided the National Socialists with the welcome pretext for staging the pogrom on November 9–10, 1938, and the subsequent intensification of the persecution of Jews in Germany: Grynszpan shot the young third secretary vom Rath in the embassy in Paris on November 7, and two days later vom

70. Quoted in Adler, *Der verwaltete Mensch*, p. 101.

71. Ben Elissar, *La diplomatie du IIIe Reich*, p. 321 regarding the limited possibilities; text of the decree in Adler, *Der verwaltete Mensch*, p. 102.

72. Report by Glicksohn, YVA 01/7, p. 2 (the price of 100 reichsmarks fell to 25 reichsmarks according to the statement by the Polish consul); report by Fritz Berger, October 6, 1948, YVA 01/4, p. 1.

Rath succumbed to his injuries. When he pulled the trigger, as well as when he was later apprehended, Grynszpan gave one motive for his actions – the deportation of Polish Jews, including his own family.

Years later, after the Vichy government had extradited him at German request and he was to stand trial in Germany, he added another story – that he had been active as a pimp for the homosexual vom Rath and had been cheated by vom Rath out of his commission or that he had even had homosexual relations himself with the diplomat. This story served to depoliticize his deed and, combined with other factors, led to a postponement of his trial, which then never materialized. In any event, this claim, which Grynszpan himself later retracted, is not credible.[73]

It can be established that Grynszpan was definitely interned at first in the camp at Sachsenhausen and then transferred to the investigative detention prison in Moabit (Berlin); after postponement of the trial, he was presumably returned to confinement in Sachsenhausen, where he was interrogated by Eichmann. While his relatives claimed that he had died, various German newspapers reported in 1960 that he was living in Paris under an assumed name, although by that time the murder fell under the statute of limitations. The historian who first researched the case also adhered to the thesis that Grynszpan was still alive and in France. On June 1, 1960, however, the Hanover district court declared him to be officially dead, with effect from May 8, 1945.[74] Ironically, if Grynszpan in fact did not perish during the war, then this one Jew who was indeed guilty of having committed a murder managed to survive the murder of the Jews unscathed. "By dint of his deed, Herschel Feibel Grünspan had become too 'prominent' for Auschwitz."[75]

73. This was first explained by Heiber, "Fall Grünspan," pp. 149–52; on the reasons for postponement, pp. 161f. An additional, painstakingly researched description of this case and the preparations for the trial in France, and so forth, is found in Thalmann and Feinermann, *Reichskristallnacht*, pp. 41–78. Also cf. Friedrich Karl Kaul, *Der Fall des Herschel Grünspan* (Berlin [East], 1965).

74. See *"Reichskristallnacht" in Hannover: Eine Ausstellung zur 40. Wiederkehr des 9. November 1938* (Hanover, 1978), p. 77 n.4. The volume also contains a photograph of Grynszpan in his classroom on p. 57, a reproduction of the family's municipal registration card on p. 59, and a photo of Grynszpan in French investigative custody on p. 60. Mendelsohn also agrees with the survival hypothesis, *Holocaust*, introd., not paginated.

75. Heiber, "Fall Grünspan," p. 134.

Shared Responsibility?

The deportation action of 1938 became a paradigm for later National Socialist actions against the Jews: it was the first large-scale deportation requiring coordination between the police, the Reichsbahn railway, diplomats, and financial authorities. The fact that Poland had not been willing or able to dissolve the camp in Zbąszyń was viewed as a symbol that Germany had been successful in making other countries partly liable for its anti-Jewish measures. Yet the international public, it was noted, had looked on with indifference.[76]

Poland's shared responsibility in the matter cannot be disputed.[77] If there was need for a final proof that not only had it failed to protect its Jewish citizens abroad, but was even prepared to sacrifice them, the following plan aired by Ambassador Lipski could serve as such proof: most of the stockholders of the Polish oil industry in Galicia were Austrian Jews. After the Anschluß, Poland feared that the shares might fall into the hands of the German Reich by confiscation. For this reason, Lipski suggested a possible compromise agreement to the Polish deputy foreign minister in July 1938. According to that proposal, Poland would assume a passive attitude regarding the confiscation of Polish-Jewish property in Germany; Germany, in turn, would refrain from deporting Jews to Poland. In addition, Germany would transfer the stock shares of former Austrian citizens to Poland. In order to instrumentalize the property of its citizens for such an agreement, the Polish government initially refrained from implementing the law on expatriation. Seen from this vantage, the ordinance on checking of passports of October 1938 specifically facilitated a further postponement of formal expatriation, keeping the path open for a clearing agreement with the German government regarding the confiscation of Polish-Jewish property.[78]

However, along with the responsibility shared by Poland, the deportation action makes something else clear: as soon as a foreign government resolutely opposed German measures, as the Polish government had done by deporting German citizens in reprisal and by insistently refusing to give any guarantee for

76. Milton, "Expulsion of Polish Jews," pp. 169, 174.
77. Likewise Thalmann and Feinermann, *Reichskristallnacht*, p.37.
78. Melzer, "Relations between Poland and Germany," pp. 217–19.

later acceptance of the Polish Jews still remaining in Germany, the National Socialist government had been forced to backtrack in respect to its objectives and lower its aims.[79] It is also significant that the deportation of the Polish Jews, which followed upon the earlier deportation of five hundred Soviet Jews in January 1938, not only suggests that the Reich felt secure enough now to take decisive steps against foreign Jews.[80] Rather, that move can be seen in another light: one might infer from the action against Soviet Jews in early 1938 a reprisal for the deportation of 150 Germans from the Soviet Union and one might infer as well from the later action against Polish Jews in Germany that the Reich was as yet not taking independent action on its own initiative against foreigners, but had only utilized an *external* occasion in order to act. The Soviet Union also denied entry to its citizens, whereupon they were promptly interned by the Germans in concentration camps.[81] For the deportation of Polish Jews a factual, though of course unintended, cooperation of two anti-Semitic regimes can be established – one of them deporting long-term foreign residents, the other one denying them the right to return to their country of origin. But in the last analysis, this provided Germany only with the chance to take a minor step toward the realization of its larger design of making Germany *judenrein*. That Poland shared responsibility for *this* step does in no way diminish Germany's responsibility for any of the steps leading up to its final aims.

Epilogue

When the German Reich attacked Poland on September 1, 1939, some of those deportees who had temporarily returned were still inside Germany.[82] They, as well as those still resident in the Reich, were now finally at the mercy of the Nazi persecutors.

79. Cf. also Adler, *Der verwaltete Mensch*, p. 100.

80. Karl A. Schleunes, *The Twisted Road to Auschwitz. Nazi Policy toward German Jews, 1933–1939* (Urbana, Chicago, and London, 1970), p. 216; on the deportation of Soviet Jews, see pp. 227f.

81. Cf. RSHA, February 15, 1938, BA, R 58/979 fols. 38f. Also Joseph Walk, ed., *Das Sonderrecht für die Juden im NS-Staat: Eine Sammlung der gesetzlichen Maßnahmen und Richtlinien – Inhalt und Bedeutung*, Motive-Texte-Materialien, vol. 14 (Karlsruhe, 1981), pp. 211, 214, 216f., 224, 226.

82. See several examples in Sauer, *Schicksale*, pp. 254f.

On September 7, the men were not interned as civilians, as was customary in dealing with citizens of enemy countries, but were sent to concentration camps. The women were registered by name, and their property was confiscated. Those who had been deported to Poland only shortly before were once again seized by the Germans, crowded together in ghettos and then, like Jews in the Reich, deported to the extermination camps, and murdered. Only a small number succeeded in saving their lives by emigrating from Poland.

Cäcilie Buchholz was deported together with other Jews from Baden to Gurs in southern France.[83] Her daughter was safe in England and was influenced there by her benefactors to give up her Jewish religion. Otto Buchholz, whose letter to relatives opened this essay, was unable in the winter of 1939 to realize his plan to arrange emigration via the American consulate in Warsaw. He was still living in the Warsaw Ghetto in 1941[84] and was later declared dead.[85]

83. On the background of this deportation, see Jacob Toury, "Die Entstehungsgeschichte des Austreibungsbefehls gegen die Juden der Saarpfalz und Badens (22./23. Oktober 1940 – Camp de Gurs)," *Jahrbuch des Instituts für deutsche Geschichte* 15 (1986): pp. 431–64.

84. See the letter by Cäcilie Buchholz to her relatives, September 11, 1941, printed in Fliedner, *Judenverfolgung in Mannheim*, vol. 2, pp. 74f.

85. *Die Opfer der nationalsozialistischen Verfolgung in Baden-Württemberg, 1933–1945: Ein Gedenkbuch*, Veröffentlichungen der staatlichen Archivdirektion Baden-Württemberg, Supplement to vol. 20 (Stuttgart, 1969), p. 43.

How Spontaneous Was the Pogrom?

Uwe Dietrich Adam

The night of Wednesday to Thursday, November 9–10, 1938, had proceeded up until then precisely according to the expectations of the three men. The program centered around the fifteenth anniversary celebration of the events of November 9, 1923, in Munich. The function took place in the "Museum," a solid, middle-class hotel with suitable facilities. Participation had been made obligatory for all members of the party, its formations, and affiliated organizations. In the smoke-filled atmosphere, fraternal feelings of old tried and tested comradeship soon welled up, fostered and bolstered by a hefty supply of alcoholic beverages. Along with private personal matters, conversations revolved principally around the brilliant deeds of the Führer: the Anschluß of Austria and the creation of "greater Germany," the Munich Conference, and the annexation of the Sudentenland into the Reich. Feelings were running high in the discussion of the latest news story, the attempted assassination of a German diplomat in Paris by a Jew.

The obligatory speeches by the local party leadership were made, followed by words of greeting from the representatives of the government, again and again with the same recollections and references to what had been achieved. Although it was a pure party function, units of the SA, SS, NSKK (National Socialist Drivers' Corps), HJ, and BDM were all dutifully present to demonstrate their respects and reverence on the day commemorating the 1923 Hitler putsch. With the exception of the Nuremberg Party Convention, there was probably no other festive function in the Nazi calendar at which members of the NSDAP, their formations, and affiliated organizations met in such a degree of unity. The official part of the meeting ended shortly after 10 P.M. with the presentation of the flags, singing of the "Horst Wessel Song," and a triple "Sieg Heil" to the Führer.

The flag delegation, consisting of three members, then hurried to return the party flag to headquarters in order to devote themselves fully to the more pleasant part of the evening's festivities. After dropping off the flag, the delegation of three proceeded immediately to a tavern, where they stayed until 2 A.M. A car approached them on the empty street as they headed for home. The subdistrict head (*Kreisleiter*) of the NSDAP ordered the three men to get in and told them that a radio message from Gauleiter Murr in Stuttgart had contained the order to set fire that night to all synagogues in the Reich. The *Kreisleiter* ordered the three nocturnal revelers to set fire to the local synagogue. So they returned to party headquarters, downed a few more beers during their deliberations, and then looked about for some flammable materials. Luckily, the synagogue was visible from party headquarters. With the aid of a withered oak-leaf wreath and a can of floor wax, they hoped to successfully accomplish their appointed task.

When the three tried to enter the synagogue, they found that the door had already been smashed in. The interior furnishings had been demolished, its windows shattered. Neighbors later reported that shortly after midnight, some eight persons in SS and SA uniforms had forced open the synagogue door and carried the interior fixtures and objects down to the Neckar River and tossed them into the water. This action, it was reported, had lasted until 1 A.M. The three arsonists, happy to be able to enter the building unimpeded, asked no further questions. After several abortive attempts, the building was brightly ablaze around 4 A.M. The firefighters, who arrived on the scene shortly thereafter, restricted their activities to securing the surrounding structures, so that by morning the synagogue had burned down to its foundation walls.

Events similar to these just described for the Swabian university town of Tübingen during the Reichskristallnacht, as based on eyewitness accounts, took place in many parts of the Reich. The Tübingen example is, in any case, well suited, in terms of the series of events and structuring of the scenario, to provide an answer to the question of just how "spontaneous" the pogrom was in reality.

Before dealing with this question, it is useful to illuminate the stage and the allocation of roles in the main production which provided the point of departure for these events. Beginning in the year 1928, an annual commemoration of the abortive putsch of November 8–9, 1923, was held by the NSDAP in Munich. Nearly all the prominent leaders of the party were present in the "movement's capital" during those few days, along with the top echelons of the SA and SS. The events, attestable by reference to reliable sources, had the sequence described below.

The Sequence of Events

Monday, November 7, 1938

During the morning, the seventeen-year-old Jew Herschel Grynszpan fires two shots at the legation secretary vom Rath in the German Embassy in Paris. The diplomat is injured in the shoulder. Another bullet penetrates his spleen and touches the wall of the stomach. Vom Rath is immediately operated on; his condition is very grave.

Late that afternoon, Hitler dispatches his personal physician, Dr. Karl Brandt, and Professor Georg Magnus from Münster to Paris to assist the French doctors.

Tuesday, November 8, 1938

The *Völkischer Beobachter* carries a first report about the assassination attempt in Paris and an editorial drawing a parallel to the murder of Gustloff in Switzerland in 1936; at the same time, it complains that "within our borders, hundreds of thousands of Jews still control entire blocks of stores." The editorial closes with the threat that "the shots fired in the German Embassy in Paris will not just mark the beginning of a new German attitude toward the Jewish question." That evening and night, there are local attacks in several German towns against Jewish businesses and homes, and several synagogues are set ablaze. These were in all instances preceded by party rallies in commemoration of the Hitler putsch and speeches of incitement by local party officials and are followed by the outbreak of "spontaneous actions" by the party and the SA.

Gauleiter Spregner in northern Hesse (Kurhesse), after learning of the violent excesses in his district, issues a secret order prohibiting all further individual actions.

9 P.M.:
Hitler delivers his traditional speech in the Bürgerbräukeller restaurant, but does not mention the assassination attempt.

Wednesday, November 9, 1938

The solemn commemorative march to the Feldherrnhalle takes place at about noon, ending with a ceremony.

5:30 P.M.:
Vom Rath, promoted by Hitler after the shooting to embassy counsellor (*Gesandtschaftsrat 1. Klasse*), dies in Paris.

8:00 P.M.:
Party leaders and "old party stalwarts" meet for an evening of comradeship in the Old Town Hall in Munich.

Almost the entire leadership of the SS is in Hotel Vier Jahreszeiten, among them the chief of the security police and the security service, SS Major General Reinhard Heydrich.

Field Marshal Göring, plenipotentiary for the Four-Year Plan, is aboard his special train returning to Berlin.

9 P.M.:
Hitler is informed of vom Rath's death during dinner. He conducts an "extraordinarily intense discussion" with the propaganda minister, Joseph Goebbels, who is sitting next to him, though even those nearby cannot understand what is being discussed.

Hitler leaves the meeting right after dinner without, as is otherwise customary, addressing those assembled. He returns to his residence on Äußere Prinzregentenstraße.

10 P.M.:
Shortly after Hitler leaves, Goebbels reports on vom Rath's death and gives a speech in which he refers to anti-Jewish rallies in Kurhesse and Magdeburg-Anhalt and adds: "The Führer has decided at his [Goebbels's] suggestion that such demonstrations should neither be prepared nor organized by the party. However, to the extent that they are spontaneous, no attempt should be made to intervene."

Those present interpret the speech to mean "that the party

should not appear from the outside to be the author of demonstrations, but in reality should organize and implement them."

10:30 P.M.:
The evening of comradeship comes to an end. The *Gauleiter* in attendance phone their district staffs or district propaganda staffs from the Old Town Hall and instruct them, in more or less precise form, to strike out, taking corresponding action against synagogues, Jewish homes, and businesses.

SA Chief of Staff Viktor Lutze gathers the SA leadership in the Old Town Hall and informs them in a brief speech about the situation.

11:00 P.M.:
The SA leaders return to their rooms in the Hotel Rheinischer Hof, from where they attempt until midnight to contact their units.

11:15 P.M.:
In Hotel Vier Jahreszeiten, Heydrich receives a call from the headquarters of State Police in Munich informing him that the district (*Gau*) propaganda staff for Munich-Upper Bavaria has issued an order for the outbreak of an action against the Jews, according to which the State Police should not interfere. Heydrich is surprised and asks SS Major General Karl Wolff to go to Himmler and request instructions.

11:30 P.M.:
Wolff meets Himmler in Hitler's apartment on Äußere Prinzregentenstraße and informs him of the situation. Himmler, who has the impression that Hitler has also been surprised by events, requests orders: "The Führer replied that the SS should stay out of this. The units of the State Police should safeguard Jewish property and take care of protecting the Jews."

11:45 P.M.:
First report of the burning of a Jewish house. Planegg Castle, which belongs to Baron von Hirsch, has been set ablaze by unknown arsonists.

11:55 P.M.:
Gestapo chief Heinrich Müller informs State Police posts by

teletype from Berlin that violence is expected against Jewish homes and businesses, adding the order that the State Police should stay out of it.

12 midnight:
Hitler and Himmler arrive at Odeonsplatz to review the midnight swearing-in ceremony for SS recruits.

Thursday, November 10, 1938

1 A.M.:
Immediately after the conclusion of the swearing-in ceremony, Himmler returns to Hotel Vier Jahreszeiten and gives Heydrich the following order: State Police posts must act in accordance with the wishes of the propaganda offices, principally to prevent looting, protect individuals, and guarantee the safety of Jewish property. Uncompromising action should be taken against looters. In the case of fires, care should be taken that the fire department control the blaze and protect nearby buildings.

1:20 A.M.:
Heydrich dictates a telex to all State Police posts containing the contents of Himmler's order and regulations regarding their sphere of authority vis-à-vis other agencies. The telex also orders that in all districts as many "especially wealthy" Jews are to be arrested as can be accommodated. Immediate contact should be established with the relevant concentration camps regarding the swiftest possible internment of these Jews.

1:25 A.M.:
Himmler assembles the General SS leaders present and briefs them on the order given by Heydrich. He forbids the deployment and participation of the General SS.

1:30 to 2:30 A.M.:
The SS leaders inform their posts through long-distance calls about Himmler's instructions.

1:40 A.M.:
Goebbels, as Reich minister of propaganda, teletypes his Old Town Hall speech to the district party offices. The propaganda

offices are specially entrusted with directing and implementing the action.

3:00 A.M.:
Himmler dictates a memo to a member of his personal staff, in which he makes brief reference to the events of the evening and notes that he has the impression Hitler was not informed about these events. Himmler closes with the words: "The order comes from the Reich Propaganda Office and I suspect that Goebbels – in his hunger for power, long since evident to me, and his blockheadedness – has given the start signal for the action; and he has done this specifically in a period that is so very difficult for us when it comes to foreign relations."

3:45 A.M.:
Heydrich sends another telex to the State Police posts in which he once again underscores the prohibition against looting and points out that the Reich Justice Ministry has instructed the district attorneys "to make no investigations regarding the business of the actions against Jews."

5:00 A.M.:
General of the Regular Police, Kurt Daluege, draws the attention of his subordinate units to the actions, stating that the police should be present at such actions "only with a small contingent, in civilian dress." The starting of fires was now to be prevented "under any and all circumstances."

Morning hours:
Economics minister Funk complains to Goebbels, who had returned in the course of the morning to Berlin, about the excesses and the damage caused to the German economy. Goebbels replies: "The Führer will give Reich Marshal Göring an order calling for the complete exclusion of Jews from the economy, and Funk will hear more about that from the Reich marshal."

Late morning:
After Hitler's arrival in Berlin, Göring complains about Goebbels who, in his economic ignorance, is not only destroying economic assets, but also destabilizing the system. Hitler excuses

Goebbels's behavior to some extent, yet agrees "on the whole that these things should not occur and mustn't be allowed to."

Afternoon:
Göring phones Goebbels and points out to him the harmfulness of his action "in no uncertain terms" and "using very harsh language." Goebbels then goes to see Hitler. Göring speaks with Hitler, whose "attitude has been somewhat changed by Goebbels." Göring did not know what Hitler discussed with Goebbels, yet remarks, "In any event, the position of the Führer was no longer what it was when I presented my first complaint to him."

Goebbels joins the discussion and, after attacking the Jews, suggests that a fine should be levied on them, to be collected by the various districts (*Gaue*). Göring disagrees: "If there is to be a fine, then only through the Reich [national] government. After a brief exchange of words regarding the amount, a billion reichsmarks is the sum decided upon. . . . The Führer then ordered that the economic solution be implemented."

Later afternoon:
The *Gauleiter* inform the subdistrict chiefs that an ordinance is anticipated stipulating that the Jews themselves will have to pay for the damage to their shops and that "in a very short period of time, there will be a number of measures instituted by legislation or decreed ordinance."

Midnight:
It is announced over the radio that the "action" has been concluded.

Evaluating the Events

It is virtually futile to attempt to eliminate historical myths. This certainly also holds true and is applicable when it comes to the events leading up to the Reichskristallnacht. In circumstances similar to the incident of the Reichstag fire, causes and effects interlock here too tightly not to assume that there is a logical, consistent connection between the two. Just as the National Socialists presumably staged the Reichstag conflagration to strike a decisive blow at the opponents of the new regime, the Reichskristallnacht appears to have been necessary to substantiate the "calculated" course and sequencing of the process within Hitler's assumed or presumed total plan to annihilate the Jews in Germany and Europe. With annual regularity, the mass media, in imperturbable obstinacy, repeated the view that the Kristallnacht was necessary, and thus even compellingly essential, in order to pave the final way to physical annihilation and to strip the Jews, already largely deprived of their civil rights and rendered penniless, of all still-remaining economic, social, and financial options. A number of persons and certain opinions expressed even go so far as to speak about "an action by those in power prepared down to the smallest detail."

Since the evidence for a "preprogrammed plan" for the Reichskristallnacht remains meager, the thesis of a planned operation is advocated all the more insistently and resolutely: thus, from the fact that new barracks were constructed in the Buchenwald concentration camp in the summer of 1938, the conclusion is drawn that they were built especially for the Jews to be arrested on November 9 and 10. Likewise, there is a statement by an official in the Reich Economics Ministry that is evaluated as a persuasive bit of evidence: in late October 1938, he advised a Jewish family not to wait until the end of November to emigrate because he had heard at a meeting in the ministry that there was a plan, even before mid-November, to "perpetrate terrible things" against the Jews in Germany. An editorial in the November 3 issue of the paper *Schwarzes Korps*, a publication of the SS national leadership, is viewed as furnishing additional evidence: in this editorial bloodthirsty threats are made against German and international Jewry. Further indications are given by supposed reports of SA members who claim they set fire as early as November 7 to synagogues, thus anticipating the surprise effect of a planned action which would have the appearance of being spontaneous in origin.

Yet it is these last references to so-called preparations for planning that are the easiest to refute. In all instances, testimony or statements regarding some sort of destructive action prior to November 8 are due to defective and mistaken memory. Even immediately after the events, it is evident that, again and again, incorrect dates and times are given for what occurred between November 8 and 10. One such example is drawn from testimony at the Nuremberg trials. The former Reich economics minister, Funk, constantly mentions November 9 in his interrogation, yet could actually only have been referring to November 10. Other witnesses also make such errors, although in not a single case did the court see fit to note this imprecision in regard to dating.

If the paper *Schwarzes Korps* is quoted as proof of plans already on the drawing boards because, as a publication of the SS national leadership, it had to be better informed than other papers, this can refer only to Himmler's knowledge and SS participation. All that is certain is that the editors of this paper had no "special inside line" either to the top echelons of the SS or to the political leadership. In addition, the paper had to constantly defend itself, especially against Goebbels, because he was full of distrust of it and attacked its editorial orientation. If the *Schwarzes Korps* threatened Jews with economic sanctions at the beginning of 1938, then that was simply because such sanctions "were in the air" – an impression shared, by the way, by many of the Jewish victims. To articulate this impression, no further knowledge was required than what you could obtain by a daily reading of the papers.

It is easy to demonstrate that the supposed construction of new barracks for prisoners in the concentration camps was little more than wishful thinking. It is a fact that new buildings were constructed during the summer of 1938 in the Buchenwald camp by a total of some 500 Jewish inmates, mainly from Berlin and Breslau, yet these structures were made of stone and were meant to replace the previous wooden barracks. Moreover, an increase in the number of barracks had become necessary due to overcrowding: the number of prisoners had nearly doubled between the fall of 1937 and the late summer of 1938, and the camps were hopelessly overcrowded.

Yet it is specifically the planned construction of barracks for inmates that is mustered as an argument (and this not by chance) to substantiate once again the thesis that the Kristall-nacht was planned in advance. The reasoning now is as follows: not only did the assassination in Paris provide a convenient propagandistic pretext, but also took place at precisely the right point in time, planned by the National Socialists for implementation of their economic measures against the Jews. This assertion is naturally designed, in turn, to strengthen the claim that the persecution of the Jews, leading up to their final annihilation, had proceeded according to a "general master plan" implemented by Hitler and his minions from 1933 to 1942, as if they were following a set script. Since our focus here is solely on planning for the ousting of Jews from the economy, an attempt will be made to describe who planned what and when.

Planning in Bureaucratic Chaos

There is no doubt that when Hitler seized power, at least two points in the party program were of overriding importance for the policy toward Jews: the revocation of equal civil rights and the ejection of the Jews from economic life. The first goal was achieved, at least in formal terms, with passage of the Nuremberg Laws in September 1935. In contrast, the elimination of the Jews from the economy proceeded at a much slower pace: in legal terms, until well into the late autumn of 1938, little had been accomplished to promote that objective. Despite the massive frontal attack launched by NS-guided economic organizations in the early summer of 1933 and despite considerable verbal threats and announcements preceding and following enactment of the Nuremberg Laws, no uniform regulations valid and binding throughout the Reich had been instituted.

For Jewish Germans, there were no legal regulations stipulating unambiguous, determinable, and generally valid restrictions on economic activity along the model of the Civil Service Law (Berufsbeamtengesetz) or the Reich Citizenship Law (Reichsbürgergesetz). What was lacking was a general law as is demonstrated by passage of the Law on the Restoration of the Professional Civil Service (Gesetz zur Wiederherstellung des Berufsbeamtentums) of April 7, 1933, or the Nuremberg Laws of September 15, 1935. However, the fact that there was no such basic law pertaining to the economy should not lead one to mistakenly conclude that Jewish Germans had been able to pursue their business affairs and occupations unharassed and without impediments. Between 1933 and 1938, the Reich instituted a substantial number of measures restricting vocational and occupational activity. Basically, one can say that all occupations requiring state approval and subject to state regulation and control were largely closed to Germans of Jewish extraction. By the late summer of 1938, the possible sphere of work and activity open to all Jewish

Germans had been hedged in and restricted to the point that any "free" practice of a profession, even in the so-called free economy, had become a virtual illusion.

One consequence of the increasingly more extensive prohibitions on professional and vocational activity was evident already in the summer of 1938, illustrating that a major slogan of Nazi propaganda had in fact never been in keeping with actual reality: a rapidly rising number of Jewish citizens found themselves having to resort to public welfare or became a burden for Jewish welfare agencies. In contradiction of all assertions of National Socialist propaganda regarding the amount of capital in Jewish hands, it became clear that the preponderant majority of the Jewish population in Germany was already dependent for survival in 1938 on savings alone, and such funds were hardly sufficient for maintaining an adequate living standard. It must also be noted that the Aryanizations of Jewish firms since 1933 had continued unabated and in virtually undiminished volume. All available statistics demonstrate that there was a constant decline in the number of Jewish businesses between 1933 and 1938.

There are many reasons for this. Even if the sale or closure and abandonment of a business was done without formal legal coercion at the time, one should bear in mind, when evaluating these events, the virtually inexhaustible possibilities that existed for harassment and discrimination, applied with especial intensity specifically in the local public sphere. Such options extended from a ban for party members on purchasing at particular stores, to harassment by the authorities using legal injunctions, all the way to the severe harassment and heavy pressure applied by banks, government, and NSDAP offices. Whoever could sell his business for a more-or-less acceptable price (under the circumstances) took advantage of that option. These "quiet" Aryanizations at the local level were not adequately registered either by the Reich Economics Ministry or the political leadership. The section for Protection against Inadmissible Interference in the Economy, the so-called Office for Protection of Jews (Judenschutzreferat) set up by Schacht, could, of course, only act in the case of formal complaints or when knowledge was available regarding infringements. In actual practice, however, this type of expropriation largely eluded the ministry's surveillance.

Thus, while a rapid retreat under coercion by Jewish proprietors was taking place, largely unnoticed by the public, the responsible ministry and the political leadership, along with the party propaganda machine, continued to spew out emotive terms like *Überfremdung* (foreign infiltration/inundation) or *Verjudung* (excessive Jewish presence) of entire commercial branches, thus overestimating the influence over and share in total national wealth that the Jews still had in the summer of 1938. Simply through continuation of the process of Aryanization which had been common enough practice, that is, without any of the draconian measures introduced in the wake of November 9, 1938, the NSDAP party program's demand for an "economy free of Jews" would have been virtually fulfilled by 1941 at the latest!

After Economics Minister Schacht's resignation (November 1937) and Göring's interim rule in that post, Funk's assumption of the ministry in February 1938 ushered in a swift and sudden tightening of anti-Jewish measures in the economy. Walther Funk, compliant and uncritically devoted to Hitler and Göring, was not the man who could set limits to the furious attacks of the party, as Schacht had done. Funk had hardly settled into his chair as minister when the Führer's deputy, his chief of staff Martin Bormann, stepped up the pressure on government agencies. Göring's announcement in late October 1938 that "the Jewish question is to be dealt with now using all means" because the Jews had to be "ousted" from the economy was reflective of its general thrust and orientation. In the Reich Economics Ministry, even before Funk took over at its helm, necessary preparations had already been made: thus, for example, the section for Protection against Inadmissible Interference in the Economy was dismantled in February 1938 and replaced by a department for Questions Pertaining to Jews.

The torrent of discriminatory measures restricting occupational/vocational activity that had descended upon the Jews from the beginning of 1938 doubtlessly derived from Hitler's intention to press on with matters after a prolonged period of external calm. For the first time since 1935, he chose the Jews as the main topic of his programmatic address at the Party Labor Convention in September 1937. In this speech he went into haranguing detail on the "Jewish actions aimed at insidious destruction and demoralization" in Germany and waxed

85

passionate on the horrific vision of a "Jewish-Bolshevik international enemy."

Hitler's threats apparently were conceptually interlinked with the plans and views regarding his next military-political objectives presented in November 1937 to an audience of top general officers. In those remarks, he also expressed his aim, which had become even more threatening since the end of World War I, that in a future war no Jew in Germany would any longer have any power and influence – or even better, that the "Jewish race" ought finally to be removed from Germany before the outbreak of such a war.

Göring's savage and violent demand voiced in October 1938 was not only in keeping with Hitler's objectives, but also reflected the wish and determination of especially active anti-Semites in the NSDAP to launch an attack finally against the Jews in the economic sphere as well, utilizing effective legal measures and regulations. Gauleiter Streicher and Joseph Goebbels became the leading spokesmen of this tack in public meetings during May and June of 1938. Due to tensions in foreign relations, the campaign could not be seen through to its conclusion, yet provided the requisite emphasis to underscore Göring's instructions announced at a ministerial meeting on April 28, 1938. The plenipotentiary for the Four-Year Plan had closed his remarks there with the call to resolve the Jewish Question through the final exclusion of the Jews from German economic life and through the transformation of Jewish capital into solid assets, which would no longer allow them to exercise any economic influence. As already noted, Göring's initiative looked quite positive. A seizure of Jewish assets had become an open option, possible at any time, facilitated by the preparatory ordinances against the "masking of Jewish firms" and the "registration of Jewish capital." A further ordinance of June 14 answered the question, Under what circumstances should a firm be regarded as Jewish?

With these decrees and ordinances, the legislative élan of the Economics Ministry appeared for the moment to be exhausted. The ministry followed the policy line "of either placing all non-Aryan businesses in Aryan hands or liquidating them within a relatively short period of time. . . . In any event, it saw no value in forced Aryanization." The numerous measures instituted by other ministries had not been coordinated beforehand with the Economics Ministry nor, in terms of objectives, do they reflect an even approximately similar orientation. A revised version of the Trade Regulations issued by the Economics Ministry itself reveals the extent to which one operated under pressure. These regulations were put together so quickly and superficially, "due to the urgent nature of regulating this sphere," that later exceptions had to be made once again for certain Jewish tradesmen.

Additional prohibitions on the practice of one's profession affected still-practicing attorneys and patent lawyers, dentists, physicians, and pharmacists, as well as a broad spectrum of other professionals. One consequence of these occupational restrictions was that the number of Jewish unemployed surged, and with it their need for financial assistance. Other ordinances stripped Jewish *Gemeinden* of their status as incorporated bodies under public law, thus depriving them of associated tax concessions. In addition, the Jewish taxpayer was automatically placed in the highest tax bracket.

The fact that these measures were instituted totally devoid of any overall conception and plan, without any coordinating agreement, and that the interests of each ministry not only clashed with those of every other but were, in their totality, pitched against the interests of the Reich, is illustrated by the proposal with which the economics minister approached the other departments in July 1938. In order to unify the *haphazard* exclusion of Jews through measures regulating taxes, finances, and professions, he recommended that in future Jews should be *forcibly* ousted from the economy and their assets confiscated. There was immediate strong and energetic disagreement. The finance minister feared large losses in tax revenues, spoke about a "destruction of the economy," and wrote a forceful objection. Schacht, who was still president of the Reichsbank, followed suit, pointing to the "dangers for the capital market," and suggested that Jews be given the opportunity to sell their enterprises within a span of ten to fifteen years "in order to receive a realistically decent price."

Along with the departments that were directly affected, one party formation, namely, the SD, also objected to "forced Aryanization." This formation, following the lead of the increasingly more powerful Reichsführer SS, was pursuing its own policy toward the Jews "on a scientific basis" and with

Hitler's approval had endorsed Jewish emigration to Palestine. The proposed plans for forced Aryanization struck at the open nerve of the SD, which is why it vehemently opposed the intentions voiced by the interior minister. In September 1938, the SD sketched two main tasks associated with the treatment of Jews in Germany: "(1) The creation of opportunities for emigration, avoiding as much as possible any costs in foreign currency; and (2) the securing of expenses for support of those Jews remaining behind through Jewish financial sources within and outside Germany." In the meantime, however, there had been a development that had deeply upset Göring in his role as the principal official responsible for the economy and rearmament. As a result of the stepped-up program for rearmament, not only had the Reich's financial situation deteriorated dramatically, but its foreign currency reserves had also been depleted. Göring thus rejected out of hand any release of foreign currency for purposes of emigration.

This was a hard blow for the SD, which was just about to introduce a new procedure to the Reich, patterned on the example of Adolf Eichmann in Vienna: as director of a Central Bureau for Jewish Emigration there, he had spurred some 50,000 of the total 190,000 Austrian Jews to emigrate within the short span of a few months. The SD was of the opinion that emigration from Germany had been relatively modest in terms of numbers: of the approximately 520,000 German Jews living in Germany in 1933, little more than 130,000 had emigrated by early 1938, so an estimated 360,000 were still living in the Altreich. Those who had emigrated included, in particular, the younger generation and persons who had not been obliged for financial reasons to remain in Germany. The SD itself calculated that some 200,000 of those Jews still in Germany would have to stay on for reasons of advanced age and lack of capital and that very difficult negotiations would be necessary to push this group within the Jewish population out of Germany as well.

Göring, with his modest knowledge of economic matters, naturally showed just as little interest in the complex problems of emigration, capital transfer, and procurement of foreign currency as did the inveterate anti-Semites within the party and government bureaucracies. These anti-Semites were more fascinated by the mere number of Jews still remaining within the Reich and their supposed property and assets. When Göring once again demanded in late October 1939 that "the Jewish Question is to be dealt with now using all means," he was thinking from his blinkered departmental perspective only of the finances of the Reich. The situation had actually become so precarious that the government had been forced to take out a special credit of four hundred million reichsmarks with the Reichsbank to assure payment of salaries for the civil service. In addition, the foreign currency accounts abroad were hopelessly overdrawn.

After the aimless and uncoordinated measures to exclude Jews from the economy in the spring and summer of 1938, the ministries once again went into action following Göring's renewed demands. Beginning in November, Jewish assets deposited with banks and savings and loan associations were reviewed; in certain cases, as when there was a suspicion of capital flight, these accounts were taken from their owners by means of so-called securing orders. In the Economics Ministry, draft plans for excluding Jews from the economy and for the confiscation of wealth that was "hostile to the state and *Volk*" existed, the implementation of which was anticipated in the near future. It was extremely unclear, given the enormous gap between the interests and intentions of the various departments and the party, however, which line would be victorious in the imminent conflict to come: a slow-paced, gradual exclusion by coercion, utilizing the option of Jewish emigration, or a ruthless and uncompromising, radical elimination of Jews from German economic life.

Motives for the Pogrom

In returning to the concrete events sketched at the beginning of this essay, at least two facts stand out: there can be absolutely no doubt that no one in Tübingen knew before midnight that actions were to take place that night against Jews and Jewish institutions. For a long time the subdistrict chief roamed helplessly through the empty streets to locate a couple of party members. Three intoxicated revelers then search laboriously for a bit of flammable material and finally come across a withered and dry laurel wreath, which they use to set fire to the synagogue. This haphazardness indeed would almost deserve the epithet grotesque, had the consequences of such action in other places not been so shocking and horrible. Similar improvisations can be observed in nearly all other localities. Nowhere is there an SA arson unit ready and on call, nowhere have measures been taken to assure a supply of flammable material, nowhere is there a party or SA functionary waiting at his phone for the relaying of the code word. Thus, one has to rule out completely the hypothesis that there was any sort of planning or even an intention to make plans.

The events at the Old Town Hall after the Goebbels speech provide emphatic substantiation of this thesis and are reflected in virtually every instance in the events taking place in pogrom localities. In Tübingen as well as in numerous other towns isolated groups are at work, groups whose orders and instructions are unknown one to the other. In Tübingen, a group of SA and SS men demolish the interior fixtures of the synagogue and ransack the building. Three hours later, a party unit swings into action and sets the fire. These separate actions reflect the different command paths that night, triggered by temporally separate waves of telephone calls or teletype messages. The *Gauleiter* commenced activities at 10:30 P.M. This was followed by the SA after 11 P.M., the State Police (Gestapo) shortly after midnight, the SS started at 1:30 A.M., and Goebbels once again at 1:40 that morning. The first two waves of telephone calls by *Gauleiter* and SA leaders, at around midnight, probably had decisive impact. Only the subsequent telexs from Heydrich, Goebbels, and Daluege brought a trace of order into that burgeoning chaos by stipulating limits of responsibility and giving detailed instructions on authority and tasks.

The SA and party acted independently of each other in those localities where the first wave of orders arrived directly and then were carried out immediately. In these instances, although the SA's initial orders were transmitted only after 11 P.M., it was generally the first actor on the scene due to the fact that its channels of command were shorter and its organization tighter and more military in character. Since the orders had only been conveyed over the telephone, the way stood wide open for all sorts of misunderstandings. It appears that the SA leadership initially appended an instruction to its orders specifying that synagogues and Jewish stores should be ransacked and demolished, while the burning of synagogues was the point emphasized in orders transmitted by the party. In any event, just as in Tübingen, this difference in orders and their interpretation could be observed in a large number of other localities as well.

In addition, these initially highly uncoordinated actions, whose sequence of events was arbitrary, not only indicate that there was a substantial lack of clarity as regards the type and scope of acts of vandalism; they also demonstrate that little information was available about the participation of various Nazi units and formations. Since the General SS did not receive an order to "refrain from involvement" in these actions until 1:30 A.M., it took an active part in the destruction in many localities. This suggests that the orders were formulated in such an indefinite and diffuse manner that every person in the NSDAP and its various associated organizations could feel that he had been called upon to act.

It was only after the teletyped messages attempting to intervene and regulate actions, sent in the early hours of November 10, that the division of tasks and demarcation of responsibility become clearly discernible, at least at the highest echelons. The responsible propaganda offices at the district and subdistrict levels (*Gau- und Kreispropagandaämter*) were supposed to act as command and coordination posts; local party offices and NS-associated organizations could then utilize their aid. The participation of SS members, which can be demonstrated in numerous instances, indicates that the district and subdistrict party offices involved in issuing orders were unaware of the orders for the SS not to participate and that they based their action on a general order. It only becomes evident through Heydrich's and Daluege's later teletype messages that there had been an effort in the meantime to limit the frenzy of destruction and the extent of the fires being set.

This points to the part played by Propaganda Minister Joseph Goebbels at this time and thus raises the question of his role as initiator and his possible motives. It cannot be disputed that with his speech, Goebbels, alone and directly, had indeed initiated the pogromlike disturbances. Testimony by witnesses indicates that he disappeared into his hotel room after the speech, presumably to pass on orders in line with his wishes personally, via the Reich Propaganda Office of the party, to the district head offices and district propaganda offices. His telex of 1:40 A.M. clearly substantiates that he was attempting to fan the flames of the action and, simultaneously, to keep control over events by means of the party offices subordinate to him.

It is highly doubtful whether Goebbels's actions that evening were motivated solely by propaganda interests. As statements by witnesses and friends and his own diaries corroborate, he was in actual fact a committed anti-Semite. Nonetheless, his outbursts were always calculated in terms of propaganda effect, so that his anti-Semitism bears a purposive character. There is no doubt that he recognized, instinctively and immediately, what opportunities for mass agitation had been made available as a result of the assassination in Paris, specifically given the state of policy toward Jews in Germany in November 1938.

Once again, as in 1933 and in connection with promulgation of the Nuremberg Laws, a moderate faction stood against an uncompromising group when it came to the question of legislation governing Jews in Germany. There was no certitude that Hitler himself was publicly in favor of a hard line, given his previous, constantly hesitating attitude and tendency to avoid clear-cut decisions. Up until then, Hitler had always understood how to hide and mask his hatred for the Jews; in all his decisions, he had repeatedly referred to the will of the people, the party, the movement. Up until November 7, such a desired, "spontaneous" expression of the will of the people had not been considered a likely prospect. Moreover, after the exhausting and disconcerting days of the Sudeten crisis, there was no reason or occasion to expect any sort of a spontaneous action on the part of the "people."

Goebbels had long known that Hitler was angry over the tedious, legalistically oriented, laborious procedural path that characterized the bureaucratic approach at the ministries. Instead, he wished to see a quick and radical solution to the economic dimension of the Jewish question, one in keeping with his thinking. Anyone who understood how to provoke this radical solution without publicly compromising Hitler, the Führer and chancellor, as the major instigator, could be assured of Hitler's gratitude and recognition. And Goebbels was very much in need of Hitler's good favor in the late autumn of 1938. His relationship with Hitler had been extremely tense over the previous months as a result of private problems. In addition, the chancellor had even begun to call the professional abilities of his propaganda minister into question by stating that he felt the manipulation of the news had lost much of its earlier verve. In any event, Herschel Grynszpan's act seemed like a handy means to solve all of Goebbels's problems in one fell swoop, if he could succeed in exploiting the assassination for propaganda purposes. There can be no doubt that Goebbels recognized immediately what a unique opportunity the assassination presented to press far ahead with Jewish policy, decisively and in intensified form.

One can certainly assume it to be an established fact that Goebbels made contact with Hitler immediately after the assassination attempt had become known to discuss appropriate options for shaping information in the press. Hitler undoubtedly avoided any immediate definite decision, saying that it was first necessary to await developments in the victim's condition. There was nothing beyond the familiar threats published in the *Völkischer Beobachter* on November 8. Neither the party, Goebbels, nor even Hitler made any statement about the situation. Not even in his obligatory speech in the Bürgerbräukeller on the evening of November 8 did Hitler mention this incident, which supposedly represented one of the most audacious provocations of world Jewry. Nonetheless, he did send his own physician Dr. Brandt to Paris, and it is likely that Brandt kept Hitler regularly informed about the patient's grave condition.

Whatever Hitler and Goebbels – or Goebbels alone – may have pondered on the day after November 7, the events in the Old Town Hall in Munich, based on their sequencing, look very much like a carefully staged production. Hitler was handed the telegram with the news of the death of the diplomat at 8:45 P.M. Whoever may have chosen this stage and audience, there is a planned, purposeful intention behind it. There can be no doubt that this announcement was consciously delayed, consciously kept back so that it would reach Hitler precisely at this place and in front of this particular audience, since vom Rath had already been dead since 5:30 P.M. at the latest. Brandt was at the hospital, and the telegraph office directed by Goebbels (Wolffsches Telegraphenbüro) was in the immediate vicinity. It is inconceivable that such news required more than three hours to reach Hitler.

The further developments of that evening clearly prove that, at least from the moment vom Rath's death was announced, Hitler and Goebbels were of the same view, and all subsequent measures were discussed and agreed upon between them. This holds true not just for the violence and rioting, but also – indeed, in particular – for the more distant objectives of the action. Perhaps Göring, in his rage, was, due to a lack of information, unaware that his statement made on November 18, 1938 ("Very critical situation in regard to Reich finances. Initial relief as a result of the one billion levied on the Jews and the Reich profits accruing from Aryanization of Jewish enterprises"), referred specifically to one of the objectives that had motivated Goebbels, together with Hitler, to instigate the Kristallnacht actions.

It had been Goebbels who, already on November 10, had suggested to Hitler the idea of an "atonement fine" (*Sühneleistung*). Moreover, Goebbels's remark that he had consciously provoked the events in order to force the hesitating economics minister, Funk, and his ministry to take some action on the Jewish Question indicates how closely Hitler was linked to the initiative for the pogrom. The Reichsführer SS confirmed that indirectly by reproaching Funk with the criticism that these excesses could have been avoided if he [Funk] had "dealt with" the Jews more harshly and energetically even earlier.

Thus, one is probably justified in proceeding on the basis of the assumption that Goebbels, along with Hitler, had been airing plans closely connected with the assassination since November 7, 1938, plans that could only be realized in combination with that event. The central objectives were two: finding a solution to the financial crisis besetting the Reich, and finally excluding and ejecting Jewish Germans from the economy. In accordance with Hitler's wishes, what was aspired to was their ousting from the German public sphere: Jews were to be marginalized, discriminated against, and branded as criminals, dislodged and pushed to the very edge of National Socialist society.

Viewed in this light, the Reichskristallnacht can hardly be regarded as a well-planned and staged action carried out by the National Socialists. Rather, it is characterized as a conscious, cleverly staged, and unscrupuluously implemented *exploitation of a situation* that had presented itself unexpectedly – an action that, by utilizing a chance opportunity, served to open further perspectives for the future. Those perspectives, at this point at the latest, provided a presentiment of the shape of things to come, revealing the dark outlines of the will to proceed even to the physical annihilation of the Jews.

The Fateful Year 1938

The Continuation and Acceleration of Plunder

Avraham Barkai

"The year 1938 signifies a historical turning point in the fate of the Jews." These were the words with which the Reichsvertretung der Juden in Deutschland opened its annual report written in early 1939.[1] In a similar vein, the Foreign Office began a lengthy report on *The Jewish Question as a Factor in Foreign Policy in 1938* with the sentence: "It is probably no coincidence that the fateful year 1938 has brought the Jewish Question closer to a solution with the realization of the conception of a Greater Germany."[2] These statements expressed the sense of consternation or satisfaction felt by contemporaries regarding the November 1938 pogrom and the measures that followed in its wake.

Historiography was unable to overlook this intensification in the harshness of the National Socialists' Jewish policy starting in early 1938, and historians thus shifted the turning point back to this juncture in the revised periodization of policy development. Yet most historians are generally agreed, even today, that Jews in Germany at the end of 1937 were still relatively well off in economic terms. The late Israeli historian Shaul Esh noted in a 1958 essay that the November 1938 pogrom had not marked the beginning or end of a period, yet had signified a stage in a new policy, which Esh believed had begun around the end of 1937. He explained the introduction of this new stage by reference to the disappointment of the National Socialist leadership over the failure of previous Jewish policy: "In the eyes of the Nazi leaders this was the only failure worth mentioning which they had suffered in their policy. After more than 50 months the number

---

1. Reichsvertretung der Juden in Deutschland, Annual Report (*Arbeitsbericht*) 1938 (hereafter: RV/AR), p. 1.
2. *IMT*, vol. 23, p. 237, PS–3358.

of German Jews had dropped about 100,000 souls, i.e. only by some 20%. Their economic position had not been shaken fundamentally. On the contrary, the more they concentrated in the big towns . . . the steadier grew their position."[3]

Helmut Genschel described "the economic repression of the Jews up until 1937" as a "creeping disease." "Success, measured against the party goal of an economy 'free of Jews,' was extremely modest."[4] Uwe D. Adam has pinpointed the beginning of the effective ousting of Jews from the economy to the autumn of 1938, positing a direct connection between this radicalization in policy and the dismissal of Schacht as economics minister in November 1937. In Adam's view, this was proof of to what extent "the implementation of racial policy could be dependent on the existence of one person."[5]

In contrast, emphasis here will be on continuity: an attempt will be made to present the events of the year 1938, especially in the economic field, as a consistent continuation of previous policy. That policy was intensified, but was by no means separated from associated developments by some sort of decisive "turning point" or "shift." New research in the historical sources suggests compellingly that the economic position of most Jews in Germany had been significantly undermined by the end of 1937. A broad stratum had already been reduced to poverty and was living on welfare. The greater part of Jewish enterprises had already been closed down or sold in the course of Aryanizations, and the proceeds concentrated in the form of liquid bank accounts and securities deposits, had been made "accessible" for the plunder and pillage to come. The economic activity of the greater majority of Jews in Germany at that juncture was limited almost exclusively to the sphere of consumption even then; their expenditures were at that time already, financed by income

3. Shaul Esh, "Between Discrimination and Extermination: The Fateful Year 1938," *Yad Vashem Studies* 2 (1958): 80, 85.

4. Helmut Genschel, *Die Verdrängung der Juden aus der Wirtschaft im Dritten Reich* (Göttingen, 1966), pp. 139f.

5. Uwe D. Adam, *Judenpolitik im Dritten Reich* 2d ed. (Düsseldorf, 1972), pp. 359, 173. Willi A. Boelcke has expressed an even more extreme view, contending that "one day after Schacht's dismissal . . . the millstone of anti-Semitism was set rolling in the direction of the economy, the last reserve of Jewish activity" (*Die deutsche Wirtschaft, 1933–1945* [Düsseldorf, 1983], p. 210). The main sources for this apologia for Schacht are the testimony given by more than 100 officials active in the Economics Ministry during the Nazi period.

from the property left to them, and even by the prin
these liquid assets. Jewish organizations for self-assista:
vided aid to make sure that a portion of this wealth and income
was also channeled to the pocketbooks of penurious Jews left
with few financial means. Thus, the greater proportion of German Jewry at this point was already living on the products and
savings of previous economic activity.

After years of successful attempts by party and government
authorities to "displace" Jews from active economic life, all the
prerequisites had been created by the beginning of 1938 for the
final removal of Jews from the German economy ("Entjudung
der deutschen Wirtschaft"). Now one could go about eliminat-
ing the remainder of any remunerative economic activity by
Jews and could prepare for the registration and seizure of their
assets. The successes of the regime in foreign policy and the
domestic consensus among the population offered highly favorable prerequisites for such a move at the end of 1937, just as the
war in the east later created suitable preconditions for the
subsequent physical extermination of the Jews. In this context,
the November pogrom was a signal to complete within the span
of a few weeks what had been set into motion many months
before.

Demographic and Social Structure

There were still between 350,000 and 365,000 Jews living in the
Altreich at the beginning of 1938. Some 165,000 to 175,000 had
emigrated or died since January 1933. The remaining Jews were
distributed among some 1,400 *Gemeinden*, of which more than
730 were classified as "communities in distress" and were in
varying stages of advanced liquidation. More than 65 percent of
all Jews were concentrated in large metropolitan areas, with
140,000 (ca. 40 percent) in Berlin alone.[6]

There are no extant supporting documents on the exact occupation and employment structure within the Jewish minority at

6. The Reichsvertretung estimated the number at the end of 1937 to be some
350,000 (RV/AR 37, pp. 14f.). In contrast, Herbert Strauss arrives at the more
plausible figure of 365,000, see Herbert Strauss, "Jewish Emigration from Germany: Nazi Policies and Jewish Responses, I/II," *YLBI* 25 and 26 (1980 and 1981):
313–58; 343–409.

this point in time. However, since Jewish blue-collar and white-collar employees at this juncture were largely able to find work only in Jewish firms, their employment situation was basically dependent on the number of existing Jewish enterprises. The available sources indicate quite clearly that of the roughly 100,000 Jewish firms in existence in January 1933,[7] some 60 to 70 percent were no longer in existence by the spring of 1938 or had been transferred to Aryan hands. This is even confirmed by the otherwise questionable figures of the *Judenreferent* (adviser on Jewish affairs) in the Economics Ministry, Alf Krüger: as of April 1, 1938, he listed a total of 39,552 Jewish firms.[8] Consequently, it is difficult to understand how Genschel, for the autumn of 1937, could have estimated "the proportion of Aryanized businesses at below 25 percent and that of manufacturing firms substantially less."[9]

The Aryanization of the retail shops had reached an especially advanced stage. Of the more than 50,000 Jewish shops and stores in existence in 1933,[10] there were, according to official statistics, only about 9,000 left in the entire Altreich in July 1938, with 3,637 of these in Berlin. The reporters considered this circumstance proof that still-existing "expectations regarding Aryanization [were] exaggerated . . . since the *Entjudung* of retail trade had . . . already reached quite an advanced point."[11]

7. Estimate, based on the census figures from June 1933. After the departure of some 25,500 to 30,000 Jews from January of that year on, there were a total of 110,669 independently employed Jews without assisting family members, see *Statistik des Deutschen Reichs*, vol. 451, no. 5 and 453, no. 2. Cf. also Esra Bennathan, "Die demographische und wirtschaftliche Struktur der Juden," in Werner E. Mosse and Arnold Paucker, eds., *Entscheidungsjahr 1932: Zur Judenfrage in der Endphase der Weimarer Republik* (Tübingen, 1965), pp. 106f. In the German statistics, all independent firms were counted as enterprises (*Betriebe*), from department stores to independent law and medical practices to itinerant trade "firms" operated by independent traveling salesmen and pedlars. If we take a limited number of partnerships into consideration, the figure of 100,000 Jewish "firms" in January 1933 hardly seems to be too high an estimate.

8. Alf Krüger, *Die Lösung der Judenfrage in der Wirtschaft: Kommentar zur Judengesetzgebung* (Berlin, 1940), p. 44. Krüger's data do not contain any source references. The survey of Jewish firms did not take place until July 1938, and the final results of that are not known.

9. Genschel, *Die Verdrängung*, p. 136.

10. Herbert Kahn, "Umfang und Bedeutung der jüdischen Einzelhandelsbetriebe innerhalb des gesamten deutschen Einzelhandels: Hauptergebnisse einer wissenschaftlichen Untersuchung (Aufgrund einer Erhebung in 69 Grossgemeinden), Im Auftrag der Reichsvertretung der Juden durchgeführt Februar 1934," mimeographed manuscript, p. 12.

11. *Textil-Zeitung*, December 3, 1938; *Berliner Morgenpost*, November 25, 1938.

Highly detailed and extensive data on the business situation of Jewish retail shops still in existence at the end of 1937 can be found in the files of the *Gauwirtschaftsberater* of the Nazi party, whose responsibility it was to supervise the Aryanizations. Thus, for example, it was noted on October 1, 1937, in Bochum that more than 50 percent of the Jewish businesses "had already been dissolved or were in the process of being Aryanized," and the situation for the remaining enterprises was "generally very bad."[12] In a survey done by the DEA of South Westphalia in June 1938, comments such as the following were generally noted next to the still-existing Jewish enterprises: "operations shut down almost completely," "nothing left but Jewish customers," "store is usually closed," etc.[13]

An instructive source of information for the Jewish economic and business situation at the time is provided by the results of the official registration of Jewish property carried out in April 1938. Jewish assets totaling some 5.1 billion reichsmarks were registered within the borders of the Altreich.[14] According to various estimates, this amounted to less than half of the total Jewish assets and property in Germany in 1933,[15] while the number of Jews had been reduced by only one third. With Austria included, only 1.195 billion reichsmarks (some 14 percent) of the registered total assets of 8.531 billion reichsmarks consisted of working capital. The remainder was made up of some 2.5 billion reichsmarks in real estate and 4.88 billion in "other types of assets." The latter consisted principally of liquid accounts in cash, stocks, or bonds. A "strictly confidential" summary by the Economics Ministry in November 1938 notably marked this part as "vulnerable assets" and "readily seizable." In this connection, it was also underscored that since the April

12. StA Münster, GW, no. 145.
13. StA Münster, GW, nos. 145 and 703 (October 1938).
14. Geheimes Staatsarchiv Preußischer Kulturbesitze Berlin-Dahlem (Secret State Archives), Rep. 151, No. 1658a, Economics Minister, Circular Letter III/Jd. 8910/38, November 28, 1938.
15. Strauss, "Nazi Policies," p. 342. Ludwig Pinner estimated total Jewish private assets in 1933 at approximately twelve billion reichsmarks, see "Vermögenstransfer nach Palästina, 1933–1939," in: *Zwei Welten: Siegfried Moses zum 75. Geburtstag* (Tel Aviv, 1962), p. 134. This would amount to 3 to 4 percent of total German capital in the period 1930–34 and appears probable as an estimate (calculated according to W.G. Hoffmann, *Das Wachstum der deutschen Wirtschaft seit der Mitte des 19. Jahrhunderts* [Berlin and Heidelberg, 1965], pp. 44, 602).

1938 survey, "substantial assets, whose amount is difficult to estimate, have been sold below their true value to non-Jewish businessmen. There is therefore certainly a possibility that liquid assets have grown as a result of the *Entjudung* which has taken place in the meantime, while nondisposable firm assets have shrunk in volume."[16]

Gainfully employed Jews were dissimilarly affected by this development. The small upper stratum of major Jewish entrepreneurs and bankers, who still maintained excellent ties to the bourgeois upper class in Germany and abroad, was able to keep its head above water longer than the more heavily endangered middle classes. Members of this upper stratum were less susceptible to the violent boycott terror of the street, and their sense of economic security stretching back over generations was still more than a mere illusion at this point in time. They appear for the most part to have successfully escaped from Germany in time. Even if they often had to leave behind most of their wealth, they had sufficient financial reserves and family connections abroad to protect them from physical distress.

The Hamburg banking family of Max Warburg can serve as an example of the bourgeois upper class. The family stood its ground, resisting various pressures until May 1938. The way in which Max Warburg explained his stubborn tenacity is significant. In his farewell speech to the assembled personnel of his firm, he stated that it had not been his wish to witness "this firm, to which our life's work has been devoted up until this very moment, being destroyed."[17] There is no doubt though that his sense of responsibility for the Jewish community was also a major factor serving to keep him in Germany until 1938. Warburg never denied his affiliation with that community, and even prior to the takeover by the Nazis, he had been a member of numerous German and international Jewish bodies. In 1933, he had been one of the initiators in founding the Reichsvertre-

16. Circular Letter, see n. 14 above. From a total of 8.531 billion reichsmarks, 1.408 billion in debts and obligations were subtracted, leaving net assets at 7.123 billion reichsmarks, some two billion of which was in Austria. Since the declaring of assets in Austria was ordered shortly after the Anschluß, it is reasonable to assume that a larger proportion of Austria-Jewish assets was within the firms; correspondingly, the percentage of "working capital" in the Altreich was under 14 percent.

17. Eduard Rosenbaum, "M.M. Warburg & Co., Merchant Bankers of Hamburg," *YLBI* 7 (1962): 147.

tung der Juden in Deutschland, and for many years he was a member of the board of the Hilfsverein. Warburg's bank also played a leading role in salvaging Jewish assets through the Haavara Agreement, which was probably another important reason for his tenacity in staying on in Germany.[18]

Less fortunate Jews had a far more difficult time mustering enough moral fortitude at the end of 1937 to keep up their courage and not fall prey to despair. Their energies were totally consumed by the struggle to survive and earn a living. Former doctors and lawyers, top-management personnel and unemployed workers were now wandering from town to town with their suitcases of samples or even with pedlars' goods; in the provinces, even that source of itinerant livelihood had been prohibited to Jews. Women let out rooms in their apartments or started serving lunch there in order to earn a meager income. Since all these activities required a trading license and each move, even the relocation of a business into the premises of one's own home, was officially regarded as a "new opening," attentive officials of the NSDAP noted with alarm at this time that there was a rise in the number of "new openings of Jewish firms."[19]

Along with the accelerated Aryanization, Jewish unemployment also showed a substantial rise in the fall of 1937. In October of that year, Jewish social workers expressed concern about the fate of thirty thousand "nonintegrable hard-core unemployed." Their numbers had doubled by the spring of 1938,[20] this at a time when the German economy as a whole was already suffering from a labor shortage. The welfare budgets of the Jewish *Gemeinden* were no longer sufficient to support all those in need. For the moment the public welfare offices were still making support payments to Jewish applicants, yet these were based on such reduced payment schedules and were subject to all sorts of possible harassment that the Jewish communities

18. Ibid., p. 146. Haavara is Hebrew for "transfer" and was the official name of a scheme for preemigration capital transfer to Palestine, see W. Feilchenfeld, D. Michaelis, and L. Pinner, *Haavara-Transfer nach Palästina und Einwanderung deutscher Juden, 1933–1939* (Tübingen, 1972); "Paltreu" was the abbreviation for Palästina-Treuhandgesellschaft (Palestine Trusteeship Corporation), the corporation set up to transfer capital for Jews emigrating from Nazi Germany to Palestine as part of the Haavara Agreement.

19. StA Münster, GW, no. 10 (1935), no. 25 (1937).

20. *Jüdische Wohlfahrtspflege und Sozialpolitik*, n.s. 8 (1938): 6, 150.

were obliged to provide ever-larger supplementary amounts of aid. The Jewish Winter Relief supported 77,200 persons in the winter of 1937/38, more than 21 percent of the Jewish population, and its expenditures amounted to 3.3 million reichsmarks.[21].

The Political Context

The intensification and worsening of the economic persecution against Jews cannot be explained by any thesis that contends that this radicalization in measures was the product of some sort of internal dynamics of uncoordinated – or even competing – initiatives flowing from a supposed "dualistic" policy toward the Jews. On the contrary, it had been planned and prepared over a long period of time, and these preparations, in the context of a step-up in rearmament and planning for war, can be traced back both to the party and to government authorities.

Hitler's memorandum on the Four-Year Plan of August 1936, in which he put the accelerated military and economic preparations for war on the agenda, had made only passing mention of the Jews. Yet the context is significant: Hitler called for ensuring, "with iron-willed determination," German self-sufficiency in raw materials and recording of "all outstanding hard currency credits held by Germany abroad." For this purpose, the Reichstag was to issue two laws: "(1) A law stipulating the death penalty for economic sabotage, and (2) a law making all of Jewry liable for any damages caused to the German economy, and thus to the German people, by individuals from this criminal element."[22] In this way, the expropriation of the Jews was clearly envisioned as a component of the accelerated preparations for war within the framework of the Four-Year Plan, and one of the pretexts for that expropriation is already hinted at here. Göring's leading role in shaping policy toward the Jews, as a result of his appointment as plenipotentiary for the Four-Year Plan, was its institutional expression.

Although Hitler's memo was marked "top secret," it soon became evident that his notions about the future treatment to be

21. RV/AR 1938, p. 22.
22. Wilhelm Treue, "Hitlers Denkschrift zum Vierjahresplan 1936," *VfZ* 3 (1955): 209f.

accorded the Jews were quite well known and were being taken seriously. On December 18, 1936, State Secretary Stuckart in the Interior Ministry had already informed the Economics Ministry that discussions were in progress regarding the "formation of a Jewish Guaranty Association." These discussions had come to the conclusion that at that time the only area where such a move could be implemented was in the field of taxation policy. It was stated that the Führer had "given basic approval to the levying of a special tax on Jews" and had ordered "preparations for such a bill to be speeded up so as to make it possible to proclaim the law soon after the end of the Gustloff trial."[23]

Despite Hitler's expressed wish, it took almost two years before the measure, conceived as "expiation" for David Frankfurter's killing of Gustloff in Switzerland, was finally made a reality after the assassination of vom Rath by Herschel Grynszpan in Paris in November 1938. The reason for this postponement sprang from certain doubts on Göring's part. Although a draft law had been finalized in June 1937 in the Finance Ministry, specifying that "a special fund for the Reich was to be set up based on taxes from Jews," State Secretary Reinhardt found it necessary to inform the Führer's deputy on December 23, 1937, that proclamation of this law had been temporarily postponed. Göring, he stated, had expressed his concern that "declaration of the law at the present time might endanger the Reich's situation in respect to raw materials and foreign currency."[24]

The planned preparations for intensified plundering of the Jews were not limited solely to this special tax. Even earlier, on September 29, 1936, a discussion had taken place among state secretaries in the Interior and Economics Ministries to prepare a top-echelon discussion on policy toward the Jews "to counter the danger that Jews might gain new positions in the economy." After detailed discussion, the participants agreed on the following points:

(1) "Economic activity by Jews could only be allowed in order to enable them to earn their own living" (that is, not become a burden to public welfare), "yet their will to emigrate should not be dampened as a result of their economic and political situation. In the final

23. BA, R 2, No. 31097.
24. Ibid.

analysis, consideration would also have to be given to carrying out forced emigration as well."

(2) Since "affluent Jews as a rule are not overly enthusiastic about emigrating," the entire population group should be allowed only limited possibilities for economic activity.

(3) The exclusion of Jews from a number of business fields was discussed, referring to a suggestion made by the interior minister in June 1936.

(4) A special identifying mark for Jewish enterprises – or alternatively, "all non-Jewish businesses" – was considered, and a decision was made to follow up the plan by putting together a special list of Jewish enterprises.[25]

Along with government offices, various NSDAP authorities had also been increasingly occupied since the end of 1936 with accelerating the process of Aryanization and the removal of Jewish competitors. In the offices of the *Gauwirtschaftsberater* separate files were opened for every Jewish business still in existence, and turnover figures and the development of the firm were carefully monitored in cooperation with the local chambers of commerce and tax offices.[26]

By the spring of 1938 all preparations had been completed, so that the forced implementation could now begin. The flood of measures instituted from that point on has often been described in the literature.[27] For that reason, only brief mention will be made of the most important laws and measures. In March, the Jewish *Gemeinden* were stripped of their status as incorporated bodies under public law, altering their tax status to make them fully liable for all taxes on their income.[28] Even before that, all tax relief benefits such as child and family allowances were canceled for Jewish business people.[29] At the end of April,

25. BA, R 18, No. 5514, pp. 199–211.

26. Hundreds of such documents can be found in the holdings under "Gau-wirtschaftsberater, Gauleitung Westfalen-Süd," in StA Münster.

27. See among others Wolfgang Scheffler, *Judenverfolgung im Dritten Reich* (Berlin, 1964), pp. 27ff.; Joseph Walk, ed., *Das Sonderrecht für die Juden im NS-Staat: Eine Sammlung der gesetzlichen Maßnahmen und Richtlinien – Inhalt und Bedeutung*, Motive-Texte-Materialien, vol. 14 (Karlsruhe, 1981), pp. 209ff.; Genschel, *Die Verdrängung*, pp. 143ff.; Adam, *Judenpolitik*, pp. 172ff. Citations to Walk hereafter are to the section and document number in his collection.

28. Bruno Blau, comp., *Das Ausnahmerecht für die Juden in Deutschland, 1933–1945*, 2d ed. (Düsseldorf, 1954), pp. 41f.; Walk II/441.

29. Walk II/416, 420, 424, 426.

Göring issued a Decree against Abetting the Disguising of Jewish Commercial Enterprises,[30] a measure that undoubtedly functioned to prepare the way for the declaration and seizure of Jewish assets and firms. This was also properly understood by the public. A Salzburg daily paper reported on the decree with the headline "Cleaning Up!" and welcomed the measure as the "prelude to the basic solution of the Jewish Question in the economy."[31]

Four days later, on April 26, Göring and the Interior Ministry issued the Decree on the Declaration of Jewish Assets. Every Jew or non-Jewish spouse of a Jew was required to declare all internal and foreign assets exceeding the value of five thousand reichsmarks. In blunt language, paragraph 8 stated the further aim of this decree: the plenipotentiary for the Four-Year Plan was "authorized to take steps to ensure the utilization of assessable assets in the interests of the German economy."[32] At the same time, an implementation decree stipulated that every sale, lease, or "order of usufructal rights" in Jewish firms required a special permit.[33] Interior Minister Frick explained the purpose of the stipulations in a secret report on *Jews in the Economy* dated June 14, 1938: this "introduces the solution to the Jewish Question in the economic sphere. In the discussion on April 29, 1938, . . . consideration was given to how to transform Jewish property in Germany into assets that would preclude any further economic influence . . . in order to achieve a final exclusion of Jews from the German economy."

For the immediate future, Frick considered "a regulation necessary aimed . . . at a *compulsory* exclusion of the Jews." After he had given a detailed presentation of his proposals in this regard and had evaluated the possibilities for emigration as being very unfavorable, aside from the option of Palestine, Frick dedicated the final section of his remarks to the question of sources of livelihood for the remaining Jews: "Insofar as Jews can live off the proceeds of their commercial and other assets, they require strict state supervision. Insofar as they are in need of financial assistance, the question of their *public* support must

---

30. Verordnung gegen die Unterstützung der Tarnung jüdischer Gewerbebetriebe, ibid., 453.
31. *Salzburger Volksblatt*, September 25, 1938.
32. Walk II/457; Blau, *Das Ausnahmerecht*, pp. 43f.
33. Walk II/458.

be solved. It will not be possible to avoid greater utilization of the relief associations."[34]

Of the "values permitting one to exercise economic influence," Frick singled out the "working capital of the Jews" in his report as the most important; for this reason, he welcomed the fact that the "report form indicates that working capital should be separately listed."[35] He may have been surprised about the survey on assets and the low proportion of working capital included. Yet there was no doubt that the decree was aimed at the more distant future and was designed to prepare the way for the "utilization" or "seizure" of all Jewish property. In a questionnaire containing many pages, highly detailed information was asked about each capital investment – be it stocks and bonds, life insurance or outstanding debts, luxury articles or art objects – so that hardly anything could be left undeclared.[36] In addition, Jews were encouraged, via semiofficial hints, intentionally directed rumor, and ambiguous newspaper reports, not to declare their assets below their full value. State Secretary Brinckmann commented in a press conference, also participated in by foreign journalists, that valuation of their assets was being left to the Jews themselves so that the owners could be compensated in case of seizure by the state.[37] Ernst Herzfeld, a Jewish observer active at the time in a leading position and well acquainted with the situation, reported that "there was a widespread suspicion, possibly spread by the Nazis, that there was an intention to 'purchase' Jewish assets in return for full or partial compensation. Naturally, nothing more than the declared value would be indemnified. . . . These considerations led a fair number of individuals to declare the value of their real estate and other assets to be higher than the actual taxable worth."[38]

In July 1938, all still-existing Jewish enterprises were registered on the basis of the Third Decree to the Reich Citizenship

34. BA, R 18, No. 5519, pp. 153–62 (emphases in original).
35. Ibid., p. 155.
36. An original example of the questionnaire is contained in the Wiener Library, Tel Aviv University, PC 3/51.
37. *Foreign Relations of the United States: Diplomatic Papers, 1938*, vol. 2, p. 366.
38. Ernst Herzfeld, "Meine letzten Jahre in Deutschland, 1933–1938," Archives, Leo Baeck Institute, New York, ME 163, p. 43 (also contained in YVA, Jerusalem 01/8).

Law.[39] This form also called for highly accurate information on one's total wealth and current business situation.[40] It is regrettable that more of this material, which gives an exact picture of the situation of Jewish enterprises, has not been preserved or has not been unearthed to date. The fact that it had to be filled out in quadruplicate clearly proves the close degree of cooperation between the tax offices, chambers of commerce, and municipal administrations and the local party authorities in connection with this "inventory." There can be no doubt that all these offices, which even earlier had been in close contact in implementing Aryanizations, were now working hand in hand.

The Law on Changes in Trade Regulations of July 6, 1938,[41] prohibited Jews from practicing all those professions and occupations mentioned in the discussion of September 29, 1936. Some of these occupations, such as marriage brokerage or professional watchman duty, had only a small number of Jewish practitioners. In contrast, the prohibition on activity in itinerant trade, as a pedlar or traveling salesman, struck especially hard. These were the most important alternative vocations taken up by dismissed white-collar and blue-collar workers, and especially by former independent tradesmen, after they had been obliged to shut down or sell their firms. The occupation of the pedlar, which already from the mid-nineteenth century was not ranked among occupations typical for Jews, became "respectable" once again in the Third Reich. The party and its affiliated small businessmen's associations viewed these developments with alarm. In their periodical *Der Aufbau*, it was claimed in early 1938 that 18 to 20 percent of all those in itinerant occupations were Jews.[42] Since there is no further evidence, this statement cannot be verified. The change in the commercial code was also designed to close this "dangerous gap" in legislation aimed at excluding Jews from economic life.

In July 1938, the approximately 3,000 Jewish doctors still active in the Altreich were prohibited from practicing their profession. Only 709 of them were allowed to continue their activities under the designation medical practitioner (*Krankenbehandler*), though such activity was restricted to the treatment of

39. *Dritte Verordnung zum Reichsbürgergesetz*, Walk II/503.
40. Wiener Library, PC 3/57.
41. Gesetz zur Änderung der Gewerbeordnung, Walk II/500.
42. *Der Aufbau*, January 1, 1938.

Jewish patients only.[43] An occupational prohibition for Jewish lawyers was introduced the following September. Of the 1,753 Jewish lawyers still active in the profession in the Reich in January 1938, only 172 were allowed to advise and represent Jewish clients using the professional title of legal counsel (*Rechtskonsulent*).[44]

Along with legislation, the administrative measures undertaken by state and party authorities perhaps quietly undermined even more the economic situation of the Jews. Ernst Herzfeld reports: "Silently and tenaciously, the conditions for Jewish economic existence were made more severe. Factory owners were denied access to raw materials, or procurement was blocked completely. . . . [O]ur grievances fell mainly on deaf ears in the ministries. . . . [T]he ministerial bureaucracy did not wish, insofar as it was in any way favorably disposed to do so, to go out of its way for Jews."[45] The difficulties of Jewish workers increased at the local level even when there was no legal basis for this. In particular, the *Gauwirtschaftsberater* made sure, even before issuance of the new commercial code of July 6, 1938, that Jews were denied licenses as pedlars or that a renewal was not granted. After the change in the code, the Office for Artisan Crafts and Trade of the NSDAP in Bochum referred to a still-existing alternative and demanded that the matter be remedied: no itinerant's license was necessary to practice the occupation of door-to-door salesman in one's own town or city. According to various sources, some ten thousand Jewish sales representatives were still able to earn something in this way in Berlin. That situation had to be remedied, it was argued, since "it is precisely the Jewish door-to-door salesman . . . who knows only too well how to touch the hearts of our housewives with tearful tales of woe about the unfortunate plight of the Jews . . . to derive profit from such tales for himself and his race."[46]

43. Vierte Verordnung zum Reichsbürgergesetz, Walk II/510; Stephan Liebfried, "Stationen der Abwehr: Berufsverbote für jüdische Ärzte im Dritten Reich, 1933–1938, und die Zerstörung des sozialen Asyls durch die organisierten Ärzteschaften des Auslands," *Bulletin des Leo Baeck Instituts*, no. 62 (1982): 11.

44. Fünfte Verordnung zum Reichsbürgergesetz, Walk II/547; Wiener Library, PC 3/61.

45. Herzfeld, "Meine letzten Jahre," p. 42.

46. StA Münster, GW, no. 139. Cf. also Peter Hanke, *Zur Geschichte der Juden in München zwischen 1933 und 1945*, Schriftenreihe des Stadtarchivs München, Heft 3 (Munich, 1967), pp. 144, 199f.

Accelerated Legislation

All legislative and administrative measures were designed to bring about an accelerated *Entjudung* of the economy – in other words, the total disappearance of Jewish firms – by means of "voluntary" sale or closure. The use of violence was employed to augment the action and help it along. Already in January 1937, the Judenreferat in SD headquarters had recommended "popular anger" as the "most effective means" to accelerate "a solution to the Jewish Question." That anger "vents itself in violent excesses of which the Jew has learned a great deal through pogroms and from which he fears nothing quite so much as a hostile mood that can turn spontaneously against him."[47]

Juilius Streicher, editor of *Der Stürmer*, seized the initiative at the end of 1937 with a Christmas boycott in Nuremberg. Other cities followed suit, and the disturbances reached a new high point in Berlin in June 1938 with the defacing of storefront windows and violent attacks against Jews. On June 22, 1938, the American ambassador sent a detailed report on these pogrom-like disturbances and added: "The present campaign against the Jews outstrips in thoroughness anything of the kind since 1933. . . . Just as the outbursts of 1935 led to the Nuremberg legislation of September of that year, it is expected that the present campaign will also result in further legislative measures."[48] The ambassador had thus clearly comprehended the tactical combination characteristic of National Socialist policy toward the Jews.

As foreseen and intended, the result was a step-up in the wave of Aryanizations throughout the entire year of 1938. Nonetheless, it must be emphasized once again that the extent of these Aryanizations should be viewed – in the context of the previous long-term sequence of developments – as the remaining step in an ongoing process of liquidation and plunder and not, as Genschel suggests, as the "boom period for Aryanizations."[49] At the beginning of 1938, Jewish retail trade and the free professions had largely been closed out of the economy and eliminated. At least half of all Jewish blue-collar and white-collar workers were unemployed. In contrast large industrial con-

47. BA, R 58, no. 956, SD-HA Ref. II/112, Zum Judenproblem, January 1937.
48. *Foreign Relations*, vol. 2, p. 382.
49. Genschel, *Die Verdrängung*, p. 218.

cerns, as well as some firms in wholesale trade and import/ export, private banks and, curiously enough, Jewish artisan crafts, had been spared this fate to a relatively large extent.

The reasons for this grace period have not as yet been fully explained. They were probably different for each of the various economic branches. The Jewish artisan crafts, the bulk of which were concentrated in the garment field, were, like retail trade, exposed to the competition from small businessmen, and it is therefore all the more astonishing that in December 1938 there were still 5,800 Jewish artisan enterprises in Germany. In mid-1935, there had been 8,500 such firms.[50] There are two plausible reasons for this: first of all, the percentage of Jews involved in the artisan crafts was much lower than in commercial retail trade.[51] Consequently, it is likely that the limited Jewish presence engendered less anti-Semitic competitive aggression in this branch. Second, the Jewish craft firms had apparently fallen upon such hard times that there were hardly any interested Aryan buyers wishing to take them over. In the main, these were mostly small tailors, furriers, or hatmakers, many of Eastern European origin, who even previously had been used to hardship and a frugal way of life. They now clung tenaciously to their modest sources of income, for which they were unable to find any alternative. This assumption is confirmed by the fact that almost all of the Jewish craft firms and shops were liquidated between December 1938 and the end of March 1939; of the 5,800 still in existence, only 345 were Aryanized.[52]

In contrast, the large Jewish concerns had been spared longer, most likely due to their economic power of resistance. In the early years of the Third Reich, considerations of employment policy had been dominant in government thinking, and that had prevented the taking of any harsh measures against labor-

---

50. 1938, according to RV/AR 1938, pp. 15f.; 1935 according to Herbert Kahn, "Das jüdische Handwerk in Deutschland: Eine Untersuchung aufgrund statistischer Unterlagen der Reichsvertretung der Juden in Deutschland, Berlin 1936," mimeographed manuscript, p. 1, Wiener Library, KY 3/W1.

51. According to the June 1933 census, 19,319 Jews were independently employed in industry and the craft trades; their representation in this branch of the economy was 0.43 percent. In contrast, 72,662 Jews were listed in the commercial branches, constituting a share of 4.25 percent of the total there. Separate figures for the artisan crafts cannot be precisely calculated on the basis of available data.

52. RV/AR 1938, pp. 15f.

intensive Jewish firms. The large concerns enjoyed an additional advantage: as long as some semblance of legality was preserved, the Aryanization of these large enterprises required substantial amounts of capital. Interested Aryan parties with the requisite capital at their disposal chose in many cases to wait until they could buy up these firms at more favorable prices due to increasing pressure on the Jews. A typical example of this is Flick's behavior in connection with Aryanization of the Simson weapons factory in 1934–35 and the Lübeck smelting plant, in which the Jewish iron-ore firm Rawack & Grünfeld AG had a working interest, in 1936–37.[53] In addition, the large Jewish concerns relied on their standing assets and their business contacts in Germany and abroad and were in no hurry to finalize sale deals under unfavorable conditions.

At the end of 1937 both sides apparently understood that the period of tedious and drawn-out negotiations was nearly over. The Jewish owners discovered too late that now they were forced to sell their property not only far beneath its value, but generally under more unfavorable terms than might have been possible only a short time before. Genschel, on the basis of data contained in the *Jüdische Rundschau*, records 796 Aryanizations for the entire German Reich for the period of January to October 1938 alone. This included 340 factories, 260 of which were in textile and garment manufacture, 30 of which were in the shoe and leather industry, and 370 of which were wholesale firms.[54] Twenty-two private banks were also Aryanized in that same time period, including such respectable old banking houses as M.M. Warburg, Bleichröder, Gebr. Arnhold, Dreyfus, and Hirschland.[55]

The competition to buy up medium-sized and smaller Jewish firms at rock-bottom prices continued. The still-existing Jewish firms, singled out as being relatively profitable objects for potential Aryanization (rather than candidates for liquidation) on the basis of inquiries by the *Gauwirtschaftsberater* and the chambers

---

53. Ibid., pp. 173ff. The Jewish press only reported on Aryanizations of large and better-known firms. According to my estimate, based on various data sources, a total of 4,500 to 5,000 Jewish firms of all sizes were Aryanized between the end of 1937 and November 1938 (see also RV/AR 1938). On Flick see my article, "Die deutschen Unternehmer und die Judenpolitik im 'Dritten Reich,'" *Geschichte und Gesellschaft* 15 (1989): 235–37.

54. Genschel, *Die Verdrängung*, pp. 173ff.

55. Ibid.

of commerce and government offices cooperating with them, brought numerous party members and other *Volksgenossen* onto the scene who had previously gone empty-handed and now wished to take advantage of this final chance to line their pockets. This was the period of the "unbridled enrichment of those who felt they had gotten a raw deal and now belonged to the ranks of the parvenus."[56] The methods of extortion became more and more brutal, and municipal authorities competed with party offices in efforts to intimidate Jewish business proprietors even further and render them tractable.

By this juncture, however, special efforts in that regard were hardly necessary. The *Gauwirtschaftsberater* for South Westphalia reported with satisfaction to the Commission on Economic Policy at Munich party headquarters on March 24, 1938, that only in rare cases was it necessary to summon Jews to appear at the mayor's office. "The Jews soften up and turn compliant as soon as they learn that the party is looking into them personally."[57] With a bit of extra pressure, the owners of businesses in the process of liquidation could be prevented, even without a legal pretext, from selling off their stock inventories separately before Aryanization or from holding liquidation sales.[58]

An instructive, though far from representative, letter by a Munich merchant who had been employed as an expert consultant in Aryanization cases, expresses the dominant atmosphere at the time. The writer, describing himself as a "National Socialist, member of the SA, and admirer of Hitler," states that "[I] was so disgusted by the brutal . . . and extortionary methods employed against the Jews that, from now on, I refuse to be involved in any way with Aryanizations, although this means losing a handsome consultancy fee. . . . As an experienced, honest, and upstanding businessman, I [can] no longer stand idly by and countenance the way many Aryan businessmen, entrepreneurs, and the like . . . are shamelessly attempting to grab up Jewish shops and factories, etc., as cheaply as possible and for a ludicrous price. These people are like vultures, swarming down with bleary eyes, their tongues hanging out

56. Ibid., p. 247.
57. StA Münster, GW, no. 682.
58. Ibid., no. 707.

with greed, to feed upon the Jewish carcass."[59]

The statistical data from Munich also indicate quite clearly that the "race for Aryanization" involved only a small number of Jewish businesses still remaining in operation. In February 1938, there were still 1,680 "Jewish tradesmen" in Munich. By October 4, that number had shrunk to 666, of whom two-thirds had a foreign passport. Hanke is correct in regarding these figures as proof that even before November 9 "the elimination of the Jews had reached its final stage."[60] In a similar vein, a newspaper article at the time observed that in retail trade "the number of businesses changing hands [was] not so great because . . . there had already been a step-up in the number of transfers in recent years." Nonetheless, during the course of 1938, a number of larger firms, "both in the industrial sector and in wholesale and retail trade, had been Aryanized," and there was "a veritable mountain of applications for permits" on the desk of the *Gauwirtschaftsberater*.[61]

In summary, a document which can be regarded as a faithful description of the situation of the Jews at that time deserves to be quoted at length. The document is entitled "Memorandum on the Treatment of Jews in the Capital in All Areas of Public Life." It is highly probable that it was prepared by one of the *Judenreferenten* in early 1938 for Julius Lippert, state commissioner and mayor of Berlin.[62] The author notes a "recent unusually strong influx to Berlin . . . attributable to the fact that Jews in outlying areas . . . see fewer and fewer possibilities for earning a living there." He recommended that this influx should not be completely prohibited since there were "better opportunities for preparing for one's emigration" in Berlin. However, a permit to move to Berlin should be restricted to certain neighborhoods in town, "with the additional stipulation that pursuit

59. Letter of April 16, 1938 to the Chamber of Industry and Commerce, Munich, given in Hanke, *Juden in München*, pp. 154f.

60. Ibid., p. 224.

61. *Fränkische Tageszeitung*, September 3, 1938.

62. "Denkschrift über die Behandlung der Juden in der Reichshauptstadt auf allen Gebieten des öffentlichen Lebens," YVA, 08/17. The date and signature are missing, but an internal source analysis makes it clear that the document was written sometime between May 1 and June 16, 1938. That its purpose was to bring together and stimulate measures that could only be decided upon at higher levels of government, that the writer was extremely familiar with the relevant legislation and all practical measures, and that he also took concerns about foreign policy into consideration are also clear.

113

of any employment in Berlin would be enjoined." "While it appeared impracticable at the moment to concentrate Berlin Jews within a ghetto, one could ensure in this way that there would be no new settlement by Jews in specific neighborhoods, thus indirectly leading to the creation of a kind of ghetto over the longer term." In contrast, the writer is less concerned about the danger that in-migrating Jews might "become a burden for public welfare" in view of the "to-date satisfactory regulation adopted by Berlin welfare offices denying Jews migrating into the city any public welfare assistance."[63]

In respect to the Jewish school system, the memorandum notes that in 1937 there were still 2,122 Jewish pupils attending public schools and that the Education Ministry was, at the moment, looking into the entire matter. "In this connection, consideration should be given to the possibility of canceling compulsory education for Jewish children altogether." This suggestion appears to have found especial favor with the official to whom the memorandum was addressed because he commented in a handwritten remark in the margin: "Yes, excellent! They don't have to be able to read because ignorance is no legal protection against being punished."[64]

Since the memorandum was apparently written before issuance of the Fourth and Fifth Decrees to the Reich Citizenship Law, the writer deals in detail with Jewish doctors and attorneys. He notes there are still 742 Jewish lawyers and 1,623 Jewish doctors in Berlin, but a number of these were "no longer practicing or had only a very limited practice left." There were an "especially large number of elderly [doctors], who were enjoined from treating welfare patients . . . and Jewish hospital doctors were only employed in Jewish hospitals at that point."[65] The memorandum goes on to deal with other professions. Its author does not regard "more extensive measures as . . . necessary," since there were only a very small number of Jews still active in these professions. However, he was alarmed about some "five hundred German Jews involved in license-free urban peddling at the Berlin markets," while "there are hardly any applications . . . for municipal permits for pedlars, . . . and the municipal administrative court is turning down all applications

63. Ibid., pp. 16f.
64. Ibid., p. 22.
65. Ibid., p. 29.

114

on principle for lack of need." He is somewhat relieved by the circumstance that a corresponding change in the law was already being considered by the Economics Ministry, although "this would mean that all Aryan itinerant tradesmen, numbering in the tens of thousands, would also be required to get a permit."[66]

The Jewish pedlars and traveling salesmen gave the author of the memorandum cause for worry since the "number of applications from Jews for licenses and peddling permits is unusually high." Attempts by police authorities "to turn down Jewish applications, in cooperation with the Gestapo, on the grounds that there is reason to assume that Jews will use the practice of their trade for subversive purposes" had not been upheld by the courts. Consequently, the author comes to the conclusion that "a change in the Reich commercial code should be recommended in this extremely important area. . . . [I]n this regard, a general restriction on freedom to trade for Jews via alteration of the existing code should also be considered."[67] As we have seen, this well-informed and anonymous Berlin expert on Jewish affairs did not need to wait all too long for this to come about.

This memorandum, to my knowledge previously unknown, sheds light on the actual economic situation of Jews even before the harshest measures instituted in 1938. One should keep in mind that the situation in Berlin was far more favorable than in other cities or even in the countryside. There can be no doubt that the intensified influx to Berlin had not only been the result of preparations for emigration. Along with the legitimate assumption made by Jews that they would be socially more secure in a large community and would be better protected against anti-Semitic attacks in Berlin, economic motives most certainly also played a significant role.

Staging the Pogrom

On October 28–29, 1938, some eighteen thousand Jews with Polish citizenship were arrested by the Gestapo and deported a short time later across the Polish frontier. They were only

66. Ibid., p. 32.
67. Ibid., p. 36.

permitted to take a small amount of hand baggage and ten reichsmarks per person. This first mass deportation to the east was an anticipation – in its manner of implementation and in the reaction of the populace and the indifference shown by foreign governments as well – of later deportations, setting the grim tone to come. The pretext for the action had been provided by an ordinance issued by the Polish government in October 1938; this stipulated that the checking of the passports of Polish citizens living abroad, ordered in March of that year, had to be completed by October 30. The German authorities consequently wished to be rid of the Eastern European Jews living in the Reich before they lost their Polish citizenship.

The Jews affected by this measure were seized in their homes or arrested on the street, herded together for a brief period in jails and at other collection points, and then loaded onto railroad cars and shipped to the Polish border. The first trainloads were allowed by the Polish authorities to pass, but soon thereafter, the government decided to close the border for these unfortunate individuals. Over eight thousand who had been shipped to the frontier were forced to stay out under the open sky, exposed to the rain and cold, in a no-man's-land between Neu-Bentschen and Zbąszyń in Posen/Poznan, until Polish and international Jewish relief organizations were able to arrange emergency housing and food for them. Also among the Jews deported to Zbąszyń was the family of Sendel Grynszpan from Hanover. Their son Herschel, who had already emigrated from Germany, fired the shots on November 7 which killed the German legation secretary vom Rath in the Paris embassy. According to Herschel's own testimony, this deed was to avenge the injustice his parents had suffered. The assassination served as the direct pretext for the November 9–10 pogrom.[68]

During that night of November 9–10, organized "popular anger" was vented against the Jews throughout all of Germany. Almost all of the still-extant synagogues, some four hundred in number, went up in flames, and approximately one hundred Jews lost their lives. Thirty thousand largely affluent Jews were sent to concentration camps, and it is not known precisely how many of these perished there. The streets were thick with the

---

68. Sybil Milton, "The Expulsion of Polish Jews from Germany, October 1938 to July 1939: A Documentation," *YLBI* 29 (1984): 169–99.

shattered plate glass from the display windows of some 7,500 Jewish shops and businesses attacked during the pogrom – according to our estimates, there cannot have been many more than this number in existence at the time.[69] This shattered glass is what gave the November pogrom the name it has since been known by in the history books and popular memory, Reichskristallnacht. Even today, the exact origin of this term is not completely clear. If it really was a popular coining, then this reflects anything but a sense of sympathy on the part of the population, or even hidden protest. The term "Crystal Night" sparkles, glistens, and gleams, as if it were a festive occasion! It is high time that this malicious and misleadingly metaphoric term, which downplays the reality it designates, should disappear, at the very least from historiographical parlance.

In the research literature, the discussion of who seized the initiative and who was directly responsible for the pogrom seems almost trivial, at least in terms of the context treated here. It is relatively securely documented that Goebbels obtained Hitler's consent at the annual meeting of the party veterans (*alte Kämpfer*) in Munich and then gave the signal for the pogrom in a speech of incitement. There is also clear evidence for the participation of the SS and the at-least passive complicity of the police. Even if it should be true that, as Göring claimed, he was taken totally by surprise when he learned of the events during an overnight train trip, he was only angry because of the destruction of valuable property that had resulted. As he expressly stated, he would have much preferred, in place of the destruction, to see two hundred Jews murdered instead.[70]

All these details do nothing to change the basic facts: from the autumn of 1937, there had been an intensification in policy toward the Jews, ordered by the top echelon, and that was implemented with growing severity during the course of 1938. Its declared aim was to prohibit any economic activity by Jews – first gradually, step-by-step, then absolutely – in order to accelerate emigration. As much of their property as possible was to be left in Germany so that it could be utilized for war preparations.

---

69. *Former Communal Property in Germany: A Questionnaire Survey by the American Federation of Jews from Germany*, [1947], p. 11; Scheffler, *Judenverfolgung*, pp. 30f.

70. *IMT*, vol. 37, PS–1816; Lionel Kochan, *Pogrom: 10. November 1938* (London, 1957), pp. 107, 131f.

The plan was to conclude this phase provisionally with the expropriation of Jewish assets; these would then be made available for immediate or later utilization to aid the Reich. This objective was prepared in detail on the basis of close cooperation between government, party, and economic authorities months before the pogrom. The following quote from a newspaper serves to substantiate that the implications of these plans had been correctly understood by contemporaries:

> For a long time now, National Socialism has been making preparations to take decisive economic steps in the wake of the political conclusions arrived at in dealing with the Jews. . . . The regulation for taking inventory introduced this year by the government [was an indication of] future efforts to enhance economic performance and to exclude Jewish influence from the economy. Thus, the special utilization of Jewish capital would have come about anyhow in one form or another sooner or later. However, the shots fired in Paris . . . have triggered an early start."[71]

The writer was mistaken in his final assertion: everything points to the fact that the assassination in Paris not only provided a propagandistic pretext, but also came at an opportune point in time for the National Socialists to implement their economic measures and was made more favorable by the political events. Two weeks after the conclusion of the Munich Agreement, Göring had declared in a closed meeting on October 14, 1938, that "Jews now must be driven out of the economy." Their assets would have to be transferred in an orderly manner to the Reich and should not be squandered as a "welfare system for incompetent party members."[72] Already on October 28, the German Federation of Banks and Savings and Loan Associations informed its members that the Foreign Currency Control Office, headed by Heydrich since July 1938, was preparing "security orders" for Jewish assets, "designed to restrict the control of the owners over their various assets."[73]

Two months earlier, the Economics Ministry had pressed all those offices dealing with registration of Jewish assets to finish the job by September 30, if necessary by engaging additional

71. *Berliner Börsen-Zeitung*, November 19, 1938.
72. *IMT*, vol. 37, PS–1301.
73. Circular Letter, October 28, 1938, quoted in Adam, *Judenpolitik*, p. 184.

personnel, "in order to make preparations for possible seizure of a portion of Jewish assets for purposes of the German economy."[74] Beginning in June 1938, a number of additional offices were zealously at work on these preparations. The tax offices and the Gestapo, assisted by the chambers of commerce and the *Gauwirtschaftsberater*, drew up various lists of affluent Jews. Fifteen hundred Jews in concentration camps who had been arrested in June 1938 were put to work building additional barracks.[75]

On the basis of these preparations, it proved possible to implement decisive measures right after the pogrom. Hitler's notion of a Jewish Guaranty Association (Judengarantieverband) could finally now be made a reality – not, as earlier plans envisioned, by introduction of a special tax, but rather by an immediate confiscation of property in the form of the so-called *Sühneleistung* ("atonement fine").[76] The organizational prerequisites for this had been created through the registration of assets and the instructions sent by the Foreign Currency Control Office to the banks. In addition to the *Sühneleistung*, which assumed the form of a one-time penalty of one billion reichsmarks, the Jews were required to "restore the appearance of the streets" at their own expense. Moreover, the insurance payments for property damage were confiscated by the Reich.[77] That same day, November 12, saw the issuance of the First Decree on the Exclusion of Jews from German Economic Life. This decree prohibited virtually all still-extant options for gainful employment and ordered the dismissal of employees without any right on their part to claim pensions or compensation.[78] The immediate issuance of these detailed regulations reflects very thorough preparations; it was by no means an improvisation as the result of a "premature start."

The first implementation decree for collecting the "atonement fine" was promulgated on November 21, 1938. It demonstrated just how much the earlier decrees for plundering the Jews could be effectively utilized. The tax was levied on each individual Jew

74. Hauptstaatsarchiv Düsseldorf, OFD Düsseldorf, Br. 1026/276, Express Letter from Economics Ministry, August 19, 1938.
75. YVA, 01/249; Scheffler, *Judenverfolgung*, pp. 28f.; Kochan, *Pogrom*, p. 34; Esh, "Between Discrimination and Extermination."
76. Walk, III/13.
77. Ibid., III/7.
78. Ibid., III/8.

on the basis of the asset declaration form of April 26, stipulating that 20 percent of the total sum of declared assets was to be paid in four installments on or before August 15, 1939.[79] Changes in assets that had occurred in the interim were taken into account by the tax offices charged with collecting this penalty tax only in the case of a special order issued by higher authorities. In October 1939, the tax was raised to 25 percent of reported assets, since the total of one billion reichsmarks had supposedly not been reached.[80]

In actual fact, 1.127 billion reichsmarks were collected, leaving aside the amount of 225 million in confiscated insurance paid to the Reich for damages caused during the pogrom. If one adds the amounts collected from the Reich capital flight tax levied on Jewish emigrants during the ten months between the pogrom and the outbreak of the war, the sum transferred from Jewish property directly to the coffers of the Reich in this period reaches a total of over 2 billion reichsmarks. This does not include profits from Aryanizations pocketed by individuals or Jewish so-called contributions to party organizations.[81] The undisguised official plundering of German Jews had thus been inaugurated long before the procedures were perfected bureaucratically in connection with the mass deportations to the east after the outbreak of the war.

The Decree on the Utilization of Jewish Assets (Verordnung über den Einsatz des jüdischen Vermögens) issued on December 3, 1938, can be viewed as marking the temporary conclusion of the intensified measures introduced in the autumn of the previous year. It stipulated the "forced Aryanization" – if necessary, using the trustees appointed by the authorities – of all Jewish firms that had still not been sold or dissolved, although those firms had been prohibited since November from operating. At the same time, an order was issued requiring the deposit of cash, securities, jewelry, and other valuables in specially supervised blocked accounts (*Sperrkonten*). Any payments from these accounts were subject to a formal special permit.[82]

79. Erste Durchführungsverordnung zum Einzug der "Sühneleistung," ibid., III/21; StA Dahlem, Rep. 151, No. 2193.

80. StA Dahlem, ibid.; Walk, IV/23.

81. Raul Hilberg, *The Destruction of the European Jews*, 2d ed. (Chicago, 1967), pp. 92f.

82. Walk III/46; Genschel, *Die Verdrängung*, p. 188.

Despite Göring's declaration of October 14, 1938, deserving party members began the "final run" to grab up Jewish businesses still considered to be interesting propositions. "Unjustified profits" as a result of *Entjudung* were not seized by the Reich until issuance of a decree to that effect in February 1939.[83] According to the available sources, it does not appear that this decree had much effect. Since it was not retroactive, it was tantamount to locking the stable door after most of the horses had already escaped – or, in this instance, had been stolen. In practical terms the decree seems to have been implemented only in respect to the *Entjudung* of urban and rural real estate because that had taken place at a relatively late date.

The tactics of the National Socialist rulers, which were aimed at inducing accelerated emigration of Jews by exacerbated economic and physical persecution, had considerable success. In 1938 and 1939, some 120,000 Jews left Germany, almost as many as during the entire preceding five years.[84] Most of them, only a short time before still relatively wealthy individuals who had hesitated to part from their possessions and emigrate without secure prospects for the future, now fled the country penniless. They were literally fleeced, stripped of their possessions by "legal" means. What was left after the tax offices were finished with them had to be deposited in blocked accounts that were virtually inaccessible. Such accounts were later confiscated by the Reich using new legislation. The henchmen of the SA and SS also got their spoils: tens of thousands of Jews in concentration camps were only able to get out, despite the fact that they had valid emigration documents, after they had left enormous amounts of money, automobiles, or other property to local party groups or even to individual Nazis as a form of "voluntary contribution."[85]

For those Jews who remained, the last chapter of their existence in Germany commenced even before the outbreak of the war. From the end of 1938, the only possibilities for gainful employment were within the framework of the Jewish community. From this point on, Jewish income flowed almost

83. Walk III/132.

84. Strauss, "Nazi Policies," p. 326; Werner Rosenstock, "Exodus, 1933–1939: A Survey of Jewish Emigration from Germany," *YLBI* 1 (1956): 377.

85. Eugen Kogon, *Der SS-Staat: Das System der deutschen Konzentrationslager*, 2d ed. (Frankfurt, 1965), pp. 193f.

exclusively from the savings funds of Jewish organizations and private individuals. The Jewish Guaranty Association planned by Hitler in 1936 was completed and made a reality with the formation of the Reichsvereinigung der Juden in Deutschland.[86] That organization was officially proclaimed on July 7, 1938, but had already been effectively established at the beginning of the year.

Under the daily supervision of the Gestapo, the Reichsvereinigung increasingly managed all areas of Jewish life and administered cemeteries and synagogues, schools, welfare institutions, and the system of medical care. After the beginning of the war, the Reichsvereinigung distributed rationed foods and provided for a constantly growing number of destitute Jews, utilizing its own monetary reserves for this purpose. These efforts were financed using the assets of the disbanded Jewish *Gemeinden* and the remainder of Jewish private property that had been seized at the order and under the surveillance of the Gestapo. Already from the beginning of 1939, the Jews lived in an almost completely closed "economic ghetto," ekeing out a living from their savings of the past, until in the end they were even obliged to pay the very costs of deportation to the extermination camps from their own meager means.

86. Walk III/211.

Depriving Jews of Their Legal Rights in The Third Reich

Jonny Moser

The violent excesses during the so-called Reichskristallnacht mark the beginning of a new chapter in anti-Jewish legislation in the Third Reich, one which ultimately was to lead to the destruction of any form of Jewish existence in Germany. Up until that juncture, legislative policy toward the Jews had proceeded in a more or less unplanned manner. Many offices in the central government had practiced their own particular Jewish policy. Laws, decrees, enactments, and orders were not only issued by central government offices, but were also interpreted and further developed by agencies at the state and local level. These authorities often overlapped and showed certain regional differences in respect to the timing of legislation as well.

From an Austrian perspective, one can distinguish three distinct phases in the Jewish policy of the Nazi state: (1) the period until early 1938, (2) from the Anschluß to the Kristallnacht, and (3) the period beginning in the aftermath of that night. The first phase served to implement and make a reality of all the points of the NSDAP Party Program of 1920, a process which climaxed with the issuance of the Nuremberg Laws[1] in 1935. The National Socialist legal conception of the Jew is clearly defined and established in those laws. Jews are degraded to the level of an inferior race and from then on form a separate segment of the population in Germany. The Jewish policy practiced during this phase humiliated the Jews, isolating them from the rest of the population. Jews were denied certain options for professional training, and earning a viable living was rendered very difficult for them. Jews were prevented from keeping various religious

---

1. The Reichsbürgergesetz of September 15, 1935 (RGBl 1935, Teil I, p. 1146) and Law on the Protection of German Blood and German Honor (Gesetz zum Schutze des deutschen Blutes und der deutschen Ehre), September 15, 1935 (RGBl 1935, Teil I, p. 1146).

123

rules[2] and customs in Judaism. Their representative organizations and religious *Gemeinden* were stripped of their status as bodies incorporated under public law and were allowed solely the status of private associations.[3]

The demand of *mittelständische* circles for the exclusion of Jews from public and economic life was, for the time being, only partially met. Their formal exclusion was implemented in public administration and the free professions: civil-service officials, lawyers, physicians, pharmacists, journalists, actors and artists, tax consultants, and university professors were hampered in the practice of their professions and were in some instances already even shut out from professional life altogether.

With the Anschluß of Austria, anti-Jewish legislation entered a second phase characterized by numerous decrees and enactments which paved the way for expropriation of Jewish property and assets and the so-called *Entjudung* of economic life. The Reich agencies, cooperating with the plenipotentiary for the Four-Year Plan, Hermann Göring, had already agreed at the end of 1937 that Jewish property and assets should be transferred to German hands, if need be even by coercion. This was a process which would, it was reasoned, serve as the basis for financing a more rapid expansion of the German armaments industry. It was no accident that Göring, during his brief tenure as economics minister, had revamped the Economics Ministry into an "executive organ for implementation of the Four-Year Plan."[4]

What the economists of the Reich had not anticipated was the surprisingly swift Anschluß of Austria and the resulting difficulties with Austrian National Socialists arising from that move: the Austrians wished to compensate their party veterans for their "years of hardship," using funds from confiscated Jewish assets.[5] In addition, many Austrian party functionaries and sympathizers had placed themselves – or had been appointed – as provisional directors in Jewish firms during the period of radical change. This resulted in the so-called provisional administrators' plague. Within a very short span of time, several

2. RGBl 1936, I, pp. 203, 212.

3. Ibid., p. 338.

4. Helmut Genschel, *Die Verdrängung der Juden aus der Wirtschaft im Dritten Reich* (Göttingen, 1966), pp. 144f.

5. Jonny Moser, "Das Unwesen der kommissarischen Leiter," in Helmut Konrad and Wolfgang Neugebauer, eds., *Arbeiterbewegung, Faschismus, Nationalbewußtsein* (Vienna, 1983), p. 89.

million reichsmarks disappeared in a multitude of ways into private pockets or, wasted on populist purposes, into various party channels and coffers. Government offices in the Reich had quickly understood that, if this practice was not stopped quickly, it would lead to the total destruction of many industrial enterprises crucially needed by Göring for the Four-Year Plan. Nothing could be done about this wantonness at first for fear of harming the outcome of Hitler's referendum on April 10, 1938. In addition, a two-week "breather period" was decreed after the vote in order to help cool feelings down. After Hitler had appointed Josef Bürckel Reich commissar for the reunification of Austria with the German Reich on April 23, 1938,[6] the central government agencies were finally free to act.

On April 28, 1938, a decree was passed calling for the registration of all Jewish assets to determine their existence and amount.[7] From that point on, it was possible for the authorities to oversee and control every sale, leasing, or reopening of a Jewish business or factory. Thus began the *Entjudung* of the economy. It now became possible to meet additional demands that had been raised by the commercial middle class. Marking Jewish firms by a visible emblem was totally in keeping with the intentions of these circles, especially since such a move could serve to weaken their annoying Jewish competition, put it at a disadvantage, and even bring it to the brink of financial ruin.[8] In addition, other Jewish competitors were excluded by changing the code of trade regulations.[9] Jews were prohibited from practicing the following professions: watchman, credit adviser, real estate agent and administrator, marriage broker, and travel guide. They were also denied the practice of various itinerant trades, such as traveling salesman, operator of a stall at an open-air market, showman, pedlar, and cattle dealer. These prohibitions on trade and professions were supplemented by terror measures by the Gestapo. In May 1938, the Gestapo sent orders by express mail "to arrest disagreeable Jews immediately, especially those with a criminal record," and to intern them in concentration camps.[10]

6. RGBl 1938, I, p. 407.
7. Ibid., I, pp. 414f.
8. Ibid., I, p. 627.
9. Ibid., I, p. 823.
10. Dokumentationsarchiv des österreichischen Widerstandes, ed., *Widerstand und Verfolgung in Wien, 1934–1945* (Vienna, 1984), vol. 3, p. 263.

The Gestapo hoped that this arrest campaign would spur more rapid Jewish emigration.

During the course of the summer 1938, a veritable torrent of discriminatory laws descended upon the Jews. They were obliged with the beginning of 1939 to add the middle name Sara or Israel to their existing names,[11] had to present special identification cards that designated them as Jews,[12] and a large *J* was stamped in their passports so as to make them recognizable as Jews even abroad,[13] a fact which significantly narrowed their options for emigration. Jewish physicians were stripped of their licenses to practice on September 30, 1938.[14] From then on, they were called *jüdische Krankenbehandler* (Jewish medical practitioners). Jewish attorneys were barred from appearing before the bench;[15] they could only act as so-called *Rechtskonsulenten* (legal counsels) for Jews. Jewish nurses were forced to work exclusively in Jewish hospitals.[16] Even the Jewish patent lawyers had not been forgotten – they lost their licenses as well.[17]

This abundance of decrees clearly demonstrates a paramount intention – to oust Jews completely in the near future from German economic life. On October 14, 1938, Göring formulated that aim as follows: "The Jewish Question should be dealt with energetically, using all means, because the economy ought to be rid of the Jews." Yet he noted that care should be taken in this connection to avoid the kind of wild, uncontrolled actions that had occurred in Austria. These were to be avoided "under any and all circumstances" because the exclusion of Jews from economic life, the so-called Aryanizations, must not become a "supply system for incompetent party members."[18] The opportunity soon presented itself to eject Jews from the German economy. After 267 synagogues along with about 7,500 businesses and factories throughout the entire Reich had been destroyed during the riots ordered from above on November 9–10, 1938, Hitler instructed Göring to "take care of the Jewish

11. RGBl 1938, I, p. 1044.
12. Ibid., I, p. 922.
13. Ibid., I, p. 1342.
14. Ibid., I, p. 969.
15. Ibid., I, p. 1403.
16. Ibid., I, p. 1310.
17. Ibid., I, p. 1545.
18. *IMT*, vol. 27, p. 163, PS–1301.

Question," coordinating the decisive steps involved.[19] Anti-Jewish legislation was now to enter its third and final phase.

Göring convened a meeting at the Reich Aviation Ministry for November 12, 1938, to which all Reich offices and agencies dealing with the Jewish Question were invited. Before the Nazi leaders and higher officials in attendance, Göring declared that it was his intention, given the order of the Führer, to unify and centralize efforts associated with the Jewish Question and to move toward an ultimate solution. German Jews as a community were to be held responsible for the act perpetrated by Herschel Grynszpan; Göring termed that deed an act reflecting a "hostile Jewish attitude toward the German people and Reich," one which demanded "harsh atonement." By the Decree on an Atonement Fine for Jews with German Citizenship dated November 12, 1938, German Jews were "levied with payment of a 'contribution' of one billion reichsmarks to the German Reich."[20] The frightened and harassed Jews, who had not only endured terrible material damage but also terrible physical and mental suffering – almost thirty thousand Jewish men had been arrested and sent to concentration camps[21] – were now also delivered over to the derision and contempt of the National Socialist rulers.

The Jews had to repair immediately "all damage" that had been done to their firms and homes during the Kristallnacht and to make sure that the appearance of the streets was restored to its previous orderliness. Costs for replacement of shattered display windows and for the repair of store fixtures had to be borne by the proprietors of the affected enterprises themselves. All insurance claims filed by Jews were confiscated for the benefit of the Reich. Amounts of compensation and indemnification were transferred by insurance companies directly to the government coffers.[22] However, the decisive measure which struck the hardest blow at the Jews was the Decree on the

---

19. *IMT*, vol. 28, pp. 499ff., PS–1816; quoted in detail in Martin Hirsch, Diemut Majer, and Jürgen Meinck, eds., *Recht, Verwaltung und Justiz des Nationalsozialismus: Ausgewählte Schriften, Gesetze und Gerichtsentscheidungen von 1933 bis 1945* (Cologne, 1984), pp. 364ff.

20. Verordnung über eine Sühneleistung der Juden deutscher Staatsangehörigkeit, RGBl 1938, I, p. 1579.

21. *IMT*, vol. 31, pp. 516f., PS–3051 and vol. 25, pp. 376f., PS–374.

22. RGBl 1938, I, p. 1581.

Exclusion of Jews from Economic Life[23] enacted on November 12, 1938. According to its stipulations, effective January 1, 1939, Jews were prohibited from operating retail firms and mail-order businesses and from practicing artisan trades. They were enjoined from offering goods for sale at open markets, fairs, and exhibitions. They were required by December 31, 1938, to resign from economic enterprises as managers and senior employees and to relinquish any membership in cooperatives.

Goebbels sneeringly noted at this meeting in the Aviation Ministry that Jews were still permitted to attend cultural events and share sleeper compartments together with Germans in long-distance trains. It was a thorn in his flesh that Jews were still allowed to sit in German parks and gardens and have contact there with Germans, and he demanded that a stop be put to this. Specific segregated parks should be set aside for Jews, with the benches marked For Jews only! He also advocated the removal of Jewish children from public schools. In future, they should be taught only in special schools for Jews.[24]

Goebbels appears to have been cut off from internal sources of information in the summer of 1938. The propaganda minister demonstrated in front of Göring that he was seriously uninformed. He apparently had virtually no contacts with the NSDAP in Austria; otherwise he would have been aware that the demands he had raised had in fact been put into practice there immediately after the Anschluß. In Austria Jewish pupils had been removed from all general schools and middle schools and had been concentrated in special segregated all-Jewish schools following the consolidation of the Nazi takeover.[25] In addition, quotas for Jews had been introduced at Austrian universities and colleges,[26] Jews had been banned from most public parks and gardens,[27] and Jews had been prohibited from frequenting all beaches.[28] Finally, they had been forbidden to wear any sort of *Trachten* (traditional Alpine costume).[29]

23. Verordnung zur Ausschaltung der Juden aus dem deutschen Wirtschaftsleben, ibid., I, p. 1580.
24. See n. 19.
25. *Völkischer Beobachter* (Vienna ed.), May 10, 1938, p. 15.
26. *Wiener Neueste Nachrichten*, March 30, 1938, p. 7.
27. *Völkischer Beobachter* (Vienna ed.), June 16, 1938, and June 25, 1938, p. 31.
28. Ibid., May 14, 1938, p. 21.
29. Ibid., June 19, 1938, p. 25 and August 21, 1938, p. 9.

Initially Goebbels appears to have only met with success among his most immediate followers. The director of the Reich Chamber of Culture issued an order on November 12, 1938, prohibiting Jews entry to theaters, motion picture houses, and concerts, as well as exhibitions.[30] The interior minister ordered Jews to surrender all firearms and sharp-edged weapons in their possession and also enjoined them from carrying any weapons on their persons.[31] Jews were even forbidden to keep carrier pigeons.[32] In a police ordinance on Jews appearing in public places, state authorities were granted the right to prevent Jews from entering certain sections of town or rural regions and the right to ban Jews from being on the street at certain specified times.[33]

The Reichsführer SS and chief of German police, Heinrich Himmler, did not want to be left out: he issued an order declaring driving licenses and vehicle registration papers in Jewish possession invalid and requiring that these documents be surrendered to the authorities. Furthermore, a police order was issued prohibiting Jews from attending cultural events, as well as exhibition halls, sports and playing fields, public bathing facilities, and outdoor swimming pools, effective December 6, 1938.[34] It should also be recalled in this connection that all Jewish periodicals still permitted in the Altreich and in Austria were banned after the Reichskristallnacht. The official organization representing Jews, the Reichsvereinigung der Juden in Deutschland, was permitted to publish the *Jüdisches Nachrichtenblatt* for announcement of official orders and information pertaining to emigration. There were Berlin and Vienna editions of this paper.

After the systematic ousting of Jews from German economic life had been initiated, legal means were to be utilized to render possible the formal expropriation of their assets. This received final codification in the Decree on the Utilization of Jewish Assets dated December 3, 1938.[35] On the basis of this decree, it

---

30. Bruno Blau, comp., *Das Ausnahmerecht für die Juden in Deutschland, 1933–1945*, 2d ed. (Düsseldorf, 1954), p. 54, no. 189.
31. Ibid., p. 56, no. 197.
32. RGBl, 1938, I, p. 1749.
33. Ibid., I, p. 1676.
34. Blau, *Das Ausnahmerecht*, p. 62, no. 201.
35. Verordnung über den Einsatz des jüdischen Vermögens, RGBl 1938, I, 1709.

was possible to order the proprietor of a Jewish commercial enterprise or farming or forestry business to sell or liquidate his firm or farm within a stipulated time period. If the Jewish owner did not respond to the order by the assigned deadline, the state then appointed a liquidating agent for liquidation or sale of the enterprise, and the proprietor was obliged to pay for the costs. The funds from such sales were deposited in special closed accounts or given to the seller in the form of German Reich bonds. The same decree also stipulated that, within a week's time, Jews were required to place all their stocks and bonds in a safe deposit box at a bank. If stocks or bonds were already deposited with a bank, the Jewish owner was obliged to inform his bank that this was Jewish property. In addition, Jews were prohibited from acquiring, pawning, or selling objects made of gold, platinum, or silver, as well as jewelry and pearls. They were allowed to offer such valuables for sale only to the public purchase offices established by the government.

Many of the questions that remained open at the conference on November 12, 1938, were presented by Göring to Hitler for a final decision. Some of these decisions can be inferred from a secret protocol by Göring of December 28, 1938: "There should be no general cancellation of renter protection laws in the case of Jewish tenants." Nonetheless, it was desirable, he argued, to concentrate the Jews in specific buildings. Moreover, the use of sleeping cars and dining cars by Jews in long-distance trains should be prohibited under all circumstances since it was out of the question for high party officials to be confronted with the presence of Jews in such places. According to Hitler, no "special compartments for Jews" should be set up. The "ban on Jews" should be in effect only for exclusive residential areas, certain public squares, and streets, as well as luxury hotels and famous restaurants. The Jewish welfare institutions should likewise not be dismantled since the Jews would then become a burden for public welfare. In contrast, patents filed by Jews were to be regarded as assets with associated property rights and should therefore be Aryanized.[36]

The discrimination against Jews intensified and was swiftly extended. Jews were banned from attendance at universities;[37]

---

36. *IMT*, vol. 25, p. 101, PS–069.
37. Blau, *Das Ausnahmerecht*, p. 62, no. 201.

midwives were no longer granted a license;[38] and the licenses to practice of Jewish dentists, veterinarians, and pharmacists were declared invalid effective January 31, 1939.[39] From that point on, Jews were also at a serious disadvantage in respect to taxation laws. They were stripped of all special benefits, reductions due to dependent children, and lower tax rates in effect for certain occupations. Instead, they had to pay the highest tax rates and were not given any child benefits, even when they were inducted into conscript labor.[40] The Third Ordinance on the Decree Pertaining to the Registration of Jewish Assets of February 21, 1939, obligated them to hand over to the public purchasing offices all objects in their possession made of gold, platinum, and silver as well as jewels and pearls within a period of two weeks. The only objects Jews were permitted to keep were their wedding rings.[41]

The Law on Renting to Jews enacted on April 30, 1939, was particularly severe.[42] It stated that "a Jew cannot have recourse to protection under the law for renters" if the landlord offers him substitute accommodations – naturally inferior in quality – upon giving him notice to vacate. Utilization of this law initiated the process of residential concentration of Jews – their creeping ghettoization. In all German towns and cities, Jews were resettled and crowded together in specific sections of town as the result of National Socialist housing policy designed to provide low-cost living space for non-Jewish Germans seeking apartments.[43] Jews were obliged, if so ordered by the municipal authorities, to accept other Jews as renters and on sublet contract. Even vacant or just-vacated rooms could only be rented after obtaining express permission from the municipal authorities.

It was clear right from the beginning that Göring would not succeed in coordinating the Jewish Question and advancing its centralized solution, especially since each individual minister

38. RGBl 1938, I, p. 1893.

39. RGBl 1939, I, p. 47.

40. RGBl 1939, I, pp. 283, 449, 503, 989; Blau, *Das Ausnahmerecht*, p. 65, no. 213.

41. Dritte Verordnung zur Verordnung über die Anmeldung des Vermögens von Juden, RGBl 1939, I, p. 282.

42. Gesetz über Mietverhältnisse mit Juden, ibid., p. 864.

43. Cf. Gerhard Botz, *Wohnungspolitik und Judendeportation in Wien, 1938–1945* (Vienna, 1975).

and *Gauleiter* was pursuing his own policy toward Jews to divert public attention from the numerous deficiencies and bottlenecks in the provision of consumer goods. And even Hitler had a firmer belief in Göring's overbearing self-importance than in his effectiveness because on January 24, 1939, he ordered Heydrich "to channel the Jewish Question toward the most favorable possible solution, in keeping with the times, in the form of emigration or evacuation."[44] Thus, responsibility for the "solution of the Jewish Question" was given to the man who ultimately was to implement the physical destruction of European Jewry.

After the ravages of the Reichskristallnacht, staying on any longer in Germany had become a vital question of sheer survival for the Jews. On top of the loss of one's professional livelihood, there was the tax pressure from the revenue authorities and the psychological terror of the Gestapo. Jews who saw any opportunity to flee the country took advantage of it and left. This was encouraged by the Gestapo, the SD, and the Security Police, especially since at that time Heydrich wanted to solve the Jewish Question by means of forced emigration. On November 12, 1938, Heydrich had proudly announced to Göring that Adolf Eichmann had succeeded, by means of the Central Bureau for Emigration which he set up in Vienna, in motivating fifty thousand Jews to emigrate from Austria in the period May to October 1938; in comparison, only nineteen thousand Jews had emigrated from the territory of the Altreich in that same time span. Yet in the following six months, Heydrich was able to exceed Eichmann's figures. By the beginning of May 1939, the number of Jews living in Germany had declined by 57 percent. On June 16, 1934, there were 502,799 persons of the Jewish faith living in Germany and 191,481 in Austria as of a count on March 22, 1934. In comparison, data from the May 14, 1939, census list a total of 213,930 Jews living in the Altreich and 81,943 in Austria.[45]

A major change in attitude toward the Jews emerged with the outbreak of World War II. If they had previously been treated as a separate segment of the population and regarded as inferior, they were now seen as the "enemy within." On the very first day of hostilities, September 1, 1939, local police authorities

44. *IMT*, vol. 26, p. 266, PS–710.
45. *Statistisches Jahrbuch für das Deutsche Reich*, 59 (1941/42) (Berlin, 1942), p. 27.

placed Jews under a night curfew. Jews were prohibited from being out in the streets from 9 P.M. to 5 A.M. during the summer and between the hours of 8 P.M. and 6 A.M. during the winter months.[46] They were prohibited from owning radios and were compelled to hand these over to the police.[47] Jews were thus cut off from any link with the outside and were totally isolated. They were also prohibited from participating, together with non-Jews, in air-raid drills.[48]

Göring handily obtained the additional finances he needed for the armaments industry by means of a Second Decree on an Atonement Fine for the Jews promulgated on October 19, 1939,[49] which increased the previous levy by 250 million reichsmarks. The minister of education, meanwhile, had nothing more important to worry about than issuing a regulation that, from then on, all writers of doctoral dissertations had to specially mark any quotations from Jewish authors.[50]

Jews were not issued ration cards for clothing.[51] They were supplied with textile goods and shoes by the Reichsvereinigung der Juden in Deutschland or the Israelitische Kultusgemeinde Wien (Jewish Community of Vienna) in Austria. These representative organizations had begun early on to store away clothing and furniture from the possessions left behind by emigrants. Jews were also permitted to cover their clothing needs by purchasing in used-clothing shops. With the start of the year 1940, ration cards for Jews were marked by an additional letter *J*.[52] They had previously been excluded from any distribution and apportioning of special goods or additional rations. Now they were compelled to shop only at specified times in the stores assigned to them – in Berlin, that time period was between 4 and 5 P.M.[53] Jews were excluded from belonging to private medical insurance plans,[54] and first-degree *Mischlinge,*

46. Blau, *Das Ausnahmerecht*, p. 79, no. 251.
47. Ibid., pp. 79f., nos. 253, 254.
48. Ibid., p. 80, no. 255.
49. Zweite Verordnung zur Sühneleistung der Juden, RGBl 1939, I, p. 2059.
50. Blau, *Das Ausnahmerecht*, p. 80, no. 258.
51. Ibid., p. 81, no. 269.
52. Joseph Walk, ed., *Das Sonderrecht für die Juden im NS-Staat: Eine Sammlung der gesetzlichen Maßnahmen und Richtlinien – Inhalt und Bedeutung*, Motive-Texte-Materialien, vol. 14 (Karlsruhe, 1981), pp. 318f., IV, no. 82.
53. Blau, *Das Ausnahmerecht*, p. 84, no. 282.
54. Ibid., p. 82, no. 275.

such as the husbands of Jewish women, were discharged from the Wehrmacht.[55]

The separation and total isolation of Jews from the German population was continued and extended in consistent fashion. In the autumn of 1940, the telephones of Jews were cancelled and disconnected – with the exception of medical and dental "practitioners," legal "counsels," and the Reichsvertretung der Juden and its associated organizations.[56] Separate air-raid bunkers had to be arranged for Jews living in "mixed" housing.[57]

In view of the fact that more and more Jews were working as laborers on road and power plant construction, the responsible government authorities pondered ways to involve Jews more generally in conscripted labor so as to derive additional benefit from the situation. In December 1940, Jews were given the same status in social legislation as Poles: if employed, they were obligated to pay the discriminatory social compensation tax (*Sozialausgleichsabgabe*), previously levied only on Polish workers. This special surtax was 15 percent of gross earnings and was deducted in addition to income tax.[58] Jewish conscript labor was "regulated" in October 1941 by decreed guidelines pertaining to the treatment of Jewish workers in German firms and factories.[59] Jews could claim wages only for work actually done. Thus, they had no right to sick pay. If they wished to have a vacation or return to see their families, they were only granted unpaid free time. Jewish workers were not given any bonuses for work on Sundays and holidays. It was also prohibited to grant Jewish employees other customary company bonuses or gifts. Jews could be fired at any time, effective at the end of the next working day. Jews were required to accept any job assigned to them by the government employment offices. They were supposed to be put to work in groups and were kept separate from German workers. Legal regulations regarding child labor and special working hours for teenage youth did not apply in the case of Jews between the ages of fourteen and eighteen. Jews were given the minimum amount of unemployment benefits.

Jews in Germany were living on the top of a volcano ready to

55. Ibid., p. 82, no. 277.
56. Ibid., p. 84, no. 284.
57. Ibid., pp. 84f., no. 291.
58. RGBl 1940, I, p. 1666.
59. RGBl 1941, I, p. 681.

erupt. The first unmistakable signs of that coming catastrophe were the deportation of Viennese Jews to Nisko in southeastern Poland in October 1939, the transfer of Stettin Jews to Lublin in February 1940, the deportation of Jews from Baden to southern France in the autumn of 1940, and the deportation of five thousand Jews from Vienna to the Generalgouvernement in Poland in February and March 1941. The solution of the Jewish Question became acute once again when Hitler instructed his generals in March 1941 to prepare an attack against the Soviet Union. For this struggle between the two opposed systems Hitler issued orders which were to have horrible consequences for the Jews. The so-called commissar order (*Kommissarbefehl*) of June 6, 1941, called for the immediate execution of all commissars of the Red Army in captivity, a task delegated to the Wehrmacht. In addition, Himmler's *Einsatzgruppen* were supposed to liquidate Jewish inhabitants during the conquest of new areas in the East. This Final Solution of the Jewish Question would soon have a grave impact on Jews in the West as well.

Although there had already been deportations of German Jews to the east, Jews in Germany and Western Europe still had the possibility until October 1941 to emigrate legally via Spain and Portugal. The prerequisite was the possession of valid travel documents and boat tickets. Yet here too there were massive restrictions: for example, Himmler issued a prohibition in August 1941 prohibiting emigration by Jewish males of working age.[60] Finally, on October 23, 1941, the ominous order was issued, putting an immediate and total halt to any further permits for Jews of any age to emigrate.[61]

On September 1, 1941, the Police Decree on the Marking of Jews was promulgated in Germany.[62] From September 19 of that month on, Jews were required to wear a yellow star. It consisted of a "black six-pointed star the size of the palm of the hand, made of yellow material, with the inscription 'Jude' in black letters"; Jews were required to display this star in a clearly visible place on the left side of the chest. Another order issued at this time stipulated that Jews were not allowed to leave the

60. *Widerstand und Verfolgung*, vol. 3, p. 276, Doc. 145.
61. Ibid., p. 277, Doc. 147.
62. Polizeiverordnung über die Kennzeichnung von Juden, RGBl 1941, I, p. 547; Blau, *Das Ausnahmerecht*, pp. 91ff., no. 339.

"area of their residential community" without express written permission from the local police authorities. In using public conveyances, Jews were forbidden to sit as long as German passengers were still standing. During rush-hour periods, when public transportation was crowded, "wearers of the star" were prohibited from getting on the vehicles. They were not allowed to enter waiting rooms, restaurants, or other shelters for passengers. They were soon forbidden from using any public transport in their residential area. They were only permitted to do so after presenting a special permit obtainable if their way to work was longer than seven kilometers or if the walk there took over an hour.[63]

In October 1941, the National Socialists initiated deportations of Jews throughout the Reich. At the same time, the small harassive discriminations against the Jews continued unabated. Jews were prohibited from using lending libraries and were forbidden to sell their own books freely on the open market.[64] Jews were stripped of any power over their movable possessions.[65] All those persons wearing the Jewish star were required to hand over any fur or woolen goods, skis, or other winter accessories. They were not allowed to use public phones and were prohibited from receiving newspapers and magazines by mail or directly from the publisher.[66]

Beginning in April 1942, the dwellings of Jews likewise had to be marked with a star;[67] keeping of pet animals was forbidden. Utilizing the services of German barbers and hairdressers was prohibited to Jews.[68] They were ordered to hand over any dispensable clothing and finally were forced to surrender any cameras, optical instruments, record players, bicycles, typewriters, and adding machines in their possession.[69] In July 1942, all Jewish schools in Germany were closed on the grounds that Jewish children did not require any formal instruction.[70] Jews were not issued ration cards for eggs or tobacco. Soon thereafter they were also deprived of all ration coupons for wheat flour

---

63. Blau, *Das Ausnahmerecht*, pp. 106f., no. 377.
64. Ibid., p. 88, no. 327, p. 98, no. 344.
65. Ibid., p. 102, no. 350.
66. Ibid., p. 103, nos. 360, 361; p. 104, no. 368.
67. Ibid., p. 105, no. 375.
68. Ibid., p. 108, nos. 380, 383.
69. Ibid., p. 108, no. 386, p. 109, no. 391.
70. Ibid., p. 109, no. 392.

and white bread, milk, fish, meat, and fresh fruit and vegetables.[71] Blind Jews were not allowed to wear the traditional yellow armband lest a German find possible cause to come to their assistance.[72] Finally, Jews were forbidden to use any titles awarded by the state – though, bizarrely enough, academic titles were excluded from this prohibition![73]

From December 4, 1941, Jews were also made subject to the Penal Code for Poles.[74] All Jews born in Poland or deported there were brought before special courts for the most minor misdemeanors and infringements and were sometimes even handed over for Nazi party drumhead court-martials (*Standgerichte*). The sentences were draconian, and the death penalty was meted out even for the most minor offenses. Six weeks before the end of their incarceration, Jewish prisoners were reported by the prisons to the Gestapo so that the Gestapo could have enough time to include them in the deportation transports.[75] Justice Minister Thierack soon agreed with Himmler's demand to subject Jews to "special treatment at the hands of the police" in cases of "insufficient judicial judgment." He also agreed to the "handing over of asocial elements," particularly Jews and Gypsies, in order to place them at the disposal of the Reichsführer SS for purposes of annihilation through labor (*Vernichtung durch Arbeit*).[76] On orders from Himmler, starting in March 1943, all Jews were sent to the concentration camps Maidanek or Auschwitz for life internment after completing their jail sentences.[77]

Although the Final Solution had already begun, the total expropriation of the Jews still presented certain problems for the administrative authorities. Finally, they agreed to issue the Eleventh Decree to the Reich Citizenship Law, dated November 25, 1941.[78] This decree stipulates the following: "A Jew shall lose German citizenship if, when this decree becomes law, he maintains his regular place of residence abroad" or if "the circumstances under which [he is staying abroad] indicate that his stay

---

71. Ibid., p. 110, no. 393; p. 109, no. 387; p. 111, no. 409.
72. Ibid., p. 110, no. 400.
73. Ibid., p. 111, no. 404.
74. Polenstrafrechtsverordnung, RGBl 1941, I, p. 759.
75. Blau, *Das Ausnahmerecht*, p. 98, no. 346.
76. Vernichtung durch Arbeit, *IMT*, vol. 26, p. 200, PS–654.
77. Ibid., p. 259, PS–701.
78. 11. Verordnung zum Reichsbürgergesetz, RGBl 1941, I, p. 722.

there is not temporary." All areas outside the borders of Germany were regarded as being "abroad" for purposes of this decree; that is, the Generalgouvernement and the Protectorate of Bohemia and Moravia were also subsumed under this category. On the basis of the Eleventh Decree, all German Jews who had been or were in the process of being deported lost their German citizenship. The decree stated that the property of these Jews "becomes the property of the Reich with the loss of citizenship." Moreover, all "claims to social welfare" in Germany, such as government pensions, pensions for war victims, and old-age pensions, likewise were rendered void with deportation. Thus, after the deportation of a Jew, the authorities could dispose freely of his or her remaining assets and property or rights to property without any special procedures – especially since the head of the Security Police and SD had the final say regarding "basis for forfeiture of property," and he certainly knew best.

The problem of the legal expropriation of Jewish property had finally been solved. What still had to be "regulated" was the status of those Jews who had remained behind. This was done by means of the Thirteenth Decree to the Reich Citizenship Law of July 1, 1943.[79] According to it, Jews were no longer subject to the Penal Code for Poles of December 4, 1941, but rather to police criminal law. They were thus rendered completely defenseless and subject to arbitrary individual will. De facto, they were outlawed, declared fair game for any perpetrator, since their ultimate annihilation had already been decided upon. Therefore, it is no accident that an administrative note remarks: "The evacuation and isolation of the Jews and Gypsies, now implemented, has made the publication of special orders, as previously practiced, meaningless, and [such publication] should cease."[80] The anti-Jewish "legislation" in the Third Reich had fulfilled its task.

---

79. 13. Verordnung zum Reichsbürgergesetz, RGBl 1943, I, p. 372. On its prehistory and history, cf. Uwe D. Adam, *Judenpolitik im Dritten Reich*, 2d ed. (Düsseldorf, 1972), pp. 292ff.

80. Blau, *Das Ausnahmerecht*, p. 117, no. 428.

To Leave or Not to Leave
The German Jews at the Crossroads

Konrad Kwiet

Decimated, a disproportionate number advanced in age, separated from family and friends, cut off from the world outside Germany, stripped of their civil rights and pauperized, deployed in forced labor, crowded together in special segregated *Judenhäuser*, undernourished, depleted, exhausted, their freedom of movement severely restricted, branded by the badge of a large, compulsory yellow star – this was the grim picture presented by a *minorité fatale* in early October 1941, some thirty-five months after the great pogrom, a minority that threatened to become a "burden" for Aryan German society and was soon slated to be silently exterminated as part of the National Socialist Final Solution. On the eve of the mass deportations, there were still some 164,000 Jews living in Germany, and none had any premonition of what fate awaited them after shipment as human freight to the east. Historical experience and the powers of the human imagination boggled at the notion that systematic destruction of human life could be feasible. And it was just as difficult then to give any credence to those first "rumors" that filtered in about mass shootings and extermination by gas. Almost everywhere, the indications regarding an organized mass murder were rejected as "war propaganda" or "figments of the imagination" among Jews and non-Jews, in Germany and abroad.

The architects and executors of the Final Solution took especial heed not to reveal their terrible secret prematurely. Thus, in October 1941, when the last avenues for emigration were finally sealed and the first transport shipments were sent east, virtually all Jews clung desperately to the official proclamations that feigned a program of "resettlement" or "evacuation" for purposes of "labor deployment." Ostracized and banished from Aryan society, they were forced to live a life on bought time, waiting until they were assigned their "place on the list." This waiting, uncertainty, and anxiety before deportation were harrowing. A total of 134,000 Jews were deported from Germany to the east and only 8,000 returned.

In 1933, some 500,000 Jews had experienced the cancellation of the contract of Jewish-German fraternity, their seemingly symbiotic community (*Lebensgemeinschaft*). During the first few years of persecution, they were at the mercy of a National Socialist regime that still allowed them a choice, albeit dubious – to be rendered déclassé or to accept expulsion. They devoted long discussions to the alternatives of "homeland or exile" and the question of "leaving or not leaving." A minority left immediately: those endangered as a result of political affiliations, Zionists, and Jews who had been ousted early on from their professions. Yet the majority chose to stay. They felt unable to bid farewell to a country they and their ancestors had lived in for generations and in which they felt at home. Their acculturation and integration made it harder for them to withdraw from their familiar life world, and they continued to insist on their rights as Germans to their *Heimat* (homeland). An organization calling itself the Reichsvertretung der Juden in Deutschland was set up soon after the Nazis took power; under the leadership of Leo Baeck and Otto Hirsch, it made great efforts to protect and maintain Jewish life and continued existence in Germany. However, right from the beginning, the German-Jewish representatives left no doubt that their strategies for defense of the community would be restricted exclusively to measures within the bounds of prevailing law.

The possibility of militant resistance was considered and rejected as illusory. Underlying that rejection was the recognition that the two key partners in any social alliance had vanished from the political arena with the abdication of liberalism and the rapid liquidation of the organized labor movement. These had been forces that formerly had played a major role in marshaling support for Jewish emancipation. An additional worry was that any open Jewish resistance might eventuate in punitive sanctions and thus lead to further dangers for the Jewish community. Their defensive struggle was shaped by one other basic conviction: most Jews believed that the Nazi regime would be short-lived, an illusion they shared with many non-Jews in Germany at the time. Their confidence that the anti-

Semitism ordained by regime decree would soon dissipate once again after the rapid return of democratic government kept large numbers of Jews from taking the step of emigration and turning their backs on Germany.

Given this perspective on the future, the Jewish representatives were neither prepared to nor able to call upon members of the Jewish community to embark upon an immediate mass exodus, taking the necessary steps to initiate the self-dissolution of German Jewry. "Each one must stick to his position" was the slogan in 1933 in the acculturated and assimilated camp. Later on, they warned about any precipitate departure, and efforts were made to arranged for an "orderly" emigration. Even the chief Zionist spokesmen did not press for an immediate mass exodus. They geared their strategy to a long-term, selective process of emigration, with Palestine granted top priority as final destination. It soon became evident that there were numerous barriers blocking this path of flight, as all others.

There was not a single country that opened wide its gates unconditionally to refugees. Immigrant quotas and other restrictions served everywhere to hold down the unwanted influx of foreigners within narrow limits. And almost universally, the expellees encountered enormous difficulties in gaining a foothold in the new and alien environment. Jews in Germany studied the immigration regulations and read the letters sent back by those who had emigrated. The conditions and reports deterred many from venturing the fateful step into exile. In many countries, the refugees felt the brunt of xenophobia or were subjected to anti-Semitic attacks. There were only a few who were fluent in the language of the prospective country. Not all were able to accommodate to the new climatic and residential circumstances. As a rule, they were prohibited from practicing their former professions. They had to switch occupations, learn new trades, look for new opportunities for income, or run the risk of venturing their luck trying to fill gaps in the market by opening up new businesses. Older persons and those in the free and academic professions found it especially difficult to adjust. Emigration meant a loss of social status and required a readiness on the part of the emigré to revise his or her patterns of behavior and "correct" previously held attitudes. The expellees were often expected to acclimatize in record time to the norms and values common in their new country.

141

This call for adaptation was often made by the Jewish communities indigenous in the countries of their emigration, especially by the Jewish establishments there. For the most part, these communities limited their assistance to calls for contributions to aid the new immigrants and left it up to the welfare organizations to provide help for the new arrivals. This manner of reception engendered various animosities. Only at a later stage did many German emigrés realize that German Jews themselves had not behaved any differently toward their fellow Jews from Eastern Europe who had sought refuge in Germany before 1933. In the Kaiserreich and the Weimar Republic, the unpopular *Ostjuden* had encountered opposition and rejection due to the fact that they were different from the established German Jews in respect to origin, language, dress, religiosity, social position, and customary occupations. As a result, their presence in Germany constituted a challenge to the positions and attitudes of German Jewry. Arguments and convictions that had been common during the "golden years" of the German-Jewish *Lebensgemeinschaft* were now repeated in the black years of exile, but this time the roles had been reversed.

After expulsion, Jews from Germany experienced what it meant to cope as a refugee, especially a refugee with a reputation for evincing a panoply of "German" failings: arrogance and hauteur, pedantry, and doctrinaire assuredness. They remained isolated for a long time and formed often-caricatured groups and grouplets in which they fostered intimate social contacts in a familiar milieu. Yet up until the last, they also maintained ties with those who had remained behind. The alarming news reports spurred them to try to persuade relatives and friends to leave the country. Many left no stone unturned in their efforts to provide friends and relatives with the requisite guarantees, immigration papers, and funds.

Emigration was expensive. The Nazi regime required the payment of a Reich flight tax (*Reichsfluchtsteuer*) and other compulsory special taxes. Up to 1940, the Reich treasury had raised some nine hundred million reichsmarks in flight tax revenues. Moreover, money had to be found to cover the costs of travel and moving. It was indispensable to be able to show that one was in possession of sufficient capital in order to be given preference for obtaining entry visas and to be able to finance the beginning of a new life in another land. Emigration presupposed compulsory sale of apartments, businesses, and other enterprises. Debts, taxes, and fees were deducted from the transaction sum, and only fragments of one's original assets could be transferred abroad after liquidation. In 1934, losses already amounted to some 60 percent and soared to 96 percent in 1939. Many Jews found it very difficult to cope with these losses. The longer they persevered, the less their chance of retaining any of their assets and property. The National Socialist policy of plunder was stepped up beginning in 1937. The seizure of "Jewish wealth," a process through which not only the government and the Nazi party but also industry and countless individual Aryan *Volksgenossen* filled their coffers as well, led swiftly to financial ruin.

Not until Jews experienced a direct threat to their lives did they finally recognize that their ties to and positions in Germany were no longer defensible. That occurred in November 1938. They reacted with anxiety and horror, dismay and desparation to the wave of destruction that swept over synagogues, homes, and businesses, to the mistreatment, murders, mass arrests, and internments in concentration camps. Acts of unbridled violence and terrorism, previously considered impossible in Germany, triggered a profound sense of shock in the German-Jewish community. The pogrom left its lasting imprint on their consciousness and memories: it marked *the* turning point in events. Most Jews now abandoned the notion that they still had some sort of right as citizens to their German homeland. The recognition spread that the Nazi regime had stabilized its rule and that a return to democratic government was not in the offing. There was no longer any reason to hope for better times. On the contrary, one measure after the next was introduced aimed at shattering their economic basis of existence, introducing forced labor, and implementing spatial and social segregation of Jews – their ghettoization.

The Jews in Germany did not simply tolerate this harassment and animosity in silent passivity. Jewish representatives repeatedly raised their voices in protest against the injustices. Members of the various Jewish communities continually spoke out against the defamations, slander, and discrimination. Yet their protests fell on silent ears among the public and the authorities. The National Socialists rigorously combatted Jewish attempts to defend themselves, branding them "nasty Jewish incitement," "conduct hostile to the state," "treachery," or "high treason." There were corresponding penalties, ranging from warnings to "protective detention" all the way to the death penalty. *J'accuse – Ich klage an!* (*I Accuse*) was the title of a protest pamphlet written by Walter Gutmann, a Hamburg Jew, in response to the November pogrom. It began with the words "I take up the battle cry of Emile Zola against anti-Semitism, this in order to call the attention of my fellow Germans and the entire civilized world to the imminent threat of destruction of five hundred thousand innocent persons." His appeal went unheard. Several hundred copies of his pamphlet, mimeographed and mailed out as a letter, were seized by the postal censorship authorities. The Gestapo was able to locate its author and call him to account.

Jews by themselves were in no position to stem the destructive course of National Socialist Jewish policy. They had to depend on the assistance of non-Jews. Their persecution and expulsion were taking place before everyone's eyes, yet did not trigger any opposition in the German public, with a few exceptions. Outside Germany, people and governments preferred to refrain from meddling in the internal affairs of the German Reich. Moreover, their national and economic interests dictated the pursuit of a restrictive refugee policy. The outbreak of war then provided the useful lever for a hermetic closure of state borders. The priority given to military war aims engendered an approach that discounted the loss of the Jews as unavoidable. The general direction events would take was already determined before 1939.

In November 1938, numerous Germans looked on with dismay and fright as "popular anger," goaded by the Nazis, was discharged in the fury of the pogrom. Many voices were raised criticizing the destruction of property or complaining about the "illegal" excesses. Yet few were courageous enough to take up the cause of the persecuted or even rush to their aid. National Socialists spoke about the "Jew lovers" amongst the German populace. Nonetheless, hardly any protest was voiced in public against ghettoization. On the contrary, Jews soon began to sense an intensification in pressure not only from above, but also from below, pressure that was pushing for some sort of "solution to the Jewish Question." The broad consensus in the population, coupled with energetic support on the part of leadership elites, contributed significantly to the fact that fanatic racists were able to introduce the final prerequisite measures and ultimately make their repeated prophecies come true.

In view of this development, the old debate about whether or not to leave Germany faded in the aftermath of the November events. It was replaced by the slogan, "Save yourself if you can." A panic-like mass flight from Germany began, and there were special rescue campaigns initiated in every Jewish community. Preference was given to sending children and teenagers to Western countries, especially England. Jewish representatives now dared to venture beyond the bounds of legality. Contributions were made to secret bank accounts to finance the mass exodus, and there was a flourishing black market in documents, genuine and counterfeit. Some Jews fell victim to swindlers, others had the good fortune to be able to purchase their path to freedom by bribing corrupt officials.

The Reichsvertretung financed the release and emigration of Jews who had been detained by the authorities, utilizing special funds earmarked for this purpose. Their money was from a fund set up by the Robert Bosch firm in Stuttgart. Between 1938 and 1940, the business magnate Hans Walz made available 1.2 million reichsmarks to be used to save Jewish lives. The acceptance and utilization of these funds, not under the watchful surveillance of the Gestapo, constituted one of the few infringements of valid law by Reichsvertretung officials.

Shortly before the outbreak of the war, the Reichsvertretung was transformed into a so-called Reichsvereinigung; that association was then compelled to furnish bureaucratic-administrative assistance in helping to carry out the ghettoization and "evacuation" of Jews. There was still resistance to the first large deportation. When the approximately seven thousand Jews resident in Baden and the Saar Palatinate were suddenly arrested and deported to southern France in October 1940, the Reichsvereinigung became highly active. Its staff members hurried to locate Jews away on trips and to warn them about returning to their homes. Otto Hirsch lodged a protest in the RSHA against the deportation and demanded the immediate return of the deportees. There was an intimated threat of mass resignation by the entire Reichsvereinigung staff, and the foreign press was secretly informed about what had transpired. A circular letter was sent to all personnel urging them to observe a day of fasting and remembrance, to cancel all scheduled events of the Jewish Cultural League for one week, and to pray and give sermons on behalf of the deportees on the upcoming Sabbath. The SS forced the Reichsvereinigung leadership to revoke its instructions. Julius Seligsohn, author of the circular letter, was arrested and put to death in Sachsenhausen. Otto Hirsch was removed from his post, and later died in Mauthausen. The resistance put up by the Reichsvereinigung was broken by means of these sanctions. Down to the bitter end – its liquidation in 1943 – that organization remained ensnared in the trap of legality.

The organization itself had aimed for the year 1943 as a target by which it still hoped that it might be able to effect and guide a self-dissolution of the Jewish community in Germany. Its assumption in late 1939 was that the dissolution and disbandment process, encompassing retraining, emigration, and welfare measures, would take three years to complete. Their appeal "not to lose another minute" in order to take full advantage of the last remaining opportunities to emigrate was unmistakable. There were urgent admonitions addressed to Jews who had already left the country and to Jewish organizations abroad to take steps to promote the emigration to those still remaining behind. There were requests for contributions, sponsorships, visas. Criticism of the conduct of foreign countries and organizations was voiced when the authorities put an abrupt end in October 1941 to feverish efforts for facilitating the emigration of the remaining German Jews. A mood of depression took hold after it became necessary to acquiesce to the dictates and regulations of the National Socialists and to devote attention to arrangements for deportations to the east.

Up until this critical juncture, some 270,000 to 300,000 Jews had left Germany. In the just under ten months from mid-November 1938 to September 1, 1939, 115,000 fled to safety. After the outbreak of the war, an additional 25,000 were able successfully to flee to freedom. Thirty thousand emigrés were taken into custody once again in the occupied territories. Thus, a total of about 50 percent of German Jews were able to find refuge abroad. The paths of flight taken by them spanned all five continents. In 1933, three-fourths of all refugees had sought refuge in other European countries; by 1937, that percentage had plummeted to one-quarter. Those who reached the United States numbered 132,000, 55,000 settled in Palestine, and 40,000 found asylum in England. Brazil and Argentina each accepted some 10,000 German-Jewish refugees. Nine thousand reached the "open" port of Shanghai, 7,000 made it to the shores of Australia, and 5,000 found refuge in South Africa. The remainder were spread across a number of countries.

The waves of expulsion receded, leaving behind a residual group in which family ties had largely dissolved, and there had been substantial structural changes in respect to age and sex. Women and the elderly were in the preponderant majority. Fully half of the 164,000 Jews remaining were fifty years of age or older, a third of them over sixty. With increasing age, there was a concomitant decline in their readiness and ability to sunder ties with their familiar surroundings. Moreover, the aged, infirm, and sick had hardly any prospect of fulfilling the entry requirements and stipulations of the countries of refuge. They found a temporary place to stay in the overcrowded *Judenhäuser*, Jewish old-age homes and hospitals. Several years before, many had already taken leave of their children and grandchildren, whose decision to emigrate had been easier for them – or, more accurately, had been *made* easier for them. In addition, they had been compelled to separate from their friends and acquaintances so that the close bonds of family and friendship had been torn asunder. What remained was their memory of those who had emigrated, the consolation that *they*, at least, had found a refuge – and the fervent desire to see them all once again some day.

More men emigrated than women. In many instances, immigration permits and transportation possibilities ruled out the option of an entire family emigrating together. Many women allowed their husbands and children to go on ahead, hoping to be able to follow them soon. Others refused to leave Germany. Their concern for their aging parents or sick relatives, the need to care for a mother or father, kept them from leaving. A large number of the female staff of the Reichsvereinigung also stayed at their jobs; these women, working either as employees or in a voluntary capacity, devoted themselves to the extensive tasks of social welfare in the remaining communities. The proportion of females was 20 percent higher than that of males.

Children and teenagers were the smallest segment in the age pyramid. In 1941, only 20,669 were under eighteen years of age – some 13 percent of the remaining *minorité fatale*. Rescue came too late for more than 10,000 children that were still on the waiting lists of the Reichsvereinigung. This was also the case when it came to the Jewish youngsters who had been gathered together in Jewish *hachshara* (training) centers to be given agricultural training and Jewish education as preparation for emigration to Palestine. The others were deployed as forced laborers in the factories.

Jewish youngsters still found strength to resist. A Zionist youth group by the name of Chug halutzi (Pioneer Circle) numbered some forty members; in 1942, together with its adult counselors Joachim Schwersenz and Edith Wolff, it disappeared into the Berlin underground. The approximately fifty members who joined the Jewish Communist resistance organization known in the history of German antifascism as the Herbert Baum Group were recruited largely from the two Jewish sections of the Siemens plant in Berlin. The spectacular, abortive sabotage attempt against the propagandistic hate exhibit "The Soviet Paradise" in the Lustgarten in Berlin in May 1942 represented the highpoint of this group's resistance activity. The Gestapo and the courts later put an end to the group's existence. Almost all of its members stemmed from modest, middle-class backgrounds. The reasons compelling their parents to stay on in Germany had been primarily financial.

An additional circle of persons stuck it out in Germany. This group encompassed the approximately fifteen thousand Jewish spouses living in so-called mixed marriages and who had brought up children the Nazis termed *Mischlinge* (persons of racially mixed background). The classification "privileged mixed marriage" did not protect these families from abuse and discrimination, but it promised the Jewish parent a chance to survive as long as there was no formal divorce decree (or forced divorce). There was also still a spark of resistance in these assimilated, German-Jewish *Lebensgemeinschaften*: only a small number of such mixed marriages were ever dissolved.

In February 1943, the Gestapo struck a blow at another category of Jews who had been largely spared up to that time, the so-called armaments Jews (*Rüstungsjuden*). Within the framework of a massive planned operation, numerous Jews married to non-Jewish spouses were also arrested. That wave of arrests triggered a unique protest demostration. In Berlin, Aryan wives appeared in front of the assembly camp and demanded the release of their husbands, chanting loud slogans. Passersby also joined in with their support. Alarmed by this spontaneous and massive resistance, the Gestapo gave in and released the Jewish spouses. This protest constituted the most vehement form of open resistance to the persecution of the Jews in Germany. Its success suggests that similar actions might well have been able to redirect the destructive course of National Socialist Jewish policy into other directions.

Christians of Jewish origin recognized only too late that the race fanatics would not take religious convictions and firm roots in German society into account in pursuing their ideologically based policies. Baptized Catholics and Protestants also discovered that they could no longer expect any sort of protection from their diocese churches. Toward the end of 1941, they were classified once again as Jews and then deported to the east.

For the Jews remaining there were only two options left in order to escape the grasp of their persecutors. One path led to suicide, the other into the underground. There are no reliable statistics on the exact number of Jewish suicides and attempted suicides in the Third Reich; the figure is estimated to be about ten thousand. Already in the early years of persecution, Nazi terrorizing had driven hundreds of Jews to suicide. The number of suicides had jumped drastically during the "boycott of Jews" in April 1933, the Austrian Anschluß, and the November 1938 pogrom. The curve peaked during the period of forced deportation. More than three thousand Jews chose at that time to put an end to their lives on their own terms, constituting some 2 percent of those summoned for "evacuation." In Berlin, that percentage of suicides even reached the figure of 4 percent. These suicides were distinguished by two characteristics: their advanced age and their high degree of assimilation. Their average age was sixty-five. Single persons and married couples (joint suicides) made up the bulk of those who committed suicide. Almost all of them waited until the very last moment – when the orders for deportation arrived. The official order to vacate their homes and prepare for "resettlement" was sufficient evidence that they had finally been ousted from their society. That sense of despair sapped and destroyed their will to go on living. In their final hours before death, memories welled up in them of their childhood and families. Their thoughts went out to their children who had emigrated, and they left them goodbye letters full of love and pain. With their suicides, they also took leave of the shattered, German-Jewish *Lebensgemeinschaft*.

Between 10,000 and 12,000 Jews found the strength to resist the orders for special marking and deportation. Most of them tried to go into hiding in the capital Berlin, in former times the veritable stronghold of German-Jewish *Lebensgemeinschaft*. There were an estimated 5,000 Jews living in hiding in Berlin in 1943, some 7 percent of all Jews registered in Berlin in 1941. After the end of the war, 1,402 Jews emerged from their hiding places there: thus, one can conclude that some 30 percent of all Jews who had gone into hiding managed to survive. They had had to overcome many barriers and mortal dangers in their struggle for survival in the very heart of the Reich. First of all, there was the network of surveillance and persecution that the Nazis had spun to entrap and encase the *minorité fatale*. There were severe penalties for anyone who attempted to avoided "registration" by the authorities. Escaping that ensnaring net presupposed overcoming the Jewish bureaucratic measures as well. The Reichsvereinigung and the Jewish communities sent out notices and information sheets and were responsible for making sure that the marking of Jews and their transport were carried out "in an orderly and proper manner." They also issued sharp warnings against resisting official orders.

Another factor was the fear of a form of existence that entailed a radical change in one's way of life and daily circumstances. To go underground meant to give up their "legal" existence and to lead an "illegal" life that promised no security or rescue, holding out only a slim chance for survival. Yet a desire to go on living spurred these persons to take the fateful step and disappear into hiding. The decision to expose themselves to certain mortal dangers was combined with the hope that the time of persecution would come to an end some day. From the beginning, they were haunted by a single thought: "I feel so hedged in, when can I get out of this hole again?" Going underground and illegal also meant finding non-Jews who were willing to risk their own skins and were prepared to take in the person for days, months, or even years. During the period of war and deportation, there were still Germans, especially in Berlin, who were active in helping to rescue Jews. Relatives, old friends, and former domestic servants often offered the first quarters where Jews could go into hiding. Some Jewish forced laborers met friends at work who suggested they go into hiding and assisted them in securing their illegal existence in the underground. The danger of being discovered in these circles was especially great since they were watched over by the Gestapo. Those who had gone into hiding were constantly on the lookout for "addresses." Attics and cellars, storerooms or sheds, workshops or garden houses served as places to sleep and live. Many such hideouts were discovered due to informers or destroyed later on during bombing raids.

Life underground demanded courage, tenacity, and a high degree of social adaptability. People had to learn to live with being alone. Since couples or small groups, strangers and friends, men and women, children and the elderly all went into illegal hiding, group tensions were unavoidable. Irritability, nervousness, and agressivity plagued interpersonal relations underground, as did sexual tensions and problems. People had to put up with limitations in hygienic conditions; toilet facilities were often inadequate or nonexistent. Illness had to be surmounted, frequently without medical assistance, since living in hiding generally ruled out visits to the doctor or a hospital. Whoever left his or her hiding place increased the risk of being discovered. Police and SS units patrolled the streets, and inspectors searched the air-raid shelters looking for illegal Jews looking for protection. Informers eagerly waited to fulfill their "duty as citizens" by filing a report with the Gestapo – and then pocketing the advertised reward. There were also a small number of German Jews who were active as Gestapo informers. These persons were dubbed grabbers (*Greifer, Schnapper*); in Berlin, they numbered some fifteen to twenty individuals. They enjoyed the privilege of being exempt from wearing the obligatory Jewish star and hoped to be exempted from deportation as well. News of their betrayal and treachery quickly made the rounds among those living in hiding.

Finally, living underground entailed finding enough funds to be able to pay for a life in illegality. Ration cards and false papers were indispensable. They were sold for high prices on the black market, and demand for them increased steadily. As the war progressed, the number of non-Jews who went into hiding also mounted. These were resistance fighters and persons from that vast horde of foreign forced laborers and POWs who had managed to escape from the camps. The Jews who went into hiding did not have any financial reserves. Their helpers and rescuers had to come to their aid, providing funds for rent and clothing, food and false papers. As far as is known, the tiny resistance and escape assistance organizations operating within Germany did not have access to the funds raised in Western Europe and distributed through the central bureaucracies for the financing of rescue operations.

In the extermination camps, there was no longer any possibility for German and foreign Jews to resist annihilation. Behind them lay a long and harrowing journey. They had been arrested in Germany and in the occupied areas and were shipped in sealed boxcars from deportation assembly points, freight stations, Jewish transit camps, and forced ghettos directly to the unloading ramps of the extermination sites. They climbed off these freight cars exhausted and broken human beings, persons who had passed through all phases of moral debasement and social discrimination and who had experienced ostracism and banishment, total ejection from society, the pain and hopelessness of their situation. In their minds and hearts, they had taken along something else as well on their way to the liquidation camps – the consciousness of having been brought together, united in a Jewish community of fate and suffering.

On the selection ramps, the aged stood side by side with children and women. The selection process broke up the deportation transport. It raised the proportion of children and aged in the group that was herded off immediately to sudden death in the gas chamber. Only a few were aware that death was awaiting them at the end of their short path. That uncertainty was maintained by SS deception up until the very last moment. Those selected were told that they had to be "disinfected" before going on to their new quarters. After surrendering their baggage, they were led over a closed-off access path to the disrobing rooms. Members of a Jewish special unit were often on hand and had been instructed to conduct themselves so as to have a pacifying effect on the victims. Then the doors of the gas chambers, disguised as "disinfection rooms," were swung open.

The small number of German Jews who, because of their youth or presumed fitness to work, had been ordered to the barracks or to labor detachments had just as little opportunity to resist. Their murder had only been postponed. They lived in an isolation that could barely be penetrated. For most prisoners, the path into organized resistance in the camps remained closed. In many cases, it was hopeless to try to overcome the barriers, animosities, and anti-Semitism that emerged from among the ranks of other prisoners and groups of inmates. Individual and open acts of resistance remained limited or were automatically ruled out because they necessarily cancelled one's "respite of time" and thus any hope for continued survival in the camp. As already mentioned, some 8,000 of the 134,000 Germans Jews who were deported ultimately survived and returned.

In 1945, those who had emigrated received news about the death of their relatives and the destruction of their communities with a sense of shock and sadness, though also frequently intermingled with feelings of guilt because of their own survival. Almost all of these emigrés remained in their new countries of emigration. The old memories of Germany resurface(d) only in photo albums, letters, and conversations, especially in the recollections of a happy childhood and period at school, fondly remembered times brought to an abrupt end by anti-Semitism. Their attitudes toward Germany were marked by a clear sense of distance and often by a sharp feeling of rejection – the experience of expulsion and the murder of their close relatives ran too deep, was too profound to permit forgetting. Most preferred to avoid Germans, particularly those in the age group of the perpetrators and those who stood idly by.

Few emigrés returned to the land of their birth. Their first visits were limited to business trips or a brief, painful return to their former neighborhoods, a reunion with school friends, a visit to the cemetery. As time passed, the numbers of those willing to renew contacts with Germans, with the postwar generation, increased. The invitations and "organized visits" arranged by West German cities for the former "Jewish friends and fellow citizens," albeit late in coming, provided one opportunity for such contacts. Yet many of their children and grandchildren have sundered all ties to Germany, totally and completely.

Recollections of a Non-Aryan Emigrant from the Third Reich

Wolf Zuelzer

My contribution to this volume of commemorative and exhortative essays on the occasion of the fiftieth anniversary of the November 1938 pogrom is to explore the question suggested by the editor, of "what the factors at that time were which ultimately induced highly assimilated German citizens to depart after all from their beloved homeland." The reference here is to persons who had "made it," so to speak, such as Jewish university graduates who had established a career and who also "felt German," that is, persons for whom the decision to emigrate was presumably very difficult. These criteria actually do not quite apply to my own case: first of all, I was not a Jew (although mainly of Jewish extraction and thus a non-Aryan in Nazi terminology); second, I had not as yet established a career (at the beginning of the Nazi era, I was a twenty-three-year-old medical student in my home town of Berlin); third, I had already left Germany (with a sigh of relief!) in October 1933 and so was not a direct eyewitness to the events of the Reichskristallnacht.

If I am nonetheless contributing here, then it is for another reason: because the fate of the so-called non-Aryans in the Third Reich has been given less attention than that of the full Jews, even though their situation was by no means less precarious. It is well known that the decisive factor was race, not religion, culture, or degree of assimilation. Objectively, that is, from the perspective of those in power, no difference existed between Jews and non-Aryans (conditions prevailing in Hitler's Germany cannot be described without resorting to this terminology). Subjectively, in the consciousness of those affected, there may have been differences, but these need not concern us here since such differences were no greater than those from case to case within the two groups. People in both categories viewed themselves as Germans and both, according to the above definition, were certainly also a part of the educated middle class. Aside from this common denominator, however, each constellation was unique. If in the following remarks I limit myself to personal experiences (my own and those of family and close friends), this does not mean to imply that I see myself as representative of one or another group. Rather, that only reflects my approach: I regard the anecdotal method as the most appropriate for my chosen topic.

Let it be left open for the present whether the concept "assimilation" is applicable to the German Jews (and non-Aryans) of that period. In any event, the degree of assimilation was less important for the decision of whether to stay on in the country or emigrate than other factors: age, profession, expectations regarding a pension, or the local atmosphere (Jews in smaller towns were more exposed and visible than Jews in large urban areas such as Berlin or Frankfurt). Older persons were less flexible than the younger generation. The creation of a new life abroad was more difficult for those who were closely bound in a professional sense to their mother tongue, such as writers, actors, teachers of academic subjects, journalists, and even lawyers, judges, and administrative officials. For doctors, engineers, or musicians, that transition was easier. Another key question was whether one had any relatives or friends over there who could be relied on for help. Finally, political and ideological ties also constituted a factor: Communists felt the pull of the Soviet Union, Zionists headed for Palestine, committed anti-Fascists were drawn into participating in the Spanish Civil War.

The category non-Aryan derived from pseudoscientific racial theories which had already provided a basis for crude anti-Semitism in the nineteenth century. A definition in accordance with the percentage of "Jewish blood" is superfluous, especially since the Nazis themselves operated in a quite arbitrary manner in this regard, as indicated by Göring's famous dictum, "I'm the one who determines who's a Jew." The category encompassed a wide spectrum: full Jews, as well as those who had been baptized and their descendants, children from mixed marriages, half, quarter, and one-eighth Jews, persons at home in German culture, language, and landscape, who had no links with Jewish religion and knew little or nothing about Jewish history and custom and did not desire to know.

Long before Hitler's seizure of power, the existence of Jewish ancestors in such families was hushed up or played down; moreover, until the National Socialists took power, there had been no reason to worry about the religious preference of past generations. And is it indeed a matter of religion, as in Lessing's *Nathan der Weise* or Karl Gutzkow's *Uriel Acosta*? This, by the way, is why non-Aryans and even Jews were able to share the prejudice, widespread in middle-class circles, against *Ostjuden*, Eastern European Jews. This prejudice, based on a total ignorance of the religious and social ethos of the Jewish communities in Eastern Europe, was not directed against religion, after all, but rather against the supposed backwardness and cultural isolation of coreligionists in Poland and Galicia. This attitude should not be equated with the virulent anti-Semitism of the Nazis and their German and Austrian precursors; nonetheless, for the great majority of German Jews, the Orthodox *Ostjude* in caftan, fur cap, and ritual sidelocks was a nightmarish figure straight from the Middle Ages.

I myself only learned at the age of fourteen or fifteen that my ancestors had not fought together in A.D. 9 with Arminius against the Romans in the Teutoburg Forest. The occasion for this insight was one of those Yiddish jokes so popular in Berlin at the time, invented by Jews themselves and circulated by them, a form of self-irony which was often interpreted by the noninitiated as being anti-Semitic. I laughed at the joke, after which my father took me aside and enlightened me as to my extraction. My grandfather Wilhelm, born in 1834 in Breslau (Wilhelm! – already by that time Jewish children were being given emphatically German names) was a Jew. As I learned many years later, our family name was geographic in origin: the Jewish community in Zuelz was considered to be especially pious and learned.

Wilhelm, an important doctor and researcher, lecturer at Berlin University, a titular professor, editor of an international professional journal, and founder of the field of medical statistics in Germany, rejected Bismarck's offer of the directorship of the Reich Public Health Department for one reason only, because he was unwilling to be baptized. My father, Georg Ludwig, born in 1870 in Berlin and educated at the famous Französisches Gymnasium there, had no such scruples. His divinity was Aesculapius, not Jehovah, his goal a teaching position and the directorship of a research institute – and for that one had to be Christian. He and his brother, later active as an orthopedist in Potsdam, converted to Protestantism after the death of their father (1893), thus putting an end to the Jewish tradition in the family. We three children were baptized in the Kaiser-Wilhelm-Gedächtniskirche by Chief Court Chaplain (!) Kessler, and I was later confirmed in that same church by Pastor Conrad (a conservative German-national cleric with duel scars!). During World War I, my father directed a field hospital in Brest-Litowsk as senior staff physician, returning as a disabled veteran (typhus, malaria) in 1918. His favorite authors, whose works he could quote for pages on end, were Goethe, Homer, Horace, and Virgil.

My maternal grandfather, Hermann Wolff (1845–1902), was likewise of Jewish extraction, but became an agnostic early on and married an Austrian Catholic, the only Aryan woman in my family tree. Their children were raised as Lutherans, an odd compromise solution. The Wolffs had come from the Rhineland to Berlin. Although decidedly Francophile, Hermann took part as a volunteer in the war against France. He was initially active as a merchant, but also wrote as a music critic for several Berlin newspapers since he had had a musical education and could play music reading notes from the page. Later he became an impresario and friend of Anton Rubinstein. In 1880, he founded the later world-renowned Konzertdirektion Wolff and became adviser to and representative of the Berlin Philharmonic. He set up the Philharmonic Concert Series, procuring Hans von Bülow as director and, after his death, Arthur Nikisch. He discovered and promoted numerous young artists such as Eugen D'Albert, Bruno Walter, Arthur Rubinstein, and Arthur Schnabel. He built the Bechstein Hall, a small architectonic jewel for chamber music and lieder evenings, dedicated by no other than Brahms, Bülow, and Joseph Joachim. Brahms, Bruckner, Bülow, Saint-Saëns, Busoni, Richard Strauss – they were all guests in the home of my grandparents. Hermann Wolff's importance for German musical life during the period cannot be underestimated.

His work was continued and expanded by my grandmother Louise Wolff, an exceptional woman, originally actress, then housewife, hostess, and matriarch, finally a combination of grande dame, mother figure, and farsighted business woman, a force in the cultural and social life of Berlin – "Queen Louise," as she was dubbed, half admiringly, half ironically. She was a close friend of Nikisch, Fritz Kreisler, Bruno Walter, and the great singers of the *kunstlied*, Elena Gerhart and Julia Culp. Her house was also frequented by diplomats and politicians, Gustav Stresemann, Prince Louis Ferdinand, the Social Democratic minister of culture Konrad Haenisch, the chief editors of the *Vossische Zeitung* and the *Berliner Tageblatt*, Georg Bernhard and Theodor Wolff, journalists from Germany and abroad, art historians, musical scholars, and actors. A regular event after the Sunday dress rehearsal of the Berlin Philharmonic was the so-called Philharmonisches Diner presided over by the conductor, to which my grandmother always invited the respective soloists as the guests of honor. At the age of twelve, I was introduced to Richard Strauss on one occasion and to Gerhart Hauptmann on another. As Louise Wolff's grandchild, I grew up precisely in the hub, so to speak, of Weimar culture.

In this milieu, no one was concerned about the religion of others and most certainly not about their race. The high school I attended (Bismarck-Gymnasium, Wilmersdorf) was also pervaded by a spirit of tolerance. We envied our Jewish fellow pupils for their special holidays, but I cannot recall ever having heard anything anti-Semitic said against them. After we graduated (1927), my father put on an evening for "fathers and sons," and everyone came, both Christian and Jewish, Deutsch nationale conservatives and Democrats (there was no one else politically further to the left, and there were no Nazis yet in respectable circles in Berlin), future doctors, lawyers, government officials, merchants, and even someone who later became a Protestant minister.

The talk with my father about my Jewish ancestors triggered an identity crisis in me. At first, I did not want to believe it; then I said to myself, OK, if I am a Jew, then I want to be one too. But that proved to be impossible: virtually all the prerequisites were lacking. I was in love with a young girl from an orthodox Jewish background and fasted for her sake on Yom Kippur, yet that was a naive romantic gesture that led to nothing. I was and remained, at least until 1933, a young, German, middle-class, university-trained intellectual, just like my friends, whether Christian or Jewish.

After graduation from high school, I went to university and studied philosophy with Karl Jaspers and romance languages with Ernst Robert Curtius in Heidelberg. Curtius was adviser to a foundation for promoting German-French rapprochement, which at his recommendation awarded me a scholarship for a year in France. Thus it was that in the fall of 1928 – as a representative of German youth! – I went to Paris. There I met many of the leading writers, such as André Gide, Roger Martin du Gard, both future Nobel laureates, Jean Schlumberger, André Maurois. I gave lectures on German literature (Remarque's *Im Westen nichts Neues* had just been published and could be cited as an example of the German desire for peace) before distrustful workers' associations and traveled the length and breadth of that beautiful country. In the autumn of 1929, I returned to Berlin to finish a doctorate. My career as a literary critic seemed assured: I had already published a few essays on modern French literature in the *Neue Schweizer Rundschau* and in the *Frankfurter Zeitung*; these were even quoted in Willi Haas's journal *Literari- sche Welt* as pointing the way. That gave me pause for thought: How could I, just turned twenty, be regarded as an authority? The intoxicating year in Paris had left a kind of hangover in its wake. I switched to medicine and thus went back to the tra- dition of my father's family, took premed examinations in Bonn, and intended to finish my studies in Berlin. But things turned out differently.

What does all this have to do with the behavior of Jewish fellow citizens in the Third Reich? My case was certainly not typical, neither for non-Aryans nor for Jews, but that is precisely the crucial point: there were no typical cases, only individual ones. I could just as easily have been a Jew. The dividing line between Jews and non-Aryans had always been a fluid one. Both groups not only felt German, they were German – not highly assimilated members of society, but rather fellow creators and representatives of German culture, and had been so for more than a century. Those of us who now know the final outcome find it incomprehensible that they actually wished to be that, and that up until 1933 they had been consciously rooted in a specifically German tradition. Yet for contemporaries that outcome, in the early years of the Nazi regime – and for many even after the November 1938 pogrom – was simply inconceiv- able. Nonetheless, their situation was, almost right from the beginning, intolerable. The first boycott action against Jewish stores, not yet violent in nature, had already taken place on

April 1, 1933. With it began the systematic harassment, intimidation, exploitation, deprivation of rights, and humiliation whose next high point was the Reichskristallnacht. Baptized or not, these persons had ceased to be fellow citizens; for those in power, they were helots, or rather lepers, who ultimately were forced to mark their stigma by wearing the yellow star and adding Israel or Sara as middle name to their given names. By then, though, the war had already started, and the mousetrap had snapped shut. The question is not why they left their homeland, but why so many stayed on for so long. Why was this?

For one thing, many clung to the illusion of the constitutional state. Hitler had come to power legally and initially adhered to the formalities of the law. The Reichstag fire, which provided him with the pretext to suspend the constitution, was blamed on the Communists, but the alleged arsonist, the Bulgarian Communist Dimitroff, was acquitted by a proper court trial. In the beginning, the concentration camps were only known through rumor. There were still the regular police, though they had to close both eyes when it came to the brutal violence of the brownshirts. The Reichstag elections on March 5, 1933, were by secret ballot, even though they proved to be an empty gesture. (I voted for the Communists, not out of a sense of conviction, but because I regarded them as the most resolute opponents of the Nazis. In actual fact, their candidates had already been sent to the concentration camps some time before.) Whoever had no "political record" could move about freely and was initially left unmolested.

Anti-Semitism had for years been a phenomenon that accompanied German political life; people had gotten accustomed to it, so to speak. One illustrative example is that of the Verein deutscher Studenten (German Students' Association), founded in 1880, whose declared objective was to "clear the universities of Jews." Up until that time, it had been possible to shake off latent anti-Semitism, to brush it aside like a dog did the rain. Was it now suddenly to be a different situation? The vulgar song "Wenn's Judenblut vom Messer spritzt" ("When Jewish Blood spurts from the knife") was considered to be the product of a sadistic imagination straight from a madhouse; no German government would ever permit its realization. It is true that the measures aimed at Jews and non-Aryans became gradually more and more threatening, but they were clothed in bureaucratic-legalistic forms, as though they were the result of a clearly limited program within the framework of the law.

The fiction of the rule of law was preserved down to the Kristallnacht. The bloodbath on June 30, 1934, was justified as a necessary defense against a supposed coup by radical elements in the SA. Whoever wished to believe that, whoever hoped (as was often the case, especially among Christian non-Aryans) that at least he or she would not be personally harmed by what was happening, stayed in the country – until it was too late. Second, there were also material reasons for staying on. Whoever emigrated lost, as a rule, all assets and property, compelled to leave what he or she owned behind. The export of money, currency, and stocks and bonds was punishable by death! Bank accounts were under strict surveillance, and whoever withdrew large amounts of cash before a trip abroad could expect a search, confiscation, and arrest at the border. I myself was witness to such an incident at the Czech border. Someone had taken along a large sum of money and had hidden it in another compartment. That car was detached from the train, and the owner, who had betrayed himself by his agitation, was led away white as a sheet. Third, it was in actual fact difficult even for clear-sighted individuals to surrender their German birthright. Who was this fellow Hitler after all – some guy who had come along, a demagogue and charlatan of the worst sort, and he wished to deny them that birthright? And who were his followers? It could not be denied that millions of decent middle-class Germans had voted for him before 1933 and, even more depressing a fact, that the majority of students and faculty at universities and other institutions of higher learning had declared their support for him.

Yet should all hope be given up on that account? Weren't these people still accessible on a personal basis? Didn't they reject the extreme anti-Semitism of the brownshirts as a passing aberration or a necessary concession to the radical wing of the party? In any event, the actual Nazis, the fanatics who had chosen Hitler as their leader, were failures, misfits from the lumpen proletariat, savage, Neanderthal. And an elite fully aware of its historical importance did not wish to retreat before such a pack of riffraff. These persons simply could not change the way they were, their German nature. The process of assimilation had been concluded by 1810 in the first generation after emancipation. Think of Heinrich Heine, the most German of German lyric poets (and the most barbed German satirist); Felix Mendelssohn, whose monument stood until 1933 before the Gewandhaus in Leipzig, the musician who resurrected the forgotten *Passion of St. Matthew*, the friend of Robert and Clara Schumann, the composer of the Reformationssymphonie; Rahel Varnhagen, née Levin, and her circle – Fichte, Schleiermacher, Wilhelm von Humboldt, the Schlegel brothers; the ultraconservative specialist on constitutional law, Friedrich Julius Stahl, and the liberal parliamentarians of the March Revolution, Eduard Simson and Ludwig Bamberger. Karl Marx and Ferdinand Lassalle also belong to this series.

The dream of the indestructible community of fate (*Schicksalsgemeinschaft*) between Germans and Jews lasted approximately four generations, encompassing almost all spheres of culture despite the restrictions which were in effect until 1918. In the field of music, there were Hermann Levi, Bruno Walter, Otto Klemperer, Kurt Weill, and if you add the Austrians, Gustav Mahler, Arnold Schönberg, Erich Wolfgang Korngold, and Arthur Schnabel. In medicine, there were figures such as Paul Ehrlich, August von Wassermann, Albert Neisser, Hermann Zondek; in chemistry, Fritz Haber, Otto Meyerhoff, O.H. Warburg, Richard Willstätter; in physics, Albert Einstein (although born a German Jew and a naturalized Swiss citizen, he was, as director of the Kaiser-Wilhelm Institute for Physics from 1914 until just before the Nazi takeover, also a German citizen), Luise Meitner, Otto Stern; in philosophy, Hermann Cohen, Georg Simmel, Ernst Cassirer, Edmund Husserl; in theater, Max Reinhardt, Fritz Kortner, Elisabeth Bergner, Ernst Deutsch; in journalism, Rudolf Mosse, Leopold Ullstein, Maximilian Harden, Georg Bernhard, Theodor Wolff, Siegfried Jakobsohn, Karl Kraus, Kurt Tucholsky; in politics, Hugo Preuss, Otto Landsberg, Walther Rathenau; in literature, Döblin, Toller, Hasenclever, Borchardt, Else Lasker-Schüler, Feuchtwanger, Emil Ludwig and – once again the Austrians – Broch, Hofmannsthal, Kafka, Schnitzler, Werfel, Stefan Zweig. The list is arbitrary and could easily be extended.

The Nazis thus were, to a certain extent, correct in saying that Jews were "overrepresented" in German culture. Yet this culture was neither Jewish nor German, but a unique amalgam whose elements formed an organic unit. To stick with the chemical metaphor, the "destructive spirit" which they alleged the Jews had, the spirit which led to an irreversible separation of these elements and thus to the destruction of that culture, was the demonic spirit of National Socialism itself. In contrast with the still relatively innocuous anti-Semitism of the nineteenth century, Hitlerism was a rebellion of the primitive against culture as such and thus against a tradition whose most visible representatives were the "successful" German and Austrian Jews and non-Aryans. Nazism was anti-Semitic because it was antirational, anti-intellectual, and anti-elitarian and fought against all forces of civilization wherever they existed. The inability to comprehend this connection in its full weight and import was one of the reasons – perhaps the main reason – why so many Jews and non-Aryans remained on for such a long time in the Third Reich.

Back to individuals and individual fates. My parents were divorced, and both had remarried. My half-Aryan mother and her non-Aryan husband, a Prussian judge (!), still refused after the Kristallnacht to leave their native country. They belonged to the congregation of believers around Martin Niemöller and also regarded themselves as being inviolable because they had friends in German-national circles. They paid dearly for this mistaken reading of their situation: during the first year of the war, they were deprived of their property, sent to forced labor in a munitions plant, and compelled to wear the yellow star. Then they were sent to the Theresienstadt concentration camp (where more "prominent" prisoners were interned), survived despite their advanced age, spent five years with me and my American family, and returned in 1951 to their undamaged house (!) in Berlin-Dahlem. They still felt German and regarded the Third Reich as an unfortunate aberration. Hitler, Goebbels, Streicher, those were riffraff, commented the former Prussian judge to one of my American friends. But Göring? A Prussian officer? That was incomprehensible!

My mother's sister, naturally non-Aryan as well, remained unmolested during the war, but died in 1945 of starvation in the misery of Vienna. Her brother, my uncle Werner Wolff, formerly well known as the conductor of the Hamburg opera and an interpreter of Bruckner, and his non-Aryan wife, the singer of Mozart, Händel, and Verdi, Emmy Land, lost their posts and pension rights and later created a modest existence for themselves at the Chattanooga Conservatory in Tennessee. A cousin, Elsa Wolff, whose correspondence with Romain Roland was posthumously published (*Lettres à Fräulein Elsa*), committed suicide before being deported to Auschwitz. Another escaped to Paris, where she illustrated childrens' books under the pseudonym La Louve (The She Wolf). A third worked as a masseuse in New York. Her son, my cousin and friend Henry Ehrmann, as a Social Democrat, was sent in 1933 to a concentration camp, but was unexpectedly released. He somehow scraped by and survived until 1940 in Paris, got away just before the Germans marched in, and made a name for himself later as a professor of political science and the author of a much-quoted book on the French political system at Dartmouth College. He was recently awarded an honorary doctorate by Mannheim University. In contrast, another of my mother's cousins, who had married a Dutchman, was arrested by the Gestapo in Amsterdam and gassed in Auschwitz.

My father, a baptized Jew, wedded an Aryan woman of Danish nationality in his second marriage. After losing his post as head physician at the Lankwitz Hospital and his right to teach at Berlin University, he had already emigrated to the United States in 1934 at the age of sixty-four. He had enough strength to rebuild a practice there once again, but had to give up the work of teacher and researcher which he so loved. His brother, orthopedist in Potsdam, found refuge with one of his daughters, who was married and lived in London. Her brother, also an orthopedist, went to the United States and later held a high post in the American occupation army. He lived in Texas before that service and after and was married twice, the second time to a German woman. The children from both marriages are Americans, just like my own children.

Undoubtedly the most tragic case in my family involved the death of my younger brother, aged twenty-two, a medical student like me, gifted, good-looking, somewhat melancholic, a passionate climber. He had belonged to some sort of left-wing radical group and was unable to sign the sworn statement every student had to give regarding political activities. He therefore left Germany in the summer of 1933, intending to continue his studies in Padua. On the way there he made a detour into the Dolomites, where he ventured a climb, against the advice of other experienced Alpine climbers, and fell to his death. He was buried in a remote mountain village, according to the Catholic rites, as a "young German hero who died in battle with the forces of nature" – so stated the local leaders of the Fascists and the representative of the NSDAP sent specially from Bozen to attend the funeral. This was a triple irony of fate: such a funeral for a young, anti-Fascist, non-Aryan agnostic.

My own story is brief to tell: before 1933, I was totally non-political, voted for the Social Democrats, opted in 1932 for Hindenburg's reelection as the lesser evil, and, like so many intellectuals, did not take Hitler seriously. He was clearly a psychopath, even if a gifted one, and would, I thought, never come to power because the Reichswehr, for one, would not tolerate it. On January 30, 1933, I woke up completely. As an eleven-year-old, I recalled the Kapp Putsch and remembered the general strike which had helped to turn the coup into a failure in a few days. Now today, I thought, the unions would strike. Instead the brownshirts marched with torches through the Brandenburg Gate and thousands gathered in front of the Chancellery to cheer the Führer.

That night I understood that as an apolitical medical student I also shared part of the responsibility for this and that now it was each individual's duty to engage in active resistance. But how? I joined a secret organization expecting to be trained for a concrete program, such as sabotage or the use of firearms. I became a member of a so-called cell. There were five of us; we knew each other only by our first names and met in remote parts of the city. Yet instead of talking about concrete possibilities for active resistance, the discussion revolved around Marxist dialectics. Was National Socialism a necessary phase in world history? Was it correct for the Communists to have aided the Nazis in the Reichstag in destroying the Republic? Was the capitalist system on the verge of collapse? And so on. I did not want to risk my skin for speculations of that ilk and left the group after about three months. What could I do now as a single individual?

Shortly thereafter, in the summer of 1933, I was expelled without reason from Berlin University. There must have been some sort of personal revenge involved here. The student in SA uniform who handed me the decision refused to give me any reason. Significantly, I had no difficulty after this in enrolling again at the University of Bonn. I would have been able to finish my studies there, but instead left Germany in October with the definite intention of never returning again. What were my reasons? First of all, I could see no future for myself as a non-Aryan in the Third Reich. Second, I was so disgusted by the carryings-on of the Nazis that I was in danger of betraying myself by some remark or gesture. Third, I felt I had done my duty as a German and could, with a quiet conscience, shake the dust of the homeland off my feet. Fourth, I was young and lucky enough to be able to continue my studies abroad. Leaving was not hard for me: I boarded the train to Prague and got off six hours later, a free man.

I almost might have stayed in Czechoslovakia. I learned the language and felt at home there. I had been given the prospect of obtaining a scholarship from the Rockefeller Foundation after finishing my medical degree and then subsequently taking over as director of child care for minorities – Sudeten Germans (!), Hungarians, Ruthenians, etc. Yet things turned out differently. My father had arranged a U.S. visa for me and urged me to come. In August 1935, I arrived in the States and received further training in Boston and Chicago. Finally I landed in Detroit, where for thirty-five years I worked as head of laboratories in the Children's Hospital and as professor of pediatrics. For the last five years of my professional career, I was director of the Department for Blood Diseases and Transfusion Research of the National Heart, Lung, and Blood Institute in Bethesda, Maryland, near Washington. An academic sabbatical year allowed me to pursue historical studies and write the biography of a forgotten German pacifist of the First World War period, Georg Friedrich Nicolai.

After arriving in the United States, I soon abandoned the idea of returning to Prague. From a distance, one could already discern at that time the direction in which Europe was going: toward barbarism, extermination of the Jews and other minorities, totalitarianism, and total war. Mussolini's Abyssinian campaign, the remilitarization of the Rhineland, the Spanish Civil War, the Moscow show trials, the Japanese incursion into China, the Anschluß and its horrible consequences for Austrian Jews, the Munich Agreement, the occupation of the Sudetenland and the dissolution of Czechoslovakia, the Hitler-Stalin Pact, and then the war. Poland, Norway, Denmark, Rotterdam and Coventry, London and Belgrade, France and Greece, Crete and North Africa, and so on, to the bitter end. And then, in a way as a postscript, the Holocaust, the pictures from Auschwitz and all the other camps: in this chain of inhumanity, the Kristallnacht was a dreadful signal.

For more than half a century I have lived in the United States. It is understandable why, so long after the end of the Third Reich, I have suppressed any recollection of my German past as radically as possible. I avoided every opportunity to speak German or even to hear others speak it, even if I was with German emigrés. When I had to return to Berlin in 1955 because of my mother's severe illness, I literally felt ill when I once again heard the sound of this language, which in spite of everything I had not forgotten. It was not until the 1970s that I voluntarily went to the Federal Republic and made contact with a new type of German, generally younger than myself – modern, Western-oriented Europeans – a generation which had experienced the catharsis of which their parents had been incapable. New friendships developed, and I felt that I could once more speak and write German again.

Hitlerism was not an aberration: it was the central catastrophe of the century, a perversion of European culture in its totality. It differed from other variants of fascism not only in the degree of its brutality, but in its absolute nihilism, its negation of all values of civilization. The capacity to commit evil – sadism and genocide – has been the heritage of mankind ever since Cain slaughtered his brother Abel. The new element in Hitlerism was the systematic employment of modern technological and organizational methods, the linking of the most base instincts with the greatest efficiency. In the age of nuclear weaponry – which threatens to become at the same time an age of nationalism and obscurantism – the continued survival of Homo sapiens is dependent on a return to rational humanism and its values.

The Genesis of the Final Solution

Hermann Graml

In his 1977 study *Hitler's War*, David Irving contends that the Führer and chancellor of National Socialist Germany did not order the extermination undertaken by the Nazi regime between 1941 and 1944 of the Jews living in the areas under German power and influence at that time. Irving maintains that Hitler was not informed about the program of murder at all until October 1943, some two years after the beginning of the Holocaust, a program which functionaries like Himmler and Heydrich had been carrying out up until that time behind his back. Yet these functionaries as well, according to the Irving thesis, had not initiated the destruction of the Jews as a consciously intended "Final Solution of the Jewish Question." Rather, they had chosen this as a way out, indeed as the most comfortable way out of the impasse of embarrassments and difficulties caused by implementation of a poorly planned program of *deportation*; that program, which was certainly approved by Hitler, had run into unforeseen obstacles.[1]

When Martin Broszat responded shortly thereafter to Irving's challenge in the pages of the *Vierteljahrshefte für Zeitgeschichte*, he unmasked the assertion of Hitler's supposed ignorance, in impressive and persuasive manner, as nothing but historiographic humbug. Nonetheless Broszat, as a result of his own analysis of events, developed the thesis that in fact no plan or even specific order could be assumed to have existed when the annihilation of the Jews began. Rather, numerous isolated actions of murder, all in fact the product of an inability to cope with the administrative problems entailed by deportation, gradually combined into a total event which the Nazi leadership ultimately sanctioned (or stylized) as the Final Solution.[2] The Holocaust ap-

---

1. David Irving, *Hitler's War* (London, 1977), esp. pp. xivf.
2. Martin Broszat, "Hitler und die Genesis der 'Endlösung': Aus Anlaß der Thesen von David Irving," *VfZ*, 25 (1977): 739–75.

pears here as the result of an improvised attempt by helpless, perplexed bureaucrats to flee from the problems and difficulties of a likewise improvised program of deportation, one which, given its desired scope and magnitude, was in any event uncontrollable.

In an essay published in *Geschichte und Gesellschaft*, Hans Mommsen emphatically defended Broszat's interpretation and explicated, with customary intellectual brilliance, why both the option of a written order and an oral command issued by Hitler must be "fundamentally excluded as a possibility" as the triggering element for the annihilation of the Jews. The "genocidal policy," the term Mommsen nonetheless uses to designate the mass murder, should by no means be understood as the realization of a program: in Mommsen's view, it should rather be viewed as a "perfect improvisation."[3]

Such interpretations are dependent on several assumptions and presuppositions, and these warrant careful scholarly scrutiny. The first and foremost assumption here is the notion that National Socialist anti-Semitism did not inevitably have to culminate in an attempt to exterminate the Jews and that basically another Final Solution of the self-created Jewish Question might also have been feasible. Hans Mommsen also says that "the step to mass annihilation" came "at the end of a complex and quite open political process."[4] This does not imply that a situation first had to come about which sanctioned the idea of genocide and seduced the National Socialists into embarking on that course.

It is a banal and uncontroversial insight that a political movement considering anti-Semitism among the central tenets of its creed can only make the progression from propaganda and individual terror to an anti-Jewish policy if it achieves state power. Equally banal and not open to serious dispute is the recognition that a political regime led by anti-Semites can only move on to more and most radical measures if it has gained the required latitude for action in domestic and foreign policy. Hans Mommsen, in contrast, considers even the combined effect of anti-Semitism and such latitude to be relatively unimportant. In

3. Hans Mommsen, "Die Realisierung des Utopischen: Die 'Endlösung der Judenfrage' im Dritten Reich," *Geschichte und Gesellschaft* 9 (1983): 381–420, here esp. 417.
4. Ibid., p. 400.

his explanation of the Holocaust, it is not simply a question of the disappearance of obstacles but also of the importance of the co-causal and co-compelling factors. In the course of the argument, these factors gradually appear to take on an almost greater significance than anti-Semitism itself, at least in respect to the genocide. Thus, for example, Mommsen speaks about the "internal antagonisms of the system," which had "increasingly acted to obstruct possible options."[5] This is not a particularly persuasive line of argumentation.

National Socialist anti-Semitism, I would contend, should be viewed as the concentration, systematization, and ideological absolutization of those various anti-Semitisms which began to penetrate into leadership strata, the middle class, the petty bourgeoisie, and the farming classes in Germany in the last three decades of the nineteenth century.[6] At that time, anti-Semitism always appeared in association with antiliberal and antimodernist currents or in combination with excessive nationalism and social-Darwinist racism, that is, with perversions of the movement for bourgeois emancipation which had failed in political terms. Anti-Semitism initially was engendered above all else by a historically explicable difference between the Christian majoritarian society and the Jewish minority. The majoritarian society, since the defeat of the Liberals in the Prussian constitutional conflict and especially since the Franco-Prussian War of 1870–71, was experiencing a profound crisis in the liberal principles that up until then had been dominant. In contrast, a majority of the Jewish minority, having finally, from the beginning of the 1870s at least achieved legal equality, welcomed virtually all forms of modernizing change, took part in modernizing processes, and actively promoted their continued expansion.

However, as a result of the crisis besetting the majoritarian society, it ultimately reacted with distrust, rejection, or even animosity toward every modernizing change in the intellectual, political, and even, to some extent, economic spheres. It viewed

---

5. Ibid.
6. See Reinhard Rürup, *Emanzipation und Antisemitismus: Studien zur "Judenfrage" der bürgerlichen Gesellschaft* (Göttingen, 1975); Werner Jochmann, "Struktur und Funktionen des deutschen Antisemitismus," in Werner E. Mosse and Arnold Paucker, eds., *Juden im Wilhelminischen Deutschland, 1890–1914* (Tübingen, 1976), pp. 389–477.

threatened imminent changes with a sense of apprehension and anxiety. This difference in direction or pace of development, namely, the Jewish lead in emancipatory thinking and action, helps to explain the fact that many Germans began to regard the Jews as symbolic figures for cultural-intellectual, political, and economic processes which, regarded with antipathy and un-comprehended, were even interpreted as signaling the patho-logical decline of the nation. Thus, numerous Germans soon came to view the Jews not just as symbolic figures reflecting such processes of presumed decline, but as the very authors and movers of those negative processes.

So it was that, already in the 1870s and 1880s, the first theoreticians of anti-Semitism had emerged onto the scene – Wilhelm Marr, Eugen Dühring, Adolf Wahrmund, and Paul de Lagarde. These men cast Judaism and Jewry in the role of the evil principle operative in world history, declaring the Jews to be pathogenetic agents infecting the body of the *Volk*, creatures undeserving of the status of human beings. In logical conse-quence, they called for a struggle against the Jews. Such struggle had little left in common even with the harshest forms of confrontation familiar to us from the most bitter group con-flicts in modern states. Rather, that struggle was envisioned as the eradication of noxious pests, the removal of an unusually dangerous cultural-intellectual and political pollution of the environment. This new anti-Semitism was totally different from the previous religiously rooted anti-Judaism which, although it kept the Jews beyond the pale of the Christian society of estates and occasionally subjected them to persecution, had always regarded them essentially as human beings, fundamentally capable of entering Christendom by the path of baptism.

Modern anti-Semitism was far more threatening to the Jews. By stamping and stigmatizing them as the causative agents, the veritable germs for the processes of decay, it necessarily denied Jews the ability and capacity to change and thus to enter the dominant society, in this case, the German nation. Conse-quently, the development of anti-Semitism did not come to an end specifically as assimilation by German Jews advanced. Whoever had come to adhere to this inhuman perversion of a political doctrine of salvation freed himself not only from the necessity of having to legitimate his own views through the existence of a concrete Jewish Question in the sense of a minority problem. He also felt himself confirmed by the positive course which assimilation was taking and was goaded into the highest degree of battle readiness because he was able to interpret such progress in assimilation solely as a progressive undermining of the body of the *Volk* and as a victory for Judaism in the struggle for power.

In particular, the essence of modern anti-Semitism was its very insatiability: it was clearly impossible to satisfy by any limited regulation of the Jewish Question that it itself had created. Neither a restraining of the so-called Jewish influence or even the total dismantling of emancipation was sufficient. It is significant that the proponents of anti-Semitism did not formulate a clear program of anti-Jewish policy. It is true they often talked about the need to place Jews under the law for aliens or put them in internment, but they left no doubt that such moves could only be a first step. As Lagarde wrote: "You do not negotiate with trichinae and bacillae. Such germs are not cultivated either; they are destroyed as swiftly and thoroughly as possible."[7] Thus from its inception, modern anti-Semitism aimed at expulsion or murder. And murder represented the more logical goal, not just because expulsion simply shifted the problem in spatial terms, thus leading perhaps to an unwelcome increase in Jewish influence in other countries, but because the anti-Semitic worldview was indeed founded upon an absolutist perception: given its proclivities, the mere physical existence of representatives of the rival race, wherever they were, necessarily had to be perceived as threatening and intolerable.

The National Socialists adopted this brand of anti-Semitism and continued its propagation, though without adding any new ideological elements. They gained several additional activating impulses by amalgamating anti-Semitism in a tight bond with a racial theory grounded in the tenets of Social Darwinism, as seen in writings by Hitler and Rosenberg. They viewed Bolshevism as the newest tool, so to speak, of the rival race and centered their entire political program around the hub of an anti-Semitic dogma, the dogma of the conspiracy by international Jewry to

7. Paul de Lagarde, *Juden und Indogermanen: Eine Studie nach dem Leben* (Göttingen, 1887), p. 339. Cf. Hermann Graml, *Reichskristallnacht: Antisemitismus und Judenverfolgung im Dritten Reich* (Munich, 1988), pp. 38ff.; cf. Helmut Krausnick, "Judenverfolgung," in *Anatomie des SS-Staates* (Olten and Freiburg, 1965), vol. 2, pp. 283–448, here 291.

destroy the Aryan race.[8] In other words, without each and every National Socialist being fully aware of the fact, the fundamental inability to arrive at a limited regulation of the Jewish Question had to be an even more solid component of the anti-Semitic doctrine of salvation of the NSDAP than it had been in the programmatic plans and drafts of its predecessors.

After January 30, 1933, when the seizure of state power transformed that doctrine of salvation, previously propagated as unbinding ideology, into a set of guidelines for concrete political action, this fact was abundantly confirmed.[9] In the subsequent eight and a half years until the beginning of the Final Solution, the characteristic feature of National Socialist policy toward the Jews was that all anti-Jewish measures or packages of measures, each presented as the "solution to the Jewish problem" and also viewed even by a segment of the Nazi movement itself in this sense, proved to be mere stages: hardly had they been reached when the contours of more "final" solutions began to emerge in their wake which, when realized, showed themselves in their true nature to be nothing more than immediate short-term objectives.

Even while the first phase of National Socialist persecution of the Jews, marked by a systematic ousting of German Jews from politics, public service, and a number of the free professions, was approaching its conclusion, demands were raised everywhere for the total isolation of German Jews.[10] When Hitler satisfied this demand in September 1935 by decreeing the Nuremberg Laws, he himself ushered in the new round during the very moment of their promulgation. Although at that time Hitler called the Reich Citizenship Law (which brought to completion the deprivation of political rights of the German Jews) and the Law on Protection of Blood (which criminalized all sexual relations between Jews and so-called *Deutschblütige* [those with German blood] as "racial disgrace") the "final regulation of the Jewish Question," he nonetheless added that if this "unique secular solution" should fail, the problem would have to be

8. Cf. ibid., pp. 305ff.
9. Raul Hilberg, *Die Vernichtung der europäischen Juden: Die Gesamtgeschichte des Holocaust* (Berlin, 1982). Cf. Graml, *Reichskristallnacht*, pp. 108ff.
10. See Lothar Gruchmann, "'Blutschutzgesetz' und Justiz: Zu Entstehung und Auswirkung des Nürnberger Gesetzes vom 15. September 1935," *VfZ* 31 (1983): 418–42.

removed from the competence of the government and transferred to that of the Nazi movement for definitive solution.[11]

In actual fact, the following years witnessed a rabid campaign under the slogan "Jews out of the economy!" and already in 1937 and 1938 one can note the presence of comprehensive preparations and practical measures for Jewish expropriation.[12] Yet comments made after the November 1938 Reichskristallnacht pogrom had given the signal to push ahead to the completion of an unbridled policy of expropriation are notable. At the close of a conference on November 12, 1938, at which the new course was charted and a large number of further discriminatory measures against the Jews were approved, the chairman, Hermann Göring, stated, "If the Reich were to become embroiled in an international conflict in the foreseeable future, it goes without saying that we here in Germany would also consider it our first task to engage in a major settling of accounts with the Jews."[13] What intensification of persecution did the number-two man in the regime have in mind at this juncture? Certainly not some sort of migratory movements of the Jews living in the territory under German control. In comparison with the existence to which Jews in Germany and Austria were in any case condemned at that point, such movements would not lead to any worsening of their situation; in fact, emigration might even constitute an improvement. It is true that during those months the regime had declared emigration to be the chief aim of National Socialist Jewish policy and had actually initiated limited expulsion actions.[14] The operative political motive in this connection was possibly to stimulate anti-Semitism in the countries targeted for emigration by exporting destitute Jews there.

However, here too the actual underlying reason probably lies in the circumstance that the urge to engage in activities against the Jewish archenemy simply could not be satisfied and satiated by any measures still framed in the form of mere laws and decrees. It is evident that expulsion in this sense was only perceived to be a stopgap solution, a restraint forced upon the

11. See Max Domarus, *Hitler: Reden und Proklamationen, 1932–1945* (Munich, 1965), vol. 1, p. 537.
12. Cf. the article by Avraham Barkai in this volume, as well as Uwe D. Adam, *Judenpolitik im Dritten Reich*, 2d ed. (Düsseldorf, 1972), pp. 166ff.
13. *IMT*, vol. 18, pp. 538f.
14. Cf. Adam, *Judenpolitik*, pp. 216ff.

regime by foreign policy considerations, namely, the hope that the British and French would condone German expansion to the east. At precisely this time, Hitler persistently rejected emigration projects worked out for all of German Jewry, using specious argumentation to defend his opposition to such draft plans, for example, in a conversation with the South African minister, Pirow, on November 24, 1938.[15] At the Wannsee Conference in January 1942, Heydrich in retrospect unambiguously characterized the policy of expulsion as a course whose "disadvantages . . . given the lack of other options for a solution, initially [would have had to be] taken into the bargain."[16] Thus, Göring's statement of November 12, 1938, can only be understood as an indication that, after their deprivation of rights and expropriation, the extermination of the Jews was conceivable and even desirable as the next and true goal, in an immediate and logical unfolding of the laws of development of National Socialist anti-Semitism. It is significant that only a few weeks after the statement by Göring, Hitler likewise spoke for the first time about the destruction of the Jews. Moreover, this was in a discussion with a foreign politician, namely, the Czech foreign minister Chvalkovsky.[17]

The various stations along the path of National Socialist persecution of the Jews are thus by no means a process of radicalization; rather, they only constitute the process of maturation and revelation of an essentially radical conviction. Yet that conviction first had to pass through all those stages which had the semblance of "radicalization," of course, before it could culminate in a complete release of its potential and achieve its actual and true destiny. Concretely, what this means is that, although neither Hitler nor any other National Socialist would have been capable as early as 1933 of issuing the command for a mass murder of the Jews, such an order, which presupposed the requisite power for its issuance, was ineluctable at a later point in time.

However, in interpretations such as those advanced by Martin Broszat and Hans Mommsen, there is not only a failure to

15. *ADAP*, D 4, pp. 291ff.

16. Hans-Adolf Jacobsen and Werner Jochmann, eds., *Ausgewählte Dokumente zur Geschichte des Nationalsozialismus, 1933–1945* (Bielefeld, 1961), vol. 2, January 20, 1942.

17. *ADAP*, D 4, p. 170.

recognize the essence of National Socialist anti-Semitism, but also an underestimation of its importance as a driving force behind Nazi policy. From their perspective, the enormous abundance of programmatic anti-Semitic statements is downplayed as metaphorics, while virtually every form of anti-Jewish activity is derivable from structural conditions within the National Socialist system. Anti-Semitism itself unintentionally contracts into a weak construct which cannot be accorded any ability to have a shaping and determinative impact on the political course and political action of the Nazi regime. However, precisely in this case, one cannot note any plausible reason why the power of conviction is doubted, almost to the point of its denial.

In his excellent essay, "Weltanschauung und Endlösung," Erich Goldhagen has mustered telling arguments and solid evidence to demonstrate that there cannot be any doubt about either the central role occupied by anti-Semitism in the National Socialist worldview or the dominating influence exercised by anti-Semitism on the thinking and action of the National Socialist top echelons.[18] Only the power of an exceptionally strong conviction was able to give Nazi persecution of the Jews a dynamism that came repeatedly into conflict with foreign-policy, economic, and military interests and often enough either damaged or completely ignored those interests. What degree of dynamism and consistency were involved can be judged from the fact that the monstrous event under scrutiny here took a total of eight and a half years from the revocation of emancipation, to deprivation and pauperization, and on to the beginning of the Final Solution. Of course, anti-Semitism and anti-Jewish activities were also utilized for the purposes of integrating the rather heterogeneous National Socialist movement and of masking or covering up the lack of political constructiveness on the part of the regime. In addition, the ambition and need for recognition of rival functionaries occasionally played a substantial role, as did the greed, both individual and governmental, in connection with the so-called Aryanization of Jewish property. Yet such phenomena should be conceptualized as secondary processes or mere concomitant aspects. They did not give rise to and create Jewish persecution; rather, they were that persecu-

18. Erich Goldhagen, "Weltanschauung und Endlösung: Zum Antisemitismus der nationalsozialistischen Führungsschicht," *VfZ* 24 (1976): 379–405.

tion's products, its creations. If they occasionally exercised a certain power, then that was only because the dynamics of development dictated by the anti-Semitic credo were in any case pushing inexorably toward ever more radical measures.

Hans Mommsen even raises doubts about the anti-Semitism of the leadership personnel who managed the implementation of the Final Solution: "We know that many of the functionaries responsible for the 'Final Solution' had not been indoctrinated primarily in anti-Semitic ideology. . . . Technocratic-subservient attitudes have just as much importance as racial-political blindness or the mere acceptance of National Socialist anti-Jewish clichés."[19] Yet if one examines the biographies of the leadership echelon in the RSHA, the *Einsatzgruppen*, and the extermination camps,[20] it is striking that a clear majority of them, from Stahlecker and Ohlendorf to Globocnik, were indeed dyed-in-the-wool Nazis, an elite of often-tested Nazi activists who obeyed orders given them with a reliability which was not merely functional, but rooted in ideology and politics. Höß, the camp commander of Auschwitz, had formed his Weltanschauung, like Bormann, in the hazy milieu of the Freikorps, Black Reichswehr, and political assassins,[21] and some idea of the brand of virulent murderous anti-Semitism present in such circles can be gathered by perusing, for example, the letters of the assassins of Matthias Erzberger, edited and published by Gotthard Jasper more than twenty years ago in the *Vierteljahrshefte für Zeitgeschichte*.[22] Adolf Eichmann, in turn, organizer of the transports to the death camps, came up through the ranks of the Austrian NSDAP, which was distinguished by an especially vicious anti-Semitism.

Hans Mommsen finds it "virtually inexplicable" that the "leaders and members of the *Einsatzgruppen* . . . let themselves be used" for their murderous craft.[23] However, in actual point of fact, one can note that such a powerful pent-up desire to engage

19. Mommsen, "Die Realisierung des Utopischen," p. 382.
20. Cf. Helmut Krausnick and Hans-Heinrich Wilhelm, *Die Truppen des Weltanschauungskrieges: Die Einsatzgruppen der Sicherheitspolizei und des SD, 1938–1942* (Stuttgart, 1981).
21. Cf. Martin Broszat, comp. and ed., *Kommandant in Auschwitz: Autobiographische Aufzeichnungen von Rudolf Höß* (Stuttgart, 1961).
22. Gotthard Jasper, "Aus den Akten der Prozesse gegen die Erzberger-Mörder," *VfZ* 10 (1962): 430–53.
23. Mommsen, "Die Realisierung des Utopischen," p. 410.

in anti-Jewish activity had accumulated among the ranks of those leadership cadres between the Kristallnacht and the outbreak of war that feverishly, impatiently, these cadres awaited instructions to take corresponding action. Thus, in the weeks and months after the attack on Poland, although there had only been an order given to liquidate the Polish leadership, there were numerous shootings of individual Jews and several larger-scale massacres. The statements made by commanders of SS and police units to army officers likewise speak a clear and unmistakable language.[24] If the discernable will to destruction was still laboriously being held in check, this presumably was due (1) to Hitler's hope, kept alive until the summer of 1940, of obtaining British recognition of German hegemony on the Continent, and (2) to the disquiet which Heydrich's activities had provoked in the army.[25]

How intense the tendency to move toward mass murder had become in the meantime is also indicated by the Madagascar Plan, conceived by the Foreign Office in the summer of 1940 and worked out in detail by the RSHA, a plan generally regarded as the final expression of the policy of forced emigration. In reality, the plan should be interpreted as a manifestation of the will to destruction, although that will at the time still wished to forego guns and gas and make do with the forces of nature. At the base of the plan was obviously the expectation that the European Jews – and it should be noted that this is the first conceptual extension of Nazi persecution of the Jews to include the entire Continent – would necessarily perish in misery if herded together, without reasonable options for employment, on one of the most unhealthy islands on the planet.[26]

Second, the explanatory models of Martin Broszat and Hans Mommsen are based, although unarticulated and possibly unconsciously, on the following central assumption: the leaders of the Nazi regime had initially considered a program of deportation, clearly distinguishable from the later genocide, to be compatible with the political and military aims of Operation

24. Cf. Krausnick and Wilhelm, *Die Truppen*, pp. 63ff., e.g., p. 83.
25. Cf. Helmut Krausnick, "Hitler und die Morde in Polen: Ein Beitrag zum Konflikt zwischen Heer und SS um die Verwaltung der besetzten Gebiete," *VfZ* 11 (1963): 196–209; Krausnick and Wilhelm, *Die Truppen*, pp. 80ff.
26. Also noted by Mommsen, "Die Realisierung des Utopischen," pp. 395, 407f.

Barbarossa. Yet even a mere deportation program is, simultaneously, a settlement program, no matter what form it assumes. But the war against Russia was conceived as a war of conquest and exploitation in the service of a biological imperialism, if one leaves aside for the moment (1) its political and military motives in the wake of Germany's defeat in the air battle for Britain and the consequent decision not to launch an invasion, and (2) the anti-Bolshevik component of the war.[27] Whoever in Germany was involved with the planning of this operation, whether in the military leadership, the associated economic staffs, the recently established Ministry for Eastern Affairs, or the RSHA, knew very well there was not only a plan to get rid of the functionaries of the Stalinist system during the process of occupying, securing, and further exploiting Soviet territory and resources, but also to decimate the population, reducing it by about forty million.[28]

And despite this decimation plan, are we to believe that Hitler and the other planners were specifically thinking of settling several million representatives of the Jewish archenemy in the areas to be conquered? This does not appear very probable. In addition, Berlin expected that military victory over the Red Army would not necessarily bring an end to all combat action. The leadership was quite prepared to have to wage a running battle for many years along an insecure border with Asiatic Russia. Are we to assume that despite all that, there was a serious plan for permanent settlement of millions of the most dangerous enemies of the Aryan race and the Third Reich behind this frontier, to relocate them in vast areas of the Soviet Union which in any case were difficult to secure even without such settlement? That is still less probable, whether one considers Hitler himself or the highly security-conscious heads of the Gestapo, the SD, and the Regular Police.

Numerous indications and simple logic force one to conclude that Himmler and Heydrich, when they now invited various government departments to be involved in a European total

27. See Jürgen Förster, "Das Unternehmen 'Barbarossa' als Eroberungs- und Vernichtungskrieg," in *Das Deutsche Reich und der Zweite Weltkrieg*, vol. 4, *Der Angriff auf die Sowjetunion*, ed. by Militärgeschichtliches Forschungsamt (Stuttgart, 1983), pp. 413–50.
28. See also Robert Gibbons, "Allgemeine Richtlinien für die politische und wirtschaftliche Verwaltung der besetzten Ostgebiete," *VfZ* 25 (1977): 252–61.

solution of the Jewish Question for the first time in the autumn of 1941 through attendance at an upcoming coordination conference, were already quite clear in their own minds – and had been for some time – about what the order and plan for the task had to be.[29] Precisely at this juncture in time, the head of the Generalgouvernement in Poland, Hans Frank, who was generally well informed about such matters, mentioned in a discussion the coming Jewish migration movement and also referred to the planned coordination conference, postponed in the meantime to January 20, 1942; he then revealed the basic objectives associated with that conference. Frank asked the question, "What should be done with the Jews?" He proceeded to provide his own answer with the rhetoric remark, "Do you think they will be housed in the East in settlement villages?" Later on, shuddering and with certain doubts about whether such a gigantic enterprise could indeed succeed, he spoke about "interventions" which would "somehow or other lead to a successful annihilation."[30]

Apparently no plans for settlement were discussed at the Wannsee Conference. Rather, what is striking in the protocol written by Eichmann is that, insofar as Heydrich's plan for the Final Solution is detailed, there is no mention whatsoever of Jews unable to work or of children.[31] Their murder was evidently an obvious component or point of departure of the plan. The concept of annihilation through labor (*Vernichtung durch Arbeit*), if taken seriously in the form in which it appears in the protocol of the conference, was limited, expressly and logically, to able-bodied Jews. The remarks by State Secretary Bühler[32] and the testimony presented many years later in Jerusalem by Eichmann[33] indicate that the other conference participants likewise viewed the murder of Jews unable to work as agreed and decided upon. In other words, there is no basic divergence between practice in camps such as Auschwitz-Birkenau or Majdanek and the sketch of draft plans which become visible in the protocol of the deliberation at Wannsee. The major ideas of this

29. Cf. Krausnick, "Judenverfolgung," pp. 360ff., 391ff.

30. Werner Präg and Wolfgang Jacobmeyer, eds., *Das Diensttagebuch des deutschen Generalgouverneurs in Polen, 1939–1945* (Stuttgart, 1975), pp. 457f.

31. Jacobsen and Jochmann, *Ausgewählte Dokumente*, January 20, 1942.

32. Ibid.

33. Eichmann trial, 106th session, July 21, 1961, prot. p. 11.

sketch must, to underscore the matter once again, have long since been fixed and definite.

The third assumption in the arguments of Martin Broszat and Hans Mommsen is their assertion that the activity of the so-called *Einsatzgruppen*, which commenced with the beginning of the attack on Russia, should not be viewed as the first phase of the Final Solution, even though that activity included the mass murder of Jews in the occupied Soviet territories. Broszat and Mommsen contend that the massacres of Jews perpetrated by the *Einsatzgruppen*, like the practice of liquidation aimed at Soviet functionaries, should still be understood as a part of the conduct of the war effort, since the National Socialists had, after all, equated Bolshevism and Jewry.[34] For that reason, they argue, the justifications given in the reports by the *Einsatzgruppen* for the shooting of Jews were absolutely necessary: the supposed hostile Jewish attitude toward the Germans, their sabotage activities, and their support for the partisans. If a planned action could not be justified by such reasoning, at least as a form of retaliation, then it was not carried out.[35] They contend that merely "racist" argumentation was carefully avoided.[36] Moreover, it was significant that the activities of the *Einsatzgruppen* had been based on the so-called commissar order (*Kommissarbefehl*), that is, on a command relating to combat and conduct of the war.[37]

The *Einsatzgruppen* had been given the oral order to shoot all Jews – men, women, and children – without distinction.[38] Before the start of a campaign it is difficult to derive the totality of such an order for annihilation from a plan for military combat, even one completely out of control, no matter how broadly its interests and conditions are interpreted. When this command was issued in the spring of 1941, there were as yet no partisans on the scene nor was there any necessity for reprisal actions. Rather, experiences with Polish Jews gathered up until that time did not indicate in any way that possible resistance by the Jews was likely. This fact reveals at the very least that the detailed

34. Broszat, "Hitler und die Genesis," p. 747; Mommsen, "Die Realisierung des Utopischen," pp. 409f.
35. Mommsen, "Die Realisierung des Utopischen," p. 397.
36. Ibid., p. 410.
37. Ibid., p. 409.
38. See Krausnick and Wilhelm, *Die Truppen*, pp. 150ff.

reasons given in the reports of the *Einsatzgruppen* were nothing but a pure and simple *Sprachregelung*, phraseology dictated from above.[39] In any case, for months these justifications remained so stereotypical that they lack any credibility whatsoever. In addition, it should be pointed out that Einsatzgruppe B, precisely during the early weeks of the campaign, before its leader was apparently warned to stick to the prescribed phraseology, engaged in wholesale shootings of Jews without actually citing any justification in the reports[40] and that during the further course of the war, starting roughly at the end of 1941 and the beginning of 1942, purely "racial" reasons do indeed make their appearance in official reports.[41]

Finally, as far as the commissar order is concerned, it should be kept in mind that it was not an order to the *Einsatzgruppen* as such, but rather an order to the army. The army was instructed that it had to shoot certain categories of political commissars. In addition, it was informed that special units of the Reichsführer SS and chief of German police, known as *Einsatzgruppen*, had "special tasks" to carry out in the eastern territories and were to do so on their own authority. Certainly this passage was also a part of the authorization that had been given to Himmler's units, but only in respect to their relation to the military commanders, to establish their independence from the military.[42] Himmler received a similar authorization in respect to the Reich and general commissars under the control of the Ministry for Eastern Affairs.[43] However, the commissar order does not specify in any way on the basis of what orders these *Einsatzgruppen* were operating or even what the content of their orders would be.

Moreover, the view the actors had of their own role should not be ignored in considering this question. On August 6, 1941, Stahlecker, head of Einsatzgruppe A, commented on provisional guidelines for dealing with the Jewish problem, which had been formulated in the Reichskommissariat Ostland.[44] In his critique of the guidelines, Stahlecker accused the Reich

39. Cf. ibid., pp. 158ff.
40. Cf. ibid., pp. 165ff.
41. Ibid.
42. Ibid., pp. 116ff.; Helmut Krausnick, "Kommissarbefehl und 'Gerichtsbarkeitserlaß Barbarossa' in neuer Sicht," *VfZ* 25 (1977): 682–738.
43. Krausnick, "Judenverfolgung," p. 369.
44. This previously unevaluated document was discovered by Gerald Fleming, author of *Hitler und die Endlösung* (Wiesbaden and Munich, 1982), in the

commissar of planning a provisional "regulating of the Jewish Question" in keeping with the situation that had arisen in the Generalgouvernement. This, he contended, was incorrect for the simple reason that trouble spots could be expected in the unsecured eastern areas for a long time to come and that Jews would undoubtedly play a role as troublemakers there. Yet the conception of the Reich commissar should, he argued, likewise be rejected, since that conception "leaves aside the matter of contemplating the radical treatment of the Jewish Question, now possible for the first time in the eastern areas." The Security Police had received "basic orders" in this regard from higher echelons; such orders could not be "discussed in writing," but rather could only be communicated orally. Stahlecker simultaneously linked those basic orders quite naturally with the "total cleansing of the European area of all Jews"; he evidently assumed that such a cleansing operation would be "definite and be ready to put into practice" within the near future.

It has always been far from plausible that the National Socialist leadership wished to eradicate the Jews of the Soviet Union, but wanted to let all other Jews in areas under German control continue to live and even use them to resettle the eastern areas just emptied by mass murder. However, Stahlecker's remarks render any reference to the internal improbability and psychological impossibility of a partial order for extermination superfluous. They are convincing proof that the leadership personnel of the Security Police, on the basis of an oral explanation of the given order, already were certain at the beginning of the Russian campaign that they were making a contribution to a new "solution to the Jewish Question" with the mass murder of Soviet Jews, quite aside from and independent of the concrete security interests of the German Reich. For this inner circle of the initiated, it was equally clear that their contribution was regarded as only the first act within a sequence encompassing a total solution on a European scale that was in principle the same in scope and character. This total solution was already in the planning stage. However, if Heydrich instructed the heads of his *Einsatzgruppen* along such lines, it was only possible for him to do so with the knowledge of and through virtue of a

Riga State Archives and placed at the disposal of Helmut Krausnick, who called it to my attention. I would like to express my sincere gratitude to him for this reference.

basic decision made by the Führer. That decision must have been a short time earlier. Such a conclusion, compelling in its cogency, is precisely in keeping with the statements made by Höß and Eichmann after the war.

It is not possible to raise convincing doubts about the thesis that Hitler – sometime in the spring of 1941, before Heydrich's notice of May and June to Stahlecker, Ohlendorf, and Blume – must have given the order for the preparation of the genocide by advancing the argument that Hans Mommsen does, that there was never any "official or private" discussion of the destruction of the Jews in Führer headquarters.[45] That argument can be easily refuted by several entries in Goebbels's diaries.[46] If Hitler in his "table conversations" spoke only in vague terms about the Final Solution and did not bring up the matter at all in conversations with many high-ranking visitors, there is a simple and plausible explanation, namely, that in the meantime the police, which by then had been absorbed into the SS, was solely responsible for dealing with the Jews. Yet it can be demonstrated on the basis of analogous notes by Himmler that Hitler did speak to him about the Final Solution and several of its component actions on November 30, 1941, October 7, 1942, and June 19, 1943.[47]

Even less valid is the argument that basically Himmler never made reference to a "Führer order" on the extermination.[48] There are at least five speeches in which Himmler stated in unmistakable terms before *Gauleiter*, generals, and others that he was acting under orders in carrying out the annihilation of the Jews.[49] If for whatever reasons one refuses to accept the

45. Mommsen, "Die Realisierung des Utopischen," p. 391.

46. L.P. Lochner, ed., *Goebbels-Tagebücher* (Zurich, 1948), for example, the entry for March 27, 1942. After a visit by Hitler in Berlin, Goebbels noted on February 14, 1942 (ibid., pp. 87f.): "The Führer once more expresses his opinion that he is ruthlessly determined to do away with the Jews in Europe. One can have no sentimental feelings when it comes to this. . . . They will experience their own destruction together with that of our enemies. We must accelerate this process with cold ruthlessness." There is no evident reason why this language should be called "metaphoric."

47. Cf. Fleming, *Hitler und die Endlösung*, pp. 33, 71, 88.

48. Mommsen, "Die Realisierung des Utopischen," e.g., p. 394.

49. For example, in mid-August 1941 in Minsk before Einsatzkommando 8; on January 26, 1944, in Posen to a group of generals; on May 5, 1944, in Sonthofen; as well as on May 24 and June 21, 1944; cf. Fleming, *Hitler und die Endlösung*, pp. 62ff.

confirming testimony of Höß and Eichmann,[50] there remain the statements by Bruno Streckenbach, departmental head of the RSHA, who was responsible for the selection of *Einsatzgruppen* personnel, and the testimony of Gottlob Berger, head of the SS Main Office: both testified that Himmler had referred in their presence to an order given by Hitler.[51] Moreover, Himmler had already stated on July 28, 1942, in a communication to the Ministry for Eastern Affairs, that "*the Führer* has placed upon my shoulders the implementation of this very difficult order."[52]

There is likewise no solid support in the realities of that time or in the available sources which might justify labeling Hitler's own use of terms such as "annihilation," "extermination," and "removal" as metaphorical usage divorced from reality[53] or as a calculated threat addressed to the Western powers, that is, as the expression of an intention to utilize the Jews as hostages.[54] The first interpretation is nothing other than an arbitrary interpretative act, a pronouncement by a historian *post festum*; and the matter of hostages only appears in internal deliberations and in a somewhat shadowy form in Hitler's speech of January 30, 1939. Otherwise it cannot be demonstrated to be an element that played any role in the foreign policy behavior of the Nazi regime. As proof in support of the hostage theory, Hans Mommsen cites the already quoted threat by Göring in case of war enunciated in the meeting on November 12, 1938. However, it is really hard to comprehend how a remark made casually at the end of an internal discussion could possibly have been aimed at Western politicians and intended for their consumption.

We would probably also argue about the order given in the autumn of 1939 for the liquidation of the Polish intelligentsia in the same way that we dispute the question of the order for the preparation and start of the Final Solution, if there were not a minute difference. The public and semipublic statements by Hitler on policy toward Poland could certainly be interpreted along the lines of the explanatory models put forward by Broszat

50. Broszat, *Kommandant in Auschwitz*, pp. 120ff., 153ff., 176; District Court, Jerusalem, Criminal Case No. 40/61, opinion 76. See also Bernd Nellessen, *Der Prozeß von Jerusalem* (Düsseldorf, 1964), pp. 237f., 246.
51. Cf. Fleming, *Hitler und die Endlösung*, pp. 63f.
52. Archives, IfZ, Nuremberg Doc. No. 626, emphasis in original.
53. Mommsen, "Die Realisierung des Utopischen," pp. 386, n. 16, 395.
54. Ibid., pp. 390, 395f.

and Mommsen, especially since, at that time, numerous officers, officials, and Nazi functionaries neither believed (nor were able to believe) in the existence of a corresponding Führer order and considered the activities of *Einsatzgruppen* then operating to be excesses committed by individual SS and police leaders.[55] Heydrich's and Himmler's reference to Hitler in 1939–40 was even a bit less definite than that of 1941, when Himmler assured the generals, "I don't do anything the Führer doesn't know."[56] Nor need it be regarded as compelling evidence for the existence of a Führer order that the opposition, which arose in the army and led to court-martial proceedings against members of the SS and police, tempted Hitler to break down some of his reserve: he quashed several of the proceedings, then issued an amnesty for violent acts, and finally removed Himmler's special units completely from the jurisdiction of the army.[57]

However, we know in this case that the order for liquidation actually stemmed from Hitler personally. Yet this is only thanks to the coincidence that witnesses above suspicion – the head of the Wehrmacht Supreme Command, General Keitel, and Colonels Warlimont and Gause – made an immediate written record of events at the meeting on October 17, 1939, and that their notes have survived.[58] They in addition are confirmed by a note of Martin Bormann written on October 2, 1941. The organizational measures taken by Hitler in 1939–40 are, moreover, a classic example of a key fact, namely, that frequently it was not structural changes which produced radicalization, but rather precisely the other way round: the implementation of radical policy made it necessary to tamper with and alter structure.

55. Krausnick and Wilhelm, *Die Truppen*, pp. 42–106.
56. Klaus-Jürgen Müller, "Zu Vorgeschichte und Inhalt der Rede Himmlers vor der höheren Generalität am 13. März 1940 in Koblenz," *VfZ* 18 (1970): 95–120.
57. Krausnick and Wilhelm, *Die Truppen*, pp. 80ff.
58. Ibid., pp. 85f.

What Did the Germans Know about the Genocide of the Jews?

Hans Mommsen

The attitude and behavior of Germans toward the implementation of the genocide against the Jews during World War II and what knowledge they were able to obtain of the scope of the crime remain pressing questions for historical research and political education. The lack of a public sphere which could articulate the streams of differing opinion in the population, and indeed facilitate the genesis of such opinion, makes it difficult in this case to talk about the Germans as a social collective. At no time in its history were the German people so fragmented and segmented as under the conditions of the National Socialist "folk community." Particularly in World War II, the individual *Volksgenosse* was ground down under the burdens of military service and labor for the war effort, and millions, not only combatants, found themselves separated from their loved ones and torn from their former social web and milieu; the upshot was that private and social communication was largely disrupted or massively reduced. The sphere of experience of the individual under these circumstances differed greatly from person to person; accordingly, the perception of the regime and its policies also ran a broad gamut. To that extent then, any statement about "*the* Germans" is only possible in a limited sense: conclusions about average behavior can be drawn, but one cannot proceed from any matching and mutually corroborative experiences by individual contemporaries.

This limiting proviso is necessary in approaching the question of what the German populace knew about the genocide perpetrated against the Jews, and how it *reacted* to this knowledge. Since the liquidation of European Jewry was carried out in strictest secrecy, information about this always had the character of something extraordinary – both in the sense of the special inside controlling knowledge of those directly involved in implementing the Final Solution as well as in the sense of a dangerous truth whose discovery would necessarily result in exposing the immorality of the regime. For the outsider, there arose the unavoidable distinction between mere rumor, knowledge based on hints and intimations, and reliable information. In view of the fact that the annihilation of the Jews was carried out without a formal order and in a gray area of governmental action, reliable knowledge existed solely in regard to partial aspects of the events, in the form of reports by eyewitnesses on massacres or shootings, circumstantial evidence of criminal plans and actions, or cluelike traces left by mass graves, facilities for murder, and the personal possessions taken from the victims before their extermination – clothing, shoes, eyeglasses, and various valuables, ultimately even gold fillings from their teeth.

Individual observations of liquidations and their accompanying circumstances were indeed possible, occurred in large number, and were vividly reported on throughout the Reich by men on leave from the front and by other visitors. Yet these did not automatically coalesce into a total picture which would necessarily have had to mobilize moral disgust and political protest. For that reason, one does not get very far by trying to reconstruct systematically the scope and abundance of publicly available partial information, since that availability says nothing about the readiness of the individual to view specific details as an indicator of the whole picture and to relate that picture to the ideological pronouncements of the regime and the experience of its concrete praxis. Quite apart from the special conditions engendered by a war for the continued survival of the nation, the mentality of the average German was hardly shaped by the need to follow up in cognitive form the clues of the crime which pressed in upon his awareness, since its amoral dimension would have had to be psychologically intolerable.

Presumably, the "normal" reaction to horrendous events – and that was the profound truth of the genocide – consists, under totally different circumstances, of repression, incredulity, and the projection of guilt feelings and images of the enemy. Right from the start the Nazi regime accommodated to this psychological makeup of the normal individual and itself unconsciously practiced the already available mechanism for repression; in terms of its own interests, the regime was extremely successful with this basically primitive approach. No explicitly developed psychological strategy was necessary for this; rather, all that was needed was the conversion of private modes of reacting into public action.[1] National Socialist policy is characterized by the simultaneous implementation and denial of the crime, which was excluded as an "act of self-defense" from the otherwise unscathed world of bourgeois morality. The phenomenon of genocide, in particular, is marked by that dualism: justified propagandistically in rhetorical-philosophical paraphrase, it was denied as political reality and thus as a responsibly committed act, with very few exceptions.

These general remarks are necessary before delving into the question of the circumstances under which the German populace, or segments of it, perceived the crime against the Jews, to what extent that perception had more than an accidental character and was potentially able to condense into knowledge of the true events, and what defensive mechanisms were operative in order to repress this horrible and morally intolerable reality. However, before probing that complex of questions, it is first necessary to characterize the relationship of the German population to the Jewish Question at the outbreak of the war. While the "Reichskristallnacht" had met largely with public disapproval – not because of its anti-Semitic orientation, but rather due to its violation of bourgeois law and order – the subsequent steps to exclude the Jews from economic life and to socially isolate them totally took place without any noteworthy resistance or protest.

The migration of the Jewish segment of the population into the anonymity of the metropolitan areas and the increased emigration of Jews reduced social relations between the Jews and the non-Jewish population to a minimum. Even in the large cities, the Jewish minority retreated entirely into the background. The introduction of the Jewish star on September 1, 1941, once again impressed on the consciousness of the populace the fact, underscored by Goebbels's sarcastic propaganda, that significant numbers of Jews were still living in their midst. The extensive legal restrictions on Jewish freedom of movement preceding the imposition of the yellow badge, including the introduction of extremely limited hours for shopping and limitations on their right to leave their apartments and homes, forced

1. Note the observation of J. Peter Stern that Hitler's public success was due in significant measure to the fact that he made the private realm a public matter, *Hitler: Der Führer und sein Volk* (Munich, 1978), pp. 22f.

the increasingly aged remaining Jewish population, of which only a small number found any gainful employment, to reduce their contacts with "Aryans" to a minimum.[2]

With the beginning of the war, many of those considerations vanished which had previously prevented the government from implementing the total removal of Jews from the areas under German hegemony and from including among those subject to the measures of persecution spouses in so-called racially mixed marriages and half Jews. A large number of the classic departments in the government bureaucracy, as well as the Reich Chancellery, were interested in putting a brake on any step-up in anti-Jewish measures and in meanwhile making possible some form of survival for the Jewish population remaining in the territory of the Reich. Yet it was precisely the resistance to Himmler's and Heydrich's intentions (in viewing the Jewish Question more and more as their very own and elemental bailiwick and field of activity) to place all Jewish affairs under the authority of the RSHA that served to escalate the legal measures increasingly circumscribing the Jewish sphere of life. Those measures were often consciously humiliating, extending to a prohibition on the keeping of pet animals, to the frequenting of weekly outdoor markets, and even to using the telephone.[3]

Thus, the torrent of anti-Jewish regulations continued in intensified form after the outbreak of the war, long before Hermann Göring, chairman of the Reich Defense Council, on July 31, 1941, formally ordered the chief of the Security Police and the SD of the SS in the Interior Ministry and head of the RSHA, Reinhard Heydrich, to begin preparations for the Final Solution of the Jewish Question. The corresponding authorization did not come from Hitler, but had been drafted by Adolf Eichmann at Heydrich's request.[4] Heydrich in particular, who in this was backed by Bormann, was pushing for Jews in general to be placed under special legislation; for revocation of the

2. See the survey of the Jewish population's rapidly deteriorating situation with the beginning of the war in Paul Sauer, *Die Schicksale der jüdischen Bürger Baden-Württembergs während der nationalsozialistischen Verfolgungszeit, 1933–1945* (Stuttgart, 1969), pp. 105ff.

3. Systematic presentation in Bruno Blau, *Das Ausnahmerecht gegen die Juden in den europäischen Ländern*, Pt. 1, *Deutschland* (Düsseldorf, ³1965). See also the article by J. Moser in this volume.

4. Raul Hilberg, *Die Vernichtung der europäischen Juden: Die Gesamtgeschichte des Holocaust* (Berlin, 1982), p. 283.

citizenship of German Jews, confiscation of their property, and divestiture of their protection under labor laws; for obligating able-bodied Jews to perform forced labor and interning them in special camps, isolated from the population. State encroachment on Jewish property and assets grew ever more intense. Even before the institution of a formal legal regulation, the Gestapo began to expropriate Jews who had been placed in concentration camps. Largely excluded from normal opportunities for employment, the Jewish segment of the populace in Germany was subject to a rapid process of pauperization that further augmented its distance from the majoritarian society.

At the same time, the *Gauleiter* were dreaming up means and ways to render their respective districts *judenfrei* by the forcible deportation of Jewish inhabitants. As early as the beginning of 1940, Jews were deported from Vienna, Prague, and Stettin into the Generalgouvernement; in October of that year, 6,500 Jews were deported from the Saar Palatinate and Baden to occupied France. Joseph Goebbels in particular, as *Gauleiter* of Greater Berlin, pressed for the deportation of Berlin Jews to the Generalgouvernement. Since the start of the war and especially after the occupation of Poland, Jewish emigration, which Adolf Eichmann, as director of the Central Emigration Office in the RSHA, was promoting through all possible means, along the lines of the Viennese and Prague examples, had practically come to a virtual halt. In place of emigration, plans for creating "reserve areas" were hatched; such reserves, it was thought, could be realized after the war. Independent of this, from mid-1941, there was a set objective to relocate Jews, at least temporarily, to the ghettos set up in the Generalgouvernement or to occupied Soviet territory. In the late autumn of 1941, the RSHA finally prohibited transporting of Jews to countries outside the German sphere of control.

In the early summer of 1940, when the regime was still expecting Britain to yield to demands, Heydrich and Eichmann seized on the suggestions of Third Secretary Fritz Rademacher in the Foreign Office: he had proposed that German Jews should be "deported and resettled" on the island of Madagascar, which was a British possession. This chimera derived from anti-Semitic tradition, whose realization would likewise have spelled the destruction of forcibly deported Jews due to the climatic conditions there, did not, in any event, initially represent some sort of cynical camouflaging of the later practice of liquidation.[5] As late as May 1940, even Himmler regarded a violent extermination of the Jewish population as being incompatible with the National Socialist idea.[6] The Russian campaign removed these inhibitions, although the transition to planned mass annihilation only took place at the beginning of 1942.

Goebbels initially reacted to what appeared to be a hopeless situation in respect to the Jewish Question by a massive increase in anti-Semitic propaganda; such propaganda brought numerous variations on Hitler's claim that the war was an unavoidable defensive struggle against world Jewry, whose goal was the extermination of the German people. While anti-Semitic films had been considered undesirable before the war, movies such as the notorious *Jud Süß* were now produced that once again served to heighten hatred of Jews in the population and were designed to create the psychological foundations for a harsher approach to those Jews remaining. The intensification of anti-Jewish propaganda coincided with the preparations for the campaign against the Soviet Union; right from the start Hitler had planned that campaign as a racial war of annihilation. The ideological equation of Bolshevism and Judaism played a decisive role in this conception. Virtually without exception, the top echelon of generals, who were largely anti-Semitic in orientation, accepted Hitler's concept of the radical war between differing worldviews.[7]

The events of the war dominated the preoccupations of the populace; the result was that the people paid virtually no attention to the Jewish Question, with which they were generally no longer directly confronted. It is difficult to estimate to what extent the population accepted the propaganda that Jews were those who were really behind the war, directing its course, and that for that reason they should be combated "ruthlessly and without mercy." The ideological equation of Bolshevism and Judaism/Jewry was linked with the propagandistic cliché of the

5. Christopher Browning, *The Final Solution and the German Foreign Office* (New York, 1978), pp. 35ff.
6. See his memorandum, "Denkschrift zur Behandlung der Fremdvölkischen im Osten," May 1940, ed. Helmut Krausnick, *VfZ* 5 (1957): 194ff.
7. Cf. Christian Streit, *Keine Kameraden: Die Wehrmacht und die sowjetischen Kriegsgefangenen, 1941–1945* (Stuttgart, 1978). Similarly, Helmut Krausnick, "Kommissarbefehl und 'Gerichtsbarkeitserlaß Barbarossa' in neuer Sicht," *VfZ* 25 (1977): 682–738.

"depraved" Eastern European Jew; that clichéd image was constantly presented by Goebbels's propaganda in films and the press after the Poland campaign. This indoctrination had a lasting impact on Polish and Russian Jewry. The heightened measures against Jews in the incorporated eastern area and in the Generalgouvernement were therefore, to the extent that news reports about them leaked through, generally condoned without protest. Many of these measures were reflected in official legislation.[8]

The question of the attitude of the German population toward German Jews requires a differentiated answer. The propagandistic equating of Jews, Judaism, and Bolshevism lost plausibility in view of the fact that the Jews remaining in Germany belonged largely to the upper middle class. Certainly there existed a layer of anti-Semitic fanatics, but the greater majority of the populace tended to react with indifference. Moreover, there were considerable regional differences when it came to attitudes toward Jews. In the areas where anti-Semitism was traditionally indigenous, there were hardly any signs of opposition to the ever-intensifying persecution; in Berlin, by contrast, there was widespread criticism, though that was only rarely transformed into concrete assistance for Jews, especially since "Aryan" partners had to reckon with the possibility that in the event the Gestapo intervened, they would themselves be interned in a concentration camp, at least temporarily. It should be recalled that approximately 25 percent of the more than five thousand persecuted Jews who went underground survived thanks to the support of "Aryan" citizens; that assistance was bound up with enormous risks for those who provided it.[9]

The great mass of the German populace in any event no longer had contact with Jews. As National Socialist propagandists noted with alarm, many younger people no longer had any notion of the "Jewish opponent" against whom one was exorted to struggle. Anti-Semitism without Jews, that is, without any social contact with Jewish groups, was not a new phenomenon in Germany. Given the circumstances in the Third Reich, such a

8. See Decree on the Application of the Penal Code in Dealing with Poles and Jews in the Incorporated Territories, December 4, 1941, RGBl 1941, I, p. 759.

9. See Leonhard Gross, *The Last Jews in Berlin* (New York, 1982); Kurt R. Grossmann, *Die unbesungenen Helden: Menschen in Deutschlands dunklen Tagen* (Berlin, [2]1961).

state of affairs held true for the preponderant majority of *Volks-genossen* who sympathized with the anti-Semitic view or were radically anti-Semitic in orientation themselves. In many instances, Jews with whom one was personally acquainted were excluded from such sweeping anti-Semitic statements. It took quite some effort to get Bavarian farmers to desist from continuing to cultivate their business connections with Jewish cattle dealers. Similarly, the NSDAP had only slow success in convincing party members to adhere to the prohibition not to buy at Jewish-owned stores. Anti-Semitism was generally not widespread among the lower middle classes and the industrial working class, only among the commercial middle class that feared Jewish competition.[10] On the other hand, the condoning of anti-Semitic currents within German society for generations had an important effect: clichés about the danger of being economically "inundated" by "alien elements" (*Überfremdungs-gefahr*) and the Jewish greed for material enrichment were accepted without any critique.

The mass prevalence of anti-Semitism is not the key to the escalation of persecution measures against the Jews. Fellow travelers and opportunists were little concerned about the fate of their Jewish fellow citizens; anti-Semitism resulting from conformity and accommodation was indeed one of the worst phenomena at the time.[11] Of decisive importance, rather, was a mechanism that emerged immediately after the January 30, 1933, takeover of power: the conservative elites within the state bureaucracy began to deflect the pent-up social energies of the National Socialist movement to the field of the Jewish Question. That issue became, as it were, the outlet through which the stepwise erosion and undermining of the constitutional state and the legality of the bureaucracy took place, with heightening intensity, until the process finally swung back to engulf the entire system. The functional elites, largely anti-Semitic in orientation, though willing to go only as far as the "dissimilation" of

10. See Sarah Gordon, *Hitler, the Germans, and the "Jewish Question"* (Princeton, 1984), pp. 152ff., 166ff.; Ian Kershaw, "The Persecution of Jews and German Popular Opinion in the Third Reich," *YLBI* 26 (1981): esp. 286ff.

11. Michael Müller-Claudius, *Der Antisemitismus und das deutsche Verhängnis*, 1st ed. (Frankfurt, 1948), pp. 169ff., estimates the percentage of militant anti-Semites in the population, independent of their affiliation with the NSDAP, was 5 percent and postulates that 69 percent were indifferent; this is based on an informal internal survey.

non-assimilated Jewish groups, later thus became the prisoners of the process of radicalization. This explains why, although many of those among the great majority in leadership positions were without a primary identification with the NSDAP and in any case were not in agreement with the hard line pursued by the party in the Jewish issue, they were no longer able to find any possibility of disentangling themselves from involvement in the policy of the Final Solution.

Down to the end of 1940, numerous top functionaries and officials, as long as they were not part of the extreme wing of the NSDAP, were prepared to assist individual Jewish acquaintances. It was understandable that this was limited to assimilated Jews. The fate of the Jewish communities was concealed from the average citizen. As long as one had no personal contact or family relations with Jews, that person likewise made no effort to try even to take mental note of the unrelenting chain of anti-Jewish decrees, although the discriminatory character and cynical inhumanity of such decrees made it clear that one could expect the worst for the future. Those social groups and political outsiders who were oppositional in their thinking or who attempted to put up resistance as a rule generally had to avoid heightening the risk of interference by the Gestapo as a result of their lending assistance to Jews. For that reason, little resistance from them could be expected against the mounting intensification of anti-Jewish measures. Although Jews played a central role in the beginning stages of Socialist resistance, as in the case of the group Neubeginnen, stepped-up surveillance by the Gestapo constituted an obstacle to establishing contact with Jewish groups.[12]

As far as the society as a whole was concerned, the constant anti-Semitic indoctrination had to function to bring about a disastrous exacerbation of already-existing anti-Jewish prejudices. Of far greater significance was the fact that the function assigned to anti-Semitism, namely, to deflect attention from the inadequacies of the political and economic system by a propagandistic *Feindbild*, found a positive echo among certain segments of the population. This is reflected in the system of informers often used against Jewish citizens; such informing

---

12. See Konrad Kwiet and Helmut Eschwege, *Selbstbehauptung und Widerstand: Deutsche Juden im Kampf um Existenz und Menschenwürde, 1933–1945* (Hamburg, 1986), esp. pp. 61ff.

ultimately took on massive proportions, so that Göring issued an order to curb the phenomenon because the Gestapo was being stretched too far. The unanticipated extent of informing was bound up with the general sense of dissatisfaction as the war continued, the creeping dissolution of the social web of relations, as well as spreading corruption. Through the act of informing to the authorities, criticism, grumbling, and the need to gain social status were directed against those who could least defend themselves against such charges. Thus, unjustified complaints lodged against Jews were not primarily a sign of intensified anti-Semitic bias.[13]

Despite these events, the Jewish issue receded far into the background in public consciousness after the beginning of the war. The existence of Jews within the population once again attracted a certain interest only after Heydrich's order in September 1941 obligating Jews to wear a distinguishing badge on their clothing. Despite statements to the contrary in the situation reports of the SD, this obligation to wear a badge appears to have met with widespread disapproval among the German population; that was also true of the later regulation stipulating that Jews had to mark their homes with an identifying sign. There were various cases in which the authorities chose not to act against infringements of the regulations, although the severest penalties could be exacted, including immediate internment in a concentration camp.

As a result of the introduction of the Jewish star, the churches once again also found themselves faced with the problem of whether to give in to the regime's demand to exclude Jews who were Christians from religious services and from the congregation.[14] During that same period, rumors spread about massacres in Poland. Those who had heard about this generally considered such massacres to be the excesses of individual commanders and not a systematically pursued policy sanc-

13. Cf. Konrad Kwiet, "Zur historiographischen Behandlung der Judenverfolgung im Dritten Reich," *Militärgeschichtliche Mitteilungen* 27 (1980): 171f. This essay appeared in a slightly abbreviated version in Dan Diner, ed., *Ist der Nationalsozialismus Geschichte? Zu Historisierung und Historikerstreit* (Frankfurt, 1987), pp. 237ff.

14. The problem of separate religious services for Jewish Christians became irrelevant in the wake of the rapidly intensified deportations; see Kurt Meier, *Kirche und Judentum: Die Haltung der evangelischen Kirche zur Judenpolitik des Dritten Reichs* (Göttingen, 1968), pp. 28f., 115 ff.

tioned from above. However, a concern among the population about "excesses" of this kind once again subsided with relative rapidity.

That did not change until systematic deportations of German Jews began definitely in the spring of 1942. The first large-scale deportations had already been carried out in October 1941. When planned liquidations associated with these deportations occurred later in Kulm and Riga, and news about that – for which even the official bureaucracies were not psychologically prepared – leaked through to the population, Göring prohibited further deportations. However, it was less the mass executions by the *Einsatzgruppen*, news of which was spread by soldiers back on leave from the front, and more the circumstances under which the deportations were carried out which sparked dissatisfaction among the German public. In place of deportations implemented spontaneously, a program of systematic deportation of Jewish groups assembled previously with the assistance of the Jewish administrative bodies was instituted starting in March 1942. The deportations themselves took place stepwise and gradually; they entailed the cooperation of the local and municipal authorities and were by no means carried out under the cloak of strict secrecy. The Jews of Heidelberg, for example, were assembled at noon in the market area and then sent from there on transports.[15]

Any thinking person must have known that the Jews were being deported. The circumstances of such deportations also made it clear that a difficult and uncertain fate awaited the deportees. Numerous suicides of Jewish families were an unmistakable sign of that. The Propaganda Ministry ultimately attempted to prevent the accumulation of such death notices in the papers.[16] The population was also aware that the Jews were forfeiting their property. The numerous requests for the yielding up of Jewish living quarters and furniture submitted to the authorities are an eloquent indication of that.[17] The measures for

15. See Arno Weckbecker, *Die Judenverfolgung in Heidelberg, 1933–1945* (Heidelberg, 1985), pp. 197ff. As a rule, the Gestapo acted more discretely in Berlin, but it was virtually impossible for anyone with open eyes at the time to overlook the deportations.

16. See Konrad Kwiet, "The Ultimate Refuge: Suicide in the Jewish Community under the Nazis," *YLBI* 29 (1984): 135–67.

17. See also Matthias Schmidt, *Albert Speer: Das Ende eines Mythos* (Berlin, 1982), pp. 216ff.

Jewish "resettlement" were officially justified by the supposed necessity of making more living space available for the "Aryan" population. Initially, the populace appears to have believed the official phraseology used, which presented the illusion that resettlement was what was involved. In any event, despite early rumors, which were to an appreciable extent fed by statements made by fanatic National Socialists not based on authentic observation, the systematic extermination of deported Jews was generally thought to be impossible.

The regime overestimated the degree of anti-Semitic indoctrination among the populace. This is indirectly reflected in the official phraseology which the party Chancellery issued in October 1942 to *Gauleiter* and subdistrict party chiefs to prevent negative reactions among the general population to the deportation of Jews. According to this formulation, the party leaders were to awaken sympathy and understanding among the population for the "very harsh measures against Jews" being taken in the eastern territories by referring to the impossibility of resolving the Jewish Question through emigration. It was argued that since the coming generation would not see the Jewish Question "with enough clarity" and would not regard it as an issue "close to their lives," the entire problem would have to be solved "by the current generation"; the objective was "the total and complete expulsion or elimination of the millions of Jews present in the European economic sphere." "It lies in the nature of the matter that these in part difficult problems can only be solved, in the interest of the final security of our people, with merciless severity."[18]

However, it is evident that the deportations had become increasingly unpopular and that the great mass of the population had no sympathy for the policy of genocide. That was not changed by Goebbels's intensified anti-Semitic propaganda beginning in 1943. Bormann consequently saw himself compelled to tone down the earlier official phraseology and formulations. An order was issued in the summer of 1943 to avoid "any mention of a future total solution" in the public treatment of the Jewish Question; remarks should be limited to the reference that

18. Printed in Hans-Adolf Jacobsen, *1939–1945: Der Zweite Weltkrieg in Chronik und Dokumenten* (Darmstadt, 1961), pp. 584f.; cf. also Marlies Steinert, *Hitlers Krieg und die Deutschen: Stimmung und Haltung der deutschen Bevölkerung im Zweiten Weltkrieg* (Vienna, 1978), pp. 252f.

Jews were being deported to the east for labor deployment (*Arbeitseinsatz*).[19] The manifest resistance among the population caused Himmler to expedite the deportation measures and, in official pronouncements, to stick to the formulation of a "transport" of Jews to transit camps. This offensive strategy proved successful inasmuch as the persecution of the Jews largely disappeared from public consciousness from 1943 on.

Yet the secrecy in which the policy of the Final Solution was shrouded was strikingly incomplete. In particular, it was hard to hush up the activities of the *Einsatzgruppen* behind army front lines. A portion of the troop commanders, caught up in the lure of Hitler's ideological illusions, expressly sanctioned the planned and systematic liquidation of the Jewish population in the region. Field Marshal von Manstein stated that Jewry constituted the "link between the enemy behind our backs and the remnants of the Red Army and the Red leadership still resisting" and that it continued to form the "cell for all disturbances and possible uprisings." In a similar vein, Field Marshal von Reichenau asked the troops for their "full appreciation of the harsh but just atonement being exacted from subhuman Jewry."[20] There were certainly also a number of protests, but these were largely the product of worries about a threat to military discipline and of apprehension about stepped-up Soviet resistance. In some cases, photographing of executions and their mention in letters to home were prohibited under the threat of severe penalties.

There is considerable evidence regarding information leaked back to the Reich about the activities of the *Einsatzgruppen*; in contrast, there is virtually no such evidence documenting knowledge of the existence of extermination camps.[21] The rumors being circulated condensed only in exceptional cases into a comprehensive picture. As a rule, the assumption was made that such measures were attributable to a one-sided initiative by the SS, one which had not been cleared and agreed upon with the Reich government. In a letter from the Protestant state bishop of Hanover, August Marahrens, to the interior minister,

19. Ibid., p. 257.
20. Quoted in Léon Poliakov and Josef Wulf, *Das Dritte Reich und seine Diener* (Berlin,[2] 1956), p. 451; Steinert, *Hitlers Krieg*, p. 251.
21. Ian Kershaw, *Popular Opinion and Political Dissent in the Third Reich: Bavaria, 1933–1945* (Oxford, 1983), p. 367.

dated December 19, 1943, the author, in connection with the persecution of "non-Aryan" Christians, mentions the duty to persuade the government leadership "to do everything to make sure that necessary political and governmental measures are not compromised by serious crimes perpetrated by irresponsible individuals, thus saddling the conscience of our people with a burden it cannot bear."[22] This petition by a clergyman reflected the effects of official propaganda. While the deportation was accepted as a necessary measure and the program of forced resettlement silently condoned by the churches, the liquidations were viewed as excesses perpetrated by Himmler, to which Hitler had the duty to call a halt.

Those whose lives were directly affected by the persecution of Jews evinced an incomparably greater sensitivity than the great mass of the population. Jochen Klepper, whose family felt such a direct impact (he was married to a Jewish woman), foresaw the calamity signaled by the intensification of anti-Jewish propaganda. He interpreted Goebbels's speeches and articles at the end of 1941, Hitler's appeal in a New Year's speech of 1942, and his address on the occasion of the ninth anniversary of the "seizure of power" to mean that the systematic annihilation of European Jewry had already been decided upon.

The average *Volksgenosse* saw in all this nothing but the repetition of the customary anti-Semitic tirades, especially since all these statements were found in a contradiction-ridden and confusing context.[23] Nowhere in public pronouncements by the government could one learn anything about the concrete fate of the deported Jews. Whoever did not wish to believe the worst regarded these statements as verbal accusations directed against the Jewish adversary. For example, Goebbels, in an editorial entitled "The Jews are Guilty" published on November 16, 1941, in the weekly *Das Reich*, stated that what was now being experienced was the realization of the Hitlerian prophecy of January 30, 1939, and that Jewry was undergoing a "gradual process

22. Quoted in Eberhard Klügel, *Die lutherische Landeskirche Hannover und ihr Bischof, 1933–1945: Dokumente* (Berlin, 1965), p. 203.

23. It is often not taken into consideration that Hitler's repeated prophecies about the end of the Jewish race were included within a broad context; they were difficult to grasp and hardly determined the tenor of his speeches, which went on constantly repeating the same notions; see Hans Mommsen, "Die Realisierung des Utopischen: Die 'Endlösung der Judenfrage' im Dritten Reich," *Geschichte und Gesellschaft* 9 (1983): 381–420, esp. 390ff.

of destruction"; Jews, he said, would have to be "isolated" and separated from the German folk community.[24] This argument was picked up again in an article by Goebbels published on May 9, 1943; it contained the prediction that the Second World War unleashed by the Jews would lead to the "extinction of the Jewish race" and that world Jewry would someday suffer the same punishment being "meted out already in Germany today." These remarks reflect the peculiar ambivalence of official positions on the Jewish Question, including speeches by Hitler, which always presented the process of destruction as a future product of a "last judgment" even at a point when the genocidal measures had largely been concluded.[25] This also holds true for Hitler's speech to the generals on June 26, 1944, in which he talked once again about Jewish intentions of exterminating the Germans, although he did not go beyond official phraseology (which only allowed for the statement that Jews were being deported to work camps) in hinting at countermeasures.[26]

It is difficult to assess the impact of the ambiguity of official propaganda. Fanatic anti-Semites read the anti-Semitic threats and took them at face value. They had no compunctions about using the most extreme violence against Jews and pushing on with systematic liquidation. To what extent a cynical hegemonial knowledge crystallized and gained frequency in the party and SS bureaucracies, a knowledge that comprehended the true meaning of the official phraseology employed everywhere, must remain an open question. It could be assumed that that segment of the SS bureaucracy directly involved with the deportation and liquidations cynically accepted the mass murder; that also could be assumed in respect to the various authorities assisting in this enterprise, although the full truth only became known there gradually. Official phraseology functioned to mask the criminal realities at every point beyond the immediate perimeter of the circle of executors in the technical sense;

24. See H.-D. Müller, ed., *Faksimilequerschnitt durch "Das Reich"* (Munich, 1965), p. 7; cf. the analysis by Hans-Heinrich Wilhelm, "Wie geheim war die Endlösung?" in Wolfgang Benz, ed., *Miscellanea: Festschrift für Helmut Krausnick zum 75. Geburtstag* (Stuttgart, 1980), pp. 136ff.

25. See Wilhelm, "Wie geheim war die Endlösung," pp. 144f.

26. See Mommsen, "Die Realisierung des Utopischen," pp. 396f. Extracts from the speech in idem, "Adolf Hitler als 'Führer' der Nation," in *Nationalsozialismus im Unterricht*, Studieneinheit 11, ed. Deutsches Institut für Fernstudien (Tübingen, 1984), pp. 176ff.

those respective groups of perpetrators, it should be noted, were by no means restricted only to SS personnel and often changed.

Consequently, there was hardly any sort of clearly demarcated "insider knowledge," if one leaves aside the responsible departments in the RSHA and the police bureaucracies assisting them. Since even the initiated communicated only in secret and camouflaged language, an insider's code, there were all the prerequisites for a collective repression. Whoever attempted to penetrate to the facts was given partial answers at best. The entire horror of the reality was disclosed even to its executors only in the form of abstract numbers which the SS statistician Korherr then assembled into a necessarily fragmentary total picture that was supposed to be presented to Hitler, but was apparently never sent.[27] It was far more difficult to gain accurate knowledge of the complex situation under the prevailing conditions of the Nazi system.

In view of the fact that for a long time the international public and even the Allied governments refused to give credence to the information being channeled to them about the policy of Final Solution being carried out in the east,[28] it is not surprising that the population in the Reich did not perceive the uncomfortable truth in its true scope and immensity. This was also true of the Jewish victims. Even Leo Baeck learned only in 1943 about the fact that the deportees from Theresienstadt were being sent to the gas chambers. He kept this truth to himself because he feared that its disclosure would threaten the ability and will to survive of his fellow sufferers.[29] In a general way, Theresienstadt indeed functioned as a masquerade of the true fate awaiting the Jews, and even the International Red Cross did not

27. On this point, one should agree with the observation by Irving; see David Irving, *Hitler's War* (London, 1977), p. 871.

28. See Walter Laqueur, *The Terrible Secret: Suppression of the Truth about Hitler's "Final Solution"* (Boston, 1980), pp. 199ff. See also his more recent study on the information obtained through the industrialist Eduard Schulte: Walter Laqueur and Richard Breitman, *Der Mann, der das Schweigen brach: Wie die Welt vom Auschwitz erfuhr* (Frankfurt and Berlin, 1986); Martin Gilbert, *Auschwitz und die Allierten* (Munich, 1981), esp. pp. 111ff.

29. On Baeck, see L. Baker, *Days of Sorrow and Pain* (New York, 1978), pp. 272, 310ff. The extensive ignorance of those affected in the Altreich is also given support by statements in Else R. Behrendt-Rosenfeld, *Ich stand nicht allein: Erlebnisse einer Jüdin in Deutschland, 1933–1944* (Mannheim, ²1965), pp. 164f.

disclose the truth behind the artificial facade.[30] The great mass of the population, long since accustomed to the existence of concentration camps, remained passive toward rumors reflecting only partial fragments of the whole reality, especially since they seemed inconsequential in comparison with the concrete events of the war. There is no doubt that the terrorizing pressure of the system contributed to this attitude, since anyone who made a critical statement about the persecution of the Jews could himself expect to be interned, at least temporarily, in a concentration camp.[31]

It is psychologically understandable that the genocidal measures only entered the awareness of the mass of the population in specific phases of development, as in the period of the initial deportations at the end of 1941. After that, this complex did not surface again until the German propaganda on the Katyn massacre appeared. This propaganda sparked numerous statements in various quarters that the government should not make such a big fuss about the murder of the Polish officer corps by the Red Army since the same thing had occurred with deported Jews.[32] Nonetheless, it is impossible to derive the existence of any general knowledge about the program of liquidation or, in any event, precise insight into the systematic character of the policy of Final Solution from these few statements that have been documented.

After the first comprehensive crisis of confidence in the regime, which peaked at Stalingrad, discussion of the genocide question receded totally from the sphere of public discussion. This is principally due to the fact that the public was largely preoccupied with coping with the effects of the war, which were increasingly impinging on the everyday life of the individual. This was supplemented by a mounting sense of fatalistic benumbedness and inurement, as impressively expressed in the words of an East Prussian farmer's wife, quoted by Hannah Arendt, to the effect that already Hitler was keeping ready a mercy death by

30. H.G. Adler, *Theresienstadt, 1941–1945: Das Antlitz einer Zwangsgemeinschaft* (Tübingen, ²1960), pp. 172ff.

31. Cf. Steinert, *Hitlers Krieg*, p. 242.

32. See Dov Kulka, "'Public Opinion' in Nazi Germany and the 'Jewish Question,'" *The Jerusalem Quarterly* 26 (1982): 38ff.; idem, "Popular Christian Attitudes in the Third Reich to National-Socialist Policies toward the Jews," in *Judaism and Christianity under the Impact of National Socialism (1919–1945)* (The Historical Society of Jerusalem, June 1982).

gassing as an option to being handed over to the Bolsheviks.[33] The expression of open public indignation was held in abeyance by the interaction of a complex of factors: widespread moral indifference, anti-Semitic indoctrination (which, however, did not extend so far among broad sections of the population as to justify open violence against Jews), and social ostracization of the "pariah" Jewish community. Parallel to all this, a conscious repression of unpleasant information was characteristic of the internal situation within the regime. This held true not only for the population directly involved, but also for the top functionaries of the regime themselves. It is significant that this process of repression played a lesser role in situations where one perceived a personal threat to one's own existence.

Critical remarks about the genocide policy were frequent after the Stalingrad debacle and the mounting fury of the Allied bombing war. The "clever ploy" of Goebbels's propaganda in portraying the bombing raids as a typically Jewish form of warfare and in labeling the Western Allies in general as forces acting to further Jewish interests now boomeranged, reverting, as reflected by the reports of the SD on the general mood, to great apprehension in certain cases resulting from the fear that the severity of the war was attributable to the German measures against the Jews and that following a defeat, now deemed possible, analogous measures against the German population could be expected from the Allies.[34]

Yet the persecution of the Jews plays a quite subordinate role in the SD reports and comparable materials.[35] The careful evaluation of local and regional reports by researchers gives the impression that anti-Jewish measures frequently enjoyed open public approval, while criticism of these measures appears only in isolated instances.[36] There is considerable evidence that criti-

33. Hans Graf von Lehndorff, *Ostpreußisches Tagebuch, 1945–1947* (Munich, 1956), p. 18, entry for January 23, 1945.

34. Kershaw, *Popular Opinion*, p. 369.

35. See Heinz Boberach, ed., *Meldungen aus dem Reich: Die geheimen Lageberichte des Sicherheitsdienstes der SS, 1938–1945* (Herrsching, 1984), vol. 1, pp. 25f.

36. Cf. Falk Wiesemann, "Judenverfolgung und nichtjüdische Bevölkerung," in Martin Broszat, Elke Fröhlich, and Falk Wiesemann, eds., *Bayern in der NS-Zeit: Soziale Lage und politische Haltung der Bevölkerung im Spiegel vertraulicher Berichte* (Munich, 1977), vol. 1, pp. 429ff.; Dov Kulka, "Public Opinion in Nazi Germany and the 'Jewish Question,'" *Zionist Quarterly for Research in Jewish History* 40 (1975): 186–290; idem, "'Public Opinion' in Nazi Germany," *The Jerusalem Quarterly* 25/26 (1982): 121–44, 34–45; Ian Kershaw, "Antisemitismus

cal statements about Katyn made after Stalingrad derived mainly from persons who had previously approved of the anti-Semitic measures and supported regime policy. The opinions of those who were reticent on principle or had misgivings for humanitarian reasons were probably almost never reflected in the reports on popular mood and morale put together by the SD since they only talked about these matters with other persons of similar persuasion. Nonetheless, the fragmentary sources do indicate that it was specifically members of lower social strata who were most likely to perceive the lethal threat to the Jews and who for that reason feared Allied reprisals.[37] In contrast, Hitler believed that the main locus of resistance was in middle-class circles, while Goebbels suspected intellectuals to be the guilty party.[38] Viewed as a whole, what is surprising is the silence of the overwhelming majority of the population in the Reich; it reflects both a sense of helplessness and resignation, as well as repression and moral desensitization.

The collective repression of the genocide was abetted by the circumstance that the official churches avoided as a rule taking any stand on this issue. If they did comment, then it was in the form of internal petitions to the government. Characteristic of this stance is the initiative undertaken in December 1943 by Theophil Wurm, the state bishop of Württemberg and one of the leading representatives of the Confessional Church. In a number of petitions to the highest authorities in Berlin, he criticized the continuation of the deportations and referred to the intolerable burden of guilt being placed upon the German people. Yet Wurm's argumentation accommodated itself to the existing constellation of circumstances and alluded to the "removal" of the Jews as a fait accompli, while his primary concern was to protect "non-Aryan" Christians.

It is undisputed that this was an unusually courageous step which was sharply rejected by the government; there probably was no massive reprimand of Bishop Wurm only out of deference for his age (born 1868). However, it should be noted that

---

und Volksmeinung. Reaktion auf die Judenverfolgung," in *Bayern in der NS-Zeit*, pp. 281–348; Lawrence D. Stokes, "The German People and the Destruction of the European Jews," *Central European History* 6 (1973): 167–91.

37. Gordon, *Hitler, the Germans, and the "Jewish Question,"* pp. 192f.; Kershaw, *Popular Opinion*, p. 369.

38. Henry Picker, *Hitlers Tischgespräche*, new ed. (Stuttgart, 1977), pp. 305f.; Steinert, *Hitlers Krieg*, p. 253.

Wurm's official communications still contained an echo of the traditionally anti-Semitic biases of German Protestantism.[39] Thus, despite the clear stance of the Confessional Church on the question of "non-Aryan" church members, that church likewise failed to articulate an unmistakable public position regarding the liquidation of European Jewry. The Twelfth Synode of the Old Prussian Union held on October 16–17, 1943, in Breslau chose not to incorporate into the text of the synode's final approved resolutions the formulations of the various draft resolutions, which were in some ways more explicit, in others reminiscent of the old Christian anti-Semitism.[40] The very general phrases critical of the inhumane treatment of Jews were insufficient to enlighten those who otherwise had no knowledge of the events taking place in the east and in the concentration camps.

It can be considered certain that influential representatives of the Confessional Church were at this point well informed about the liquidation program and the systematic mass murders, due in part also to internal information acquired by Kurt Gerstein.[41] Yet the total picture of the Final Solution remained hidden even to these immediately affected contemporaries, although information had in the meantime been broadcast on the foreign radio and in the foreign press.[42] The caution even within oppositional church circles in dealing with this distressing information (which they only utilized in the form of hints contained in internal petitions to government offices) indicates that, in addition to the undeniable personal danger in the event of open protest, the generally widespread social-psychological need to

---

39. Kurt Meier, *Kirche und Judentum*, pp. 39ff. Hermann Diem composed an Open Letter to Bishop Meiser in opposition to the compromising position taken by Wurms (cf. H. Diem, *sine vi – sed verbo* [Munich, 1965], pp. 108ff., and Gerhard Schäfer, *Landesbischof Wurm und der nationalsozialistische Staat, 1940–1945* (Stuttgart, 1968), p. 165, n. 34. Cf. also Dov Kulka, "The Churches in the Third Reich and the 'Jewish Question' in the Light of Secret Nazi Reports on 'Public Opinion,'" *Miscellanea historiae ecclesiasticae* 9 (1984): 490–505.

40. See materials and resolutions of the Twelfth Confessional Synode, autumn 1943, Archiv der Evangelischen Kirche der Union, Berlin, KKKA I 616 a.

41. Gerstein had contacts with Niemöller and other members of the Confessional Church and attempted to call his apparently highly precise and accurate information to the attention of the Swedish ambassador, Baron von Otter, the Swiss embassy in Berlin, and the Vatican, as well as an unspecified number of other personalities, but most responded with incredulousness, cf. Eugen Kogon, Hermann Langbein, Adalbert Rückerl et al., eds., *Nationalsozialistische Massentötungen durch Giftgas* (Frankfurt, 1983), pp. 171ff.

42. Gilbert, *Auschwitz und die Allierten*, pp. 58ff., 62ff.

repress these events played a major role. It was significant that internal criticism was restricted to demands for a halt to previous measures. The silence of the Catholic Church in Germany,[43] which was informed at a relatively early point about the genocide taking place through the excellent contacts of the curia with bishops in southeastern Europe,[44] cannot serve to justify or excuse the lack of willingness even by large segments of the Confessional Church to speak out.

An SD report from Lemgo dated July 1942 illustrates the mixed attitude of the population to the deportations. Objections were raised against the deportation of older Jews, women, and children, since they could not harm a fly and had even done good things too; moreover, the aged would die soon in any case.[45] These statements of opinion become meaningful only when viewed against the backdrop of anti-Jewish propaganda; they reflect the tendency to distinguish between the largely assimilated German Jews and the imaginary enemy of Eastern Jewry or world Jewry. A December 1941 report from Minden/Bielefeld contained, on the one hand, a mention of criticism directed against the deportation of Jews long resident in the area, based on humanitarian grounds; on the other, it carried a rumor that, as a reprisal measure, Germans in America were being forced to wear the swastika on their chests.[46] The racist

43. See Guenter Lewy, *The Catholic Church and Nazi Germany* (New York, 1964), pp. 264–93. The complaints lodged by Cardinal Bertram and Bishop Preysing did not differ in tendency from those of their Protestant partners, but they did place greater stress on the question of mixed marriages. The uncompromising stance of the dean of the Berlin Cathedral, Bernhard Lichtenberg, is an exception; he died in October 1943 during internment in Dachau. Lichtenberg represents the exceptional case of consistent protest directed also against the deportation of non-Christian Jews.

44. See Lewy, *The Catholic Church*, pp. 293ff. and John S. Conway, "Catholicism and the Jewish People during the Nazi Period and Afterwards," in *Judaism and Christianity under the Impact of National Socialism (1919–1945)* (The Historical Society of Jerusalem, June 1982), pp. 347–75.

45. Otto Dov Kulka, "The 'Jewish Question' in the Third Reich: Its Significance in National Socialist Ideology and Policy and Its Role in Determining the Status and Activities of the Jews," vol. 2, Documents, Ph.D. diss., Hebrew University, Jerusalem, 1975. See also Ian Kershaw, "German Popular Opinion during the 'Final Solution': Information, Comprehension, Reaction," unpublished manuscript, p. 14.

46. Ian Kershaw, "German Popular Opinion and the 'Jewish Question,' 1939–1943: Some Further Reflections," in Arnold Paucker, ed., *Die Juden im nationalsozialistischen Deutschland/The Jews in Germany, 1933–1943* (Tübingen,

ideology was the implicit basis for most oppositional statements, but the domestic German-Jewish population was generally exempted from that demonization of Jews, as were those who were guilty of having unleashed the war. Misgivings about deportation measures also primarily concerned the disgusting circumstances accompanying such deportations, while deportation measures as such were not rejected.

Feelings of injustice arose in connection with the persecution of individual, identifiable groups of persons, while such feelings were rare when it came to victims crammed into ghettos or railroad boxcars. Evidently, the mechanisms of moral inhibition regarding the destruction of human life largely eroded when it came to the sea of victims forced to vegetate under inhuman conditions in the camps. Propaganda films functioned to assure that this view was also inculcated in those persons who had no direct contact with the railway transports, the assembly points, the ghettos, and the living conditions of those Jews who had remained in Germany. After the total isolation and segregation of Jews from the majority population, open resistance against the anti-Jewish measures had become a practical impossibility for the individual citizen because there was a silent majority that regarded the action of the government and the Gestapo measures as justified from the standpoint of state policy.

One exception to this was the protest by three hundred non-Jewish spouses against the deportation of their Jewish husbands on Rosenstraße in Berlin in March 1943. In actual fact, the SS gave in in this specific case.[47] However, it was only a question of time as to when they would have their way using the instrument of individual arrests, which were far less spectacular. Those who were opposed sensed how totally helpless they were. Ruth Andreas-Friedrich noted on February 28, 1943: "Should we go and challenge the SS? Should we storm their trucks and pull our friends down off the vehicles? The SS has weapons – we have none. . . . We have reverence for life. That

---

1986), pp. 365–408, here p. 376. See also Otto Dov Kulka and Aron Rodrigue, "The German Population and the Jews in the Third Reich: Recent Publications and Trends in Research on German Society and the 'Jewish Question,'" *Yad Vashem Studies* 16 (1984): 421–35.

47. Ruth Andreas-Friedrich, *Der Schattenmann: Tagebuchaufzeichnungen, 1938–1945* (Berlin, 1947), new ed. (Frankfurt, 1983), pp. 103f, and Gerhard Schoenberner, *Wir haben es gesehen: Augenzeugenberichte über Terror und Judenverfolgung im Dritten Reich* (Wiesbaden, 1981), pp. 282ff.

is our strength – and our weakness."[48] The fear of getting into trouble was an additional factor. In Heidelberg, Pastor Hermann Maaß was the only person who dared to offer assistance, at a great risk to himself, although he proved unable to accomplish very much.[49] More successful were attempts by individual factory managers and entrepreneurs to protect their Jewish workers from deportation.[50]

The causes underlying the moral indifference evident here are diverse. These events presumably show that, even under normal circumstances, it is unlikely that third parties will intervene on behalf of the persecuted. In the case of the German populace, an additional factor was the presence of a solid authoritarian disposition which automatically attributed legality to action taken by government bodies, nipping any thought of resistance in the bud. There was no one who was not clear about the fact that an uncertain fate awaited Jews in the east. Likewise, many had heard that there had been shootings and that large numbers of Jews had not survived the deportation. However, very few had a clear picture of the systematic mass extermination at the time of the deportations. They were certainly aware that there had been individual massacres. Nonetheless, rumors that went beyond this were all too easily rejected as Allied atrocity propaganda. This facilitated the repression of the actual events, and such repression was inherent in National Socialist propaganda itself. There can be no doubt that the great mass of the German population gained a concrete picture of the existence of the concentration camps and the systematic mass extermination only after the collapse of the regime.[51] In the later war criminal trials, it also proved to be extremely difficult to derive

48. Andreas-Friedrich, *Der Schattenmann*, pp. 102f.
49. See Weckbecker, *Judenverfolgung*, pp. 200f.
50. See the case of Schindler in Grossmann, *Die unbesungenen Helden*, pp. 147ff.
51. Characteristic examples of the "lack of knowledge" on the part of normal *Volksgenossen* are given in Milton Mayer, *They Thought They Were Free: The Germans, 1933–1945* (Chicago, [3]1966), esp. pp. 125ff. Based on my own personal experience, I can attest that my father Wilhelm Mommsen must have learned about the extermination of the Jews via contacts with Ludwig Bergstraesser, who in turn cooperated with Leuschner. In any event, he forbade his sons from having any closer contact with the Pfannenstiel children of their same age because Professor Pfannenstiel was implicated in the policy of the Final Solution.

knowledge of the liquidation from contemporary knowledge about the deportations.

On the other hand, there is no lack of evidence indicating that those who tried to get information were able to obtain it relatively easily and without any great personal risk. A striking proof of this is offered by the notes recorded by Karl Dürkefälden, who was employed in a machine factory in Celle as chief designer after a lengthy period of unemployment. Yet it is significant that he derived the most important information on the genocide from listening to BBC in the summer of 1942; this information allowed him to take other news and piece together a picture of what was happening.[52] The psychological predisposing factor for this was his fundamental opposition to the regime.

In contrast, the average *Volksgenosse* clung to the fiction that things were going along properly in the Third Reich aside from certain exceptions due to the war, at least as far as Hitler was concerned. Only the process of developing a more sober picture of realities in the last phase of the war changed this tenaciously held view; that attitude contained a kind of double moral standard and was bound up with a selective perception of reality. There is considerable evidence suggesting that, beginning in the second half of 1942, rumors and fragments of information coalesced and condensed into the impression that the murder of deported Jews was highly likely. This is why critical statements on the deportations came relatively late, culminating in 1943; by that juncture, such rumors had largely become a fact of death, at least as far as German Jewry was concerned, and most victims were no longer alive.

Whether one wishes to speak of a genuine "passive complicity"[53] or a partial perception of the mass murder,[54] there can be no doubt that a vague consciousness of injustice was generally present, which National Socialist propaganda attempted to counter. At the same time, there was a notably high degree of moral indifference among the mass of the population and among leading non-National Socialist officials. The typical rep-

52. Herbert and Sybille Obenaus, eds., *"Schreiben, wie es wirklich war!" Aufzeichnungen Karl Dürkefäldens aus den Jahren 1933–1945* (Hanover, 1985), pp. 111f.; cf. Herbert Obenaus, "Haben sie wirklich nichts gewußt? Tagebuch vom Alltag, 1933–45," gives a clear answer in *Journal für Geschichte* 2 (1980): 26–31.
53. Kulka and Rodrigue, *The German Population*, p. 343; cf. Kulka, "'Public Opinion' in Nazi Germany," p. 45.
54. Kershaw, "German Popular Opinion," p. 370.

ression mechanism was necessarily facilitated by the nationally motivated bond of the population to the regime and the person of the Führer. That mechanism was also based in part on the circumstance that reliable information was unobtainable or, if acquired and accepted in its full implications, at the very least presupposed an inner willingness to engage in treason. Even under other political circumstances, it is difficult to demand that from the ordinary person.

It is indisputable that numerous bits of evidence can be mustered to show approval among certain segments of the population of the anti-Semitic measures. They reflect the dominant propagandistic indoctrination and do not necessarily indicate readiness to take active action against Jews – if one leaves aside those persons who, quite apart from any ideological biases, were releasing their aggressions on defenseless persons, either in their fantasy or directly, like many (though by no means all) of the guards. It is noteworthy that secondary justifications of a purposive nature predominated among defenders of National Socialist policy toward the Jews, as they had already on the occasion of the November 1938 pogroms; strict racial-theoretical arguments, in contrast, were only advanced by a small circle, even within the ranks of the NSDAP.[55]

The main psychological obstacle consisted in the danger of the individual's being branded as a *Judenfreund* if he expressed support for Jews, even if only advocating their "correct and proper" treatment. Conscious or risked infringements of racial legislation, including the law on "protection of German blood," were far from rare; racial-political indoctrination indeed had very shallow roots. Yet it was enough to stigmatize any opposition voiced against the persecutions. The passivity of the population is also explained by the circumstance that rumors about the murder of the "deported and resettled" Jews only condensed at a relatively late juncture in a development against which, by that time, there was no immediate occasion for protest. Although there is certainly also evidence for pro-Jewish sympathies which were at the same time expressions of protest against the regime by the opposition, the great majority, who as a rule had supported demands for "removal of the Jews" from

55. See Michael Müller-Claudius, *Der Antisemitismus*, p. 166 and the evaluation in Kershaw, "German Popular Opinion," manuscript (see n. 45 above), pp. 32ff.

Germany, became a silent accomplice, an accessory to genocide.[56]

Finally, one should not overlook the background against which the deportations and liquidation took place. Even without the addition of Nazi propaganda, the intensification of the war necessarily had to lead to a numbing, yes, even brutalization and mounting indifference toward violence and the countless and uncounted numbers of dead, as well as to moral indifference toward crimes that appeared to be connected with combat warfare. In its final stages, genocide was only one of many aspects of a salient phenomenon: the total loss of respect for one's fellow man. This was all the more so in view of the course of a war which even the German civilian population perceived as growing ever more cruel and horrible. However, the more profound basis for the lack of protest should be sought elsewhere, namely, in the decay and collapse of the moral foundations of society as a whole. We have already touched on the problematic attitude of the churches, who should have been the first to protest against the deportations. There is no need for a detailed description of how the justice system indirectly placed itself at the service of genocide,[57] although it cannot be demonstrated that the policy of genocide was explicitly referred to in talks with the presidents of district appellate courts. Rather, even in 1942, in legal questions regarding Jews, the courts proceeded as if the problems to be adjudicated were not about to be rendered irrelevant by the deportations already underway.[58]

It is significant in this connection that the national-conservative opposition did not obtain precise knowledge about the extermination of the Jews until 1943, concurrently with the

56. See Inge Deutschkron, *Ich trug den gelben Stern* (Cologne, 1983), p. 106.

57. See Diemut Majer, *"Fremdvölkische" im Dritten Reich: Ein Beitrag zur nationalsozialistischen Rechtssetzung und Rechtspraxis in Verwaltung und Justiz unter besonderer Berücksichtigung der eingegliederten Ostgebiete und des Generalgouvernements* (Boppard, 1981), pp. 317ff., 459ff.; see also Uwe D. Adam, *Judenpolitik im Dritten Reich*, 2d ed. (Düsseldorf, 1972), pp. 280ff., 350ff., and passim.

58. Note the discussion between the heads of the superior district courts and the district attorneys in the Justice Ministry on March 31, 1942. At this conference Freisler, who had participated in the Wannsee Conference, urged the court heads to make sure Jewish defendants received stiff penalties in accordance with the desire of the party Chancellery (BA R22/4162, fols. 55f.). The Justice Ministry authorized the heads of the superior district courts on November 5, 1942, to place a "Jew knowledgeable about the law" at the disposal of the Jewish *Rechtskonsulenten* as assistants (cf. communication of Justice Minister to Heads of Superior District Courts, "'Handakten' des Oberlandesgerichts Köln 'Jüdische Konsulenten,'" OLG Köln).

petitions of Bishop Wurm, even though there was knowledge, at an early point, of massacres in Polish areas. Helmuth James von Moltke, in particular, proved able to gain a comparatively exact picture on the basis of his work in counterespionage.[59] In the case of Ulrich von Hassell and Carl Goerdeler, considerations tending in this direction apparently did not arise until raised in connection with the Katyn massacre. At the latest, Klaus Schenk von Stauffenberg was enlightened by Henning von Tresckow about the methods being employed by the SS *Einsatzgruppen* behind the front lines, but probably knew of these directly from his own experience.[60] Moltke knew early on about the Wannsee Conference, though he did not attribute any fundamental importance to it, as was the case with other government departments. At the end of 1942 and once again in early 1943, Johannes Popitz briefed his coconspirator Hassell in comparatively detailed form, though he only dropped a few hints about the mass gassings.[61] The impression can be gained from this evidence that the systematic character of the process of annihilation was not even fully known within the resistance and that people were increasingly thinking along the lines of more and more frequent violent actions carried out by Himmler. The leaflets of the oppositional group White Rose constituted a certain exception: they made reference to the murder of hundreds of thousands of Polish Jews, thus informing a limited

59. See Freya von Moltke, Michael Balfour, and Julian Frisby, *Helmuth James von Moltke, 1907–1945: Anwalt der Zukunft* (Stuttgart, 1975), pp. 215f. In the letter dated March 25, 1943, reproduced there, which had been written in Stockholm, Moltke stated that he believed that "at least nine-tenths of the population does not know that we have killed hundreds of thousands of Jews. People continue to believe that they have only been segregated and are living more or less the same life as before, only further east, where they come from, in conditions possibly more wretched, but without bombing raids." In addition, Moltke had reliable information about sixteen concentration camps equipped with crematoria and had heard about "the construction of a large concentration camp in Upper Silesia, planned for forty to fifty thousand inmates, of whom three to four thousand a month are to be killed." Although he had attempted to learn more, he had obtained this information only in a quite vague, unclear, and inaccurate form.

60. See Christian Müller, *Oberst i.G. Stauffenberg: Eine Biografie* (Düsseldorf, n.d.), p. 382.

61. See "Die Hassel-Tagebücher, 1933–1945," in Ulrich von Hassell, *Aufzeichnungen vom anderen Deutschland*, ed. Friedrich Freiherr Hiller von Gaertringen, new ed. (Berlin, 1988), pp. 81f., 339f., 365; cf. information in Christof Dipper, "Der deutsche Widerstand und die Juden," *Geschichte und Gesellschaft* 9 (1983): 359f.

public of these deeds.[62] Strangely, the deportation of Jews from western European and southwestern European countries is given only marginal mention in the preserved notes and sketches of the members of the July 20th conspiracy.[63]

The immediate link between deportation, selection, and extermination appears not to have been sufficiently clear even to persons in Berlin government circles with whom members of the national-conservative resistance had close contacts. This was probably due less to any policy of strict secrecy, which was basically impractical, and more to the systematic failure in communication between various governmental departments and the other bureaucracies of the regime. When Ministerial Director Wilhelm Kritzinger, later state secretary of the Reich Chancellery, attempted during 1939–40 to learn more exact details about the actions of the SS in the Generalgouvernement, he was prevented by Himmler from doing so. Even his participation in the February 1942 Wannsee Conference did not mean that he was reliably informed about the program of the Final Solution whose contours were then emerging.[64]

The fact that the opposition did not receive reliable information about the policy of the Final Solution until comparatively late in its development can be explained less by an effective system of secrecy and far more by another feature of Nazi bureaucratic behavior, namely, the system of lack of communication between the chief authorities in the top government echelons so characteristic of the regime. The top officials in the Foreign Office, including State Secretary Ernst von Weizsäcker, were far more precisely informed.[65] The lack of opposition in the

62. See Inge Scholl, *Die Weiße Rose*, rev. ed. (Frankfurt, 1985), pp. 102, 116.

63. In contrast, already in 1941 there were clearly articulated protests against liquidation measures, as in the case of Freiherr von Gersdorff; see Stokes, "The German People and the Destruction of the European Jews," p. 101. Von Hassell constitutes an exception; on September 26, 1942, he noted in his diary: "Geißler [Popitz] confirmed horrible things from the east, especially the brutal killing of many thousands of Jews. A Swiss lawyer, who had rescued several Dutch Jews after being bribed, remarked to an acquaintance: 'You Germans are such great organizers. Why do you go to the trouble, with all the transport problems you have, of first shipping so many thousands east instead of killing them right away here in the west?'" See "Die Hassel-Tagebücher," p. 330.

64. Cf. Hans Mommsen, "Aufgabenkreis und Verantwortlichkeit des Staatssekretärs der Reichskanzlei Dr. Wilhelm Kritzinger," *Gutachten des Instituts für Zeitgeschichte* 2 (Stuttgart, 1966): 380ff.

65. See Christopher Browning, *The Final Solution and the Foreign Office*, pp. 74f.

Foreign Service appears problematic because, on the one hand, that branch was indispensable for the preparation of deportations from the satellite states and was involved in the corresponding negotiations and discussions; moreover, it would have had quite solid opportunities to sabotage the deportation program, had it so desired. Significantly, those who were sufficiently informed about the objectives of the deportations were in many cases career diplomats, not National Socialist functionaries who had been channeled into the Foreign Service by Ribbentrop or had been taken on as a result of pressure from Himmler.[66] The Foreign Office had been exposed to severe pressures from the NSDAP for a long time. Yet even apart from that, it had shown tendency early on not only to condone the anti-Semitic measures of the regime, but to support them actively. That had already been evident at the time of the April 1, 1933, boycott. Initially the predominantly conservative-oriented officials of the Foreign Office had been able to register their misgiving about the constant heightening of measures against the Jews. There were individual cases in which an attempt was made to save Jewish colleagues from the worst.

When the policy of genocide was initiated, a changed constellation arose. The Foreign Office had been belatedly surprised by the ease with which the deportation program was transposed to the countries under German occupation and the satellite states, for whose inclusion in the program the cooperation of the Foreign Office was absolutely essential. The participating officials appear at first to have had only a blurred and fuzzy view of the objectives pursued by Heydrich with his authorization for working out a Final Solution and became entangled in its implementation before realizing its full implications. They therefore no longer saw any possibility for openly disassociating themselves from the program or refusing to cooperate in its execution.[67] This was probably also true of what happened in the case of the key officials of the Reichsbahn railway administration.

The Reich Transport Ministry, which was essential for implementation of the transports, was prepared to cooperate closely with Adolf Eichmann, who was responsible for the deportation

---

66. See Hans-Jürgen Döscher, *Das Auswärtige Amt im Dritten Reich: Diplomatie im Schatten der "Endlösung"* (Berlin, 1987), pp. 103ff.

67. Ibid., pp. 213ff.

program, but handled the matter as a routine affair. It is therefore impossible to speak about any preference given to transports of Jews or any special secrecy in regard to them. It is difficult today to clarify the extent to which the officials involved knew about the objective of murder. Even the director general of the German Reichsbahn, Albert Ganzenmüller, appears to have repressed the truth when finally informed about it. It remains incomprehensible why the responsible authorities permitted the transports to be carried out under ever more cruel and terrible conditions. Here too the factor of habituation appears to have played a role because the initial transports from the Altreich were still implemented, in part, in a form that appeared externally to be tolerable given prevailing wartime circumstances.[68] Bureaucratic perfectionism, which reasoned only in terms of categories of transport capacity, prevented railroad officials, who were in addition kept at a distance from the deportees by SS guard personnel, from expressing moral misgivings and becoming aware of the actual fate awaiting the deportees. However, they must have realized that several of the destinations should long since have become large cities if people there had not been murdered by the hundreds of thousands.

Yet even the minister for armaments and munition, Albert Speer, directly associated with the construction of the camps, attempted after 1945 to persuade the world that he had not been informed about the program of the Final Solution.[69] The evidence attesting to the involvement of his ministry in the utilization of vacated Jewish apartments and homes and the construction of concentration camps renders a lack of knowledge on the part of the minister virtually inconceivable.

The will and readiness to repress knowledge were not phenomena which arose in the period after defeat; rather, they began simultaneously with the events themselves.[70] This is also the case when it comes to the greater majority of the generals.[71]

68. See Raul Hilberg, *Sonderzüge nach Auschwitz* (Mainz, 1981).
69. Note the discussion triggered by Erich Goldman's article "Albert Speer, Himmler, and the Secrecy of the Final Solution," *Midstream* (October 1971): 43–50; on this, cf. Hans Mommsen, "Spandauer Tagebücher: Bemerkungen zu den Aufzeichnungen Albert Speers im internationalen Militärgefängnis, 1946–1966," *Politische Vierteljahresschrift* 17 (1976): 111f.
70. Cf. Schmidt, *Albert Speer*, pp. 216ff.
71. See Wilhelm, *Wie geheim war die Endlösung?* pp. 131ff. Dönitz likewise denied any knowledge of the genocide, see Walter Lüdde-Neurath, *Regierung Dönitz: Die letzten Tage des Dritten Reiches* (Göttingen, ³1964), pp. 91f.

Even if the claims of ignorance made after 1945 hold true only in a very limited way, they attest to the rulers' social-psychological tendency, so characteristic of behavior in the Third Reich, to repress uncomfortable truths. That tendency is reflected in the schizoid quality of Rudolf Höß's life-style[72] and was clearly manifest in the trial against Adolf Eichmann in Jerusalem.[73] It appears at least plausible, on the basis of the available sources, that even the top personnel in the departments involved had no comprehensive knowledge of the program of the Final Solution, with the exception of the Foreign Office and the Interior Ministry.

Right from the start, the representatives of the classic departments tried to limit Heydrich's objectives by defining the concept of Jew in as narrow a way as possible and by attempting to exclude the assimilated groups of Jews from deportation. In the Interior Ministry Bernhard Lösener, the official for racial matters, in particular, and State Secretary Wilhelm Stuckart, to a certain degree as well, attempted to prevent Jewish *Mischlinge* from being included in the deportations. In any case, they achieved a temporary victory: in 1942, Hitler decided to defer temporarily the deportation of *Mischlinge*, whose forced sterilization was proposed instead. This did not stop the Gestapo from deporting at least the Jewish spouses of so-called privileged mixed marriages whom the Interior Ministry also wished to protect.[74] At the time that the Wannsee Conference was convened, there was strong opposition from various government departments. However, the apparent upshot was that Himmler simply ignored them; there were no formal complaints lodged with Hitler and no unambiguous ruling by the Führer on the matter.[75]

72. See Martin Broszat, comp. and ed., *Kommandant in Auschwitz: Autobiographische Aufzeichnungen von Rudolf Höß* (Stuttgart, 1958), pp. 17ff.
73. Hannah Arendt, *Eichmann in Jerusalem*, new ed. (Munich, 1986), pp. 53ff. and the introduction by Arendt, p. viii.
74. See Adam, *Judenpolitik*, pp. 316ff.
75. The files of the Justice Ministry contain notes composed by State Secretary Freisler on November 21, 1941; according to this record, Minister Lammers presumably informed Schlegelberger that "the Führer had repeatedly said to him that it was his wish that the solution to the Jewish Question be postponed until after the end of the war. Accordingly, the current deliberations [apparently the program of deportation later presented at the Wannsee Conference] had, in Lammers's view, nothing but theoretical value. In any case, he will make sure that fundamental decisions are not made suddenly through an initiative coming from the other side without his knowledge" (BA R 22/52, fol. 153). The note evidently alludes to Himmler. On the basis of events a bit later (ibid., fols. 155f.) on March 18, 1942, one can conclude that Schlegelberger had intervened with

Even if the departments were not informed in detail about the actual events, it is surprising that, after the collapse, the fact is that it proved possible to demonstrate conclusively concrete individual knowledge only in occasional instances. After all, the Final Solution, carried out with such bureaucratic perfectionism, resulted in a wide-reaching net of complicity: a large number of governmental departments were either directly or indirectly involved with the liquidations, be it only for purposes of the administration and disposal of Jewish property or the registration of the gold from the teeth of the victims given to the Reichsbank.[76]

However, the pervasive tendency of the ministerial bureaucracy was to keep its distance from the legislation designed to prepare or supplement the genocide as much as possible and to pass on responsibility to the Gestapo, even at the risk of a loss of authority in certain spheres.[77] This contradictory attitude present even among the top echelon of officials can be clearly seen from the diary kept by Jochen Klepper, who lived in a so-called privileged mixed marriage and was fearful about the fate of his daughter, brought into the marriage by his wife and considered Jewish under NS racial law. Klepper had relatively close ties to government circles as well as to the executive committee of the Jewish community; that committee had been given responsibility by the Gestapo for registering those to be deported and was often provided with secret instructions. Through this avenue, Klepper gained knowledge of the orders sent by Section IV of the RSHA to the Reichsvereinigung and its subordinate local associations; these orders were issued largely through internal channels. This allowed him to piece together unusually precise, albeit still fragmentary, information pertaining to the escalation of the persecution measures. Consequently he was able at a relatively early juncture to assemble a basically accurate picture of what was really going on.[78] Klepper was personally

Lammers. It is significant that there is no discussion of content in regard to the "program for the Final Solution," which, if a comment at the same time by Alfred Rosenberg is correct, was being discused precisely during that period; see Robert Kempner, *Eichmann und Komplicen* (Zurich, 1961), pp. 86f. and Mommsen, "Die Realisierung des Utopischen," pp. 399f.

76. Hilberg, *Die Vernichtung der europäischen Juden*, pp. 647f.

77. Adam, *Judenpolitik*, pp. 273ff., 344ff. and Mommsen, "Aufgabenkreis," pp. 389ff.

78. Even Ruth Andreas-Friedrich was still talking at the end of 1942 about the

acquainted with the interior minister and sought his support in order to avert the imminent deportation of his daughter. Wilhelm Frick, who initially appeared ready to help and promised further assistance, admitted in his last discussion in early December 1942 that he was unable to protect any Jew. "According to the nature of the matter, such things cannot take place secretly. The Führer will get wind of them, and then all hell will break loose."[79] The helplessness of moderate functionaries extended from the municipal level up to the top ministerial echelons. The decisive motive of the interior minister, who had lost virtually all power to influence domestic political decisions, was not his racial-political convictions, but rather a timidity to take resolute action against the wishes of Himmler, who was a feared figure. As an old anti-Semite, the interior minister cut a sad figure in this situation. And it was not an isolated case. Everywhere one could hear disapprobation whispered when it came to the violent measures practiced by Himmler and radical party circles, along with the regretful complaint that there was no possibility available to counter these measures.

If this was the situation at the top echelon of the regime, it was not surprising that subordinate officials likewise failed to resist and hid behind the excuse of supposed orders; indeed, these officials did not even attempt to make suitable use of the latitude remaining for judgment and action. Nor did it matter much in this respect whether such officials were members of the NSDAP or not. There were no longer any groups within the society able to prevail in support of previously valid moral norms against fanatic National Socialists and dangerously self-important government officials. Even personages who belonged to the inner leadership circle of the regime (or had been a part of the circle in the past), such as Hans Frank or Wilhelm Kube, were unable to stand up to Himmler's thugs in their attempt to save the Jewish workers employed in their sphere of activity from annihilation, though their actions were most certainly not for humanitarian motives. To seek Hitler's intervention was

terrible "rumors," though she was otherwise quite well informed. See *Der Schattenmann*, p. 102 and Stokes, "The German People and the Destruction of the European Jews," p. 181, n. 57.

79. Jochen Klepper, *Unter dem Schatten Deiner Flügel: Aus den Tagebüchern. Die Jahre 1932–1942* (Stuttgart, 1956), p. 1130. Eichmann, who had authority in the matter, rejected the exit permit that had been approved by the Swedes. The only alternative left to the family was suicide.

useless.[80] To whom could one turn, when now even the Reich Chancellery was only trying, defensively, to prevent the worst from occurring and saw no chance to catch Hitler's ear and interest when it came to the main matter. When the situation arose, the Führer feigned deafness.

If one takes this total constellation into account, there is no need to assume a thorough anti-Semitic indoctrination of broad circles of the population to explain the helplessness, passivity, and pretended ignorance regarding the crimes against the Jews. It was sufficient that a relatively small, fanatic minority needed to fear no sanctions as it pushed ahead with the process of radicalization. The genocide question was influenced by another factor, the peculiar atmosphere of semidarkness, the cloak of obscurity in which deportation and liquidation took place. The government's failure to enunciate a formal position strengthened many in their fanciful belief that, in the last analysis, what was involved were only isolated excesses by Himmler and Heydrich, not a systematic program of extermination.

Consequently, it may be false to frame the question in terms of knowledge, that is, in terms of what the individuals involved, what the German people as a whole *knew* about the Final Solution. There can be no doubt that many had no knowledge of the events taking place in the extermination camps, whether they were anti-Semites or not. But each person could sense the burden of the crime being committed against the Jewish people, just as the sickeningly sweet odor from the chimneys at Auschwitz was noticed by those living in the vicinity without their delving into the causes of that odor.[81] The plan hatched in November 1941 by Himmler and Heydrich to push ahead with rapid extermination of the Jews, using the pretext of the Russian campaign, and to try later to cover this action up appears in retrospect to be sheer grotesquerie.

The policy of secrecy, coupled with repression, had a key effect: most National Socialist functionaries attempted to blame Himmler, saddling him with all responsibility for the Holocaust. Himmler therefore felt obliged to present the fact that Jews were being killed and to describe the circumstances of and motives for

80. Cf. Mommsen, "Die Realisierung des Utopischen," p. 415.
81. A contemporary witness who had lived in the immediate vicinity of Auschwitz as a young man told me, in a highly credible form, that his family had not had any knowledge of the mass extermination.

the mass extermination openly at two meetings – probably called especially for this purpose – a gathering of *Gauleiter* and national functionaries in Posen on October 6, 1943, and a meeting with commanders of the navy in Weimar on December 16 of that year.[82] His revelation of this state secret had a key purpose – to rid himself of the burden of sole responsibility, while simultaneously extricating the SS from the "dirty corner" it had been forced into. The National Socialist satraps to whom Himmler revealed the awful truth had little inclination to pass on any more than the barest essentials of that knowledge to others.

Thus, the full scope of the genocide – the murder of more than 4.5 million European Jews – remained hidden from the view of most contemporaries. Yet the majority of German adults at the time were probably aware in one form or another of various details of this state secret in its variegated facets. The enormity of the crime and its moral dimension rendered it incomprehensible. This was also true when it came to foreign public opinion and to the Allied governments, which hesitated to give full credence to the information they were receiving. Yet it did not take much effort or imagination to surmise the probable fate of the deported Jews. Those who had struggled to the point where they could recognize the fundamental injustice of the NS system of rule were able to learn enough to assure themselves of the probable veracity of such information. However, that was a tiny minority. The great majority went along with the collective repression offered to it as palliative by the regime.

82. See F. Bradley Smith and Agnes Peterson, eds., *Heinrich Himmlers Geheimreden, 1933 bis 1945, und andere Ansprachen* (Frankfurt, 1974), pp. 162ff., 201; in his speech to the SS elite leadership on December 4, he mentioned the genocide in connection with the question of maintenance of the internal morale of the SS, but did not give it any special emphasis; on this, see Mommsen, "Die Realisierung des Utopischen," p. 384.

Liberated But Not Free
Jewish Displaced Persons in Germany after 1945

Abraham J. Peck

Today Holocaust survivors are for many only an "interesting phenomenon." They are sought out by oral historians wishing to record their memories and by school systems requesting their presence in classrooms where the Holocaust is studied and discussed. The survivors continue to gather to hallow the memory of six million dead, to ask their children to continue to bear witness, and to demonstrate that revisionist historical efforts to prove the Holocaust a myth are vicious lies. Whenever they are in our presence, they inevitably are figures of reverence and mystery. They are like no other people we know. This is not a new feeling.

In the spring of 1945, when the first concentration camps were being liberated, one American Jewish GI who was among the liberators of Nordhausen, where V-2 rocket parts were manufactured, wrote the following: "There was a great barrier between us. . . . I really felt alien, more than alien, it was through a wish that I wasn't fully aware of to disassociate myself: That is different . . . those people are different . . . I don't belong there."[1] Elie Wiesel, himself a survivor, feels that survivors constitute a "separate, doomed rapidly disappearing species, an isolated and tragically maligned species." He quotes a survivor living in Oslo, Norway: "In 1945 I had a purpose: It has been turned into ridicule."[2]

---

1. This paper is dedicated to the memory of my mother, Anna Peck, of blessed memory, a part of the voice of the She'erit Hapletah, whose spirit is scattered to the winds. The basic research for this article was made possible by a grant from the Memorial Foundation for Jewish Culture. Morris Parloff, quoted in Robert H. Abzug, *Inside the Vicious Heart: Americans and the Liberation of Nazi Concentration Camps* (New York, 1985), p. 42.
2. Elie Wiesel, *A Jew Today* (New York, 1978), pp. 185–208.

Who are the survivors? Although many possess an external sense of success, the survivors remain a subgroup within the Jewish communities in which they live. They prefer to live in close proximity to each other, worship in their own synagogues, and participate in their own social organizations. They remain possessed by the transition from the harrowing experience of being an "individual in the concentration camp," to finding themselves victims of the "concentration camp within the individual," a situation where stress and suffering over a long period of time have left many with an inner isolation, unable to respond normally to a "normal" postcamp experience.

The children of survivors share with them this often unnatural world. Their condition is less well known than that of the survivor. It is only within the last decade that some of these children have begun to come to grips with the reality of their situation. They have often lived in the eye of a hurricane, surrounded by the shadows of the "war." They know that the war is a part of their being, but do not know why. "I've asked next to nothing," writes one survivor's child, "also worried about my own suffering in (my parent's) response. I want to know very badly, yet I dread the moment of having to raise the issue, although I realize that it is my duty to learn and to be able to retell their stories to my children."[3]

And occasionally, when survivors are pressed to go beyond the retelling of their experiences, certain feelings emerge about the survivor relationship to the "world," that vast body of humanity, Jew and non-Jew, which knew of the relentless Nazi drive to annihilate European Jewry. That sense that the world knew, writes Dorothy Rabinowitz, who has studied survivors, "coexisted side by side with their perception that 'people' [in America and elsewhere] rejected the facts about the holocaust, which had been widely published after 1945."[4] There is a story here, one which has just begun to emerge and one which I have been fortunate enough to discover.

In April of 1945, the late American Jewish novelist Meyer Levin was a war correspondent traveling with the Fourth

3. Abraham J. Peck, "The Children of Holocaust Survivors," in Allon Schoener, ed., *The American Jewish Album, 1654 to the Present* (New York, 1983), pp. 309–10.
4. Dorothy Rabinowitz, *New Lives: Survivors of the Holocaust Living in America* (New York, 1976), p. 196.

Armored Division as it made its way east around the German town of Gotha. He and his companions came upon some "cadaverous refugees" along the road. "They were like none we had ever seen," Levin wrote later, "skeletal, with feverish sunken eyes, shaven skulls." They identified themselves as Poles and asked Levin and the others to come to the site where they had been held prisoner. They spoke of "people buried in a big hole" and "Death commando." They described a camp but the Americans did not want to go there during the oncoming darkness for fear of enemy attack. They would wait for light.

What they found the next morning at a camp called Ohrdruf, named for and just outside a small town near Gotha, were scenes that had not been seen before – not in the quantity, not in the form of death, not in the manner of killing. As Levin drove through the gate he saw piles of dead prisoners, all in striped uniforms. The corpses were fleshless, and at the back of each skull was a bullet hole. A shack held a stack of stiff and naked men. "The bodies were flat and yellow as lumber," Levin remembered.[5]

This was only the beginning. During the next several weeks, camp after camp was liberated by the Americans, the British, and the Russians. We know best what the American liberators felt at the moment of liberation of such camps as Nordhausen, Buchenwald, Dachau, and Mauthausen in Austria: "Oh the odors," wrote one, "well there is no way to describe the odors. . . . Many of the boys I am talking about now – these were tough soldiers, there were combat men who had been all the way through on the invasion – were ill and vomiting, throwing up, just the sight of this. . . ."[6] Another wrote: "These Jewish people . . . were like animals, they were so degraded, there was no goodness, no kindness, nothing of that nature, there was no sharing. If they got a piece of something to eat, they grabbed it and ran away in a corner and fought off anyone who came near them."[7] Finally, a third wrote: "[The prisoners] were so thin they didn't have anything – didn't have any buttocks to lie on; there wasn't any flesh on their arms to rest their skulls on . . . one man that I saw there who had died on

---

5. Meyer Levin, quoted in Abzug, *Inside the Vicious Heart*, p. 21.
6. C.W. Doughty, quoted in ibid., p. 31.
7. Samuel Glasshow, quoted in ibid., p. 63.

his knees with his arms and head in a praying position and he was still there, apparently had been for days."[8]

These were some of the physical reactions and impressions of tough American GIs, farm boys from Iowa, streetwise New Yorkers, and mountain men from Appalachia. But it took the sensitivity of a literary imagination like Meyer Levin's to give it the perspective, the meaning, which defines the Holocaust for our time. Levin wrote: "We had known. The world had vaguely heard. But until now no one of us had looked on this. Even this morning we had not imagined we would look on this. It was as though we had penetrated at last to the center of the black heart, to the very crawling inside of the vicious heart."[9]

The gulf of experience and expectations that lay between liberators and survivors, the different world that made battle-weary Americans innocent by comparison, disoriented and disturbed even those most ready to embrace the victims of Nazi terror. Speaking to an international conference of liberators in 1981, Elie Wiesel spoke of the American soldiers who liberated him from Buchenwald on April 11, 1945. "You were our liberators," Wiesel said, "but we, the diseased, emancipated, barely human survivors were your teachers. We taught you to understand the Kingdom of Night." What the liberators learned and what the survivors already knew would force both to confront a world which suffered from what Robert Abzug has called a case of "double vision," of seeing the reality of newsreel films, which showed a pile of bodies stacked as they were described "like cordwood" at Dachau, hundreds of corpses laid out in rows before the ruins of buildings at Buchenwald, bulldozers filling mass graves at Bergen-Belsen, but at the same time of not seeing these things, of not believing that they were possible.[10] The result was a world which shut it all out, a world which was silent.

But not entirely. The New York intellectual Dwight Mac-Donald, writing in 1945, reflected on the events in Europe from 1933 to 1945. "Something has happened. What is it? Who or what is responsible? What does it mean about our civilization,

---

8. William B. Lovelady, quoted in ibid., p. 33.
9. Meyer Levin, quoted in ibid., p. 19.
10. See Abzug, *Inside the Vicious Heart*, chap. 7, "Telling the Story."

225

our whole system of values?"[11] For MacDonald, indeed for the major portion of American and European liberals, a great catastrophe had taken place. Their world view of rationality and progress toward international peace had been smashed to pieces, victims of the "belief that humanity had set limits to the degradation and persecution of one's fellow man."[12] Those inside the vicious heart, even for a short time, already knew this much earlier. The Viennese Jewish writer, Stefan Zweig, writing about the new order of things as a refugee from Nazism in Brazil, knew. "We of the new generation," Zweig wrote, "in opposition to that idealistically blinded generation [prior to World War I]. . . have learned not to be surprised by any outbreak of bestiality; we who each new day expect things worse than the day before, are markedly more skeptical about a possible moral improvement of mankind."[13] Zweig's skepticism drove him and his wife into suicide a few short months later.

But such despair was not evident for the Jewish survivors of the Holocaust at the moment of liberation. Simon Schochet was a prisoner in Dachau:

"When I awoke, morning had finally come and the pains subsided. At the window Alexis and the other man suddenly began to shout that they saw some vehicles which did not look German. We crawled to the window and peeked out. A long column of tanks moved slowly down the road below us. They were marked with white stars. We stared at each other in disbelief. Was it true? Were we suffering a collective hallucination brought on by the events of the previous day? Perhaps the Germans had captured those tanks . . . but against these fears, a single thought, hope, belief overwhelmed us, a single unvoiced thought sounded and echoed in our confused and tortured minds: We are free! Free! I saw this in Alexis' eyes and in the eyes of all the men. And so, clutching our aching stomachs we turned toward the door and began to climb down the attic steps. . . .

They were waiting for us in front of the villa, where Alexis said we should turn in our uniforms to the proper side. And so, having undressed and dressed again, we walked down the middle of the open road on this cool May morning to meet our liberators."[14]

11. Quoted in Alfred Gottschalk, "Religion in a Post-Holocaust World," in Abraham J. Peck, ed., *Jews and Christians after the Holocaust* (Philadelphia, 1981), p. 2.

12. Alexander Donat, quoted in Henry L. Feingold, "Who Shall Bear Guilt for the Holocaust: The Human Dilemma," *American Jewish History* 68 (March 1979): 281.

13. Stefan Zweig, *The World of Yesterday* (Frankfurt, 1981), pp. 171ff.

14. Simon Schochet, *Feldafing* (Vancouver, 1983), pp. 14–15.

And on that cool morning in May, a group of perhaps as many as 100,000 Jewish survivors found themselves among the eleven million uprooted and homeless people wandering throughout Germany and central Europe. Many of these DPs sought to return home to rebuild their lives and their nations.[15]

Not so the Jews. As one Jewish survivor wrote: "The Jews suddenly faced themselves. Where now? Where to? For them things were not so simple. To go back to Poland? To Hungary? To streets empty of Jews. To wander in those lands, lonely, homeless, always with the tragedy before one's eyes . . . and to meet again, a former Gentile neighbor who would open his eyes wide and smile, remarking with double meaning, "What! Yankel! You're still alive!"[16]

These Jews, later to be joined by 150,000 others from Russia and Poland, formed the She'erit Hapletah (Hebrew for the "saving remnant"). We are not even certain when the term came to be applied to those who survived Hitler's war against the Jews. It is a biblical term appearing in 1 Chronicles 5, which refers to the Jewish remnant that survived the Assyrian conquest. It reappears in the list of survivors which was published in July 1945. More important, the term was both a description and a source of identity for those surviving the death camps, those who were partisans in the forests, and those who took refuge from Hitler in the deepest reaches of Russian Siberia. It was an identity which would give birth to a revolutionary ideology created from the inner being and experience of the She'erit Hapletah.

We know little about the hopes and aims of the Jewish DPs beyond their need to leave *Galut* (exile) for the land of Eretz Israel and other nations. Marie Syrkin has recently written that the "Displaced Person is a savage euphemism." "By now," she contends, "a DP is an almost forgotten term as is DP camp." Yet the period between liberation and the establishment of Israel, during which survivors of the Nazi death camps became DPs, represents for Syrkin a grim epilogue to the Holocaust and a

15. See Wolfgang Jacobmeyer, *Vom Zwangsarbeiter zum heimatlosen Ausländer* (Göttingen, 1985) and "Jüdische Überlebende als 'Displaced Persons': Untersuchungen zur Besatzungspolitik in den deutschen Westzonen und zur Zuwanderung osteuropäischer Juden, 1945–1947," *Geschichte und Gesellschaft* 9 (1983): 421–52.

16. "Homecoming in Israel," in Leo W. Schwarz, *The Root and the Bough* (New York, 1949), p. 310.

227

coda to its meaning.[17] Marie Syrkin is surely correct: DP is an almost forgotten term. Indeed, when we think or read of the Jewish DPs they are inevitably portrayed as the passive objects of history, awaiting with resignation and despair the acting out of a drama in which they could play little, if any, role.

Yet this is simply not true. From the very beginning of their liberation, Jewish DPs sought to recapture their sense of humanity and their sense of Jewishness, aspects of an identity which had been systematically taken away by the Nazis. "The Jews who have been liberated in the camp want to catch up," wrote one observer. "They are starving for a word of Judaism."[18]

But this was not an easy task. The American and British military authorities, in their efforts to bring order to the chaos of postwar Europe, set up DP camps in Germany and Austria. In those camps, Jews were thrown together with their former persecutors. Often ex-Nazis were put in charge of the DP camps, which were patrolled by armed guards. One American report noted that the hard core of the non-Jewish DPs "[has] been proved to be a criminal and fascist group, many of whom left their countries voluntarily to work for Hitler."[19] Perhaps most shocking was the attitude of General George S. Patton, who led the Third Army in southern Germany, which contained most of the DPs in the American zone. Patton insisted that every camp be surrounded by barbed wire and manned by armed guards to watch the survivors as if they were the vanquished enemy. Patton wrote in his diary on September 15, 1945, that others "believe that the Displaced Person is a human being, which he is not, and this applies particularly to Jews who are lower than animals."[20]

Word of these conditions soon reached American government authorities. Jewish leaders in America and abroad asked President Harry Truman to investigate the situation. Truman approved an investigation headed by Earl G. Harrison, the dean of the University of Pennsylvania Law School. Harrison's subsequent report on the conditions of the Jewish DPs shocked officials at the highest levels of the American government and

17. Marie Syrkin, *The State of the Jews* (Washington, D.C., 1980), p. 11.
18. H. Leivick, *Mit der She'erit Hapletah* (Toronto, 1947).
19. Ira Hirschmann, quoted in Leonard Dinnerstein, *America and the Survivors of the Holocaust* (New York, 1982), p. 22.
20. Ibid., pp. 16–17.

military. A portion of his report stated that "as matters now stand, we appear to be treating the Jews as the Nazis treated them except that we do not exterminate them. They are in concentration camps in large numbers under our own military guards instead of the SS troops. One is led to wonder whether the German people seeing this, are not supposing that we are following or at least condoning Nazi policy."[21] Within months Jewish DP camps were created in both the American and British zones of Germany and Austria. In addition, an adviser for Jewish affairs, Chaplain Judah P. Nadich, was added to the staff of General Dwight D. Eisenhower, the commander of the Supreme Headquarters of the Allied Expeditionary Forces in Europe.[22]

Jewish DP camps were established on or near the sites of former concentration camps. By May of 1947 there were at least sixty of these camps. Among the most important were Bergen-Belsen, in the British zone of Germany, and Landsberg, Feldafing, and Föhrenwald in the American zone.[23] There were also numerous Jewish children's centers, hospitals, and agricultural training centers. The latter prepared Jewish survivors for eventual immigration to Palestine. Ironically, two of these centers were located on estates once belonging to the notorious Julius Streicher, the editor of the fanatically anti-Semitic newspaper, *Der Stürmer*, and to Hermann Göring, one of Hitler's most important lieutenants. Perhaps even more ironic, the nucleus of the Jewish DP community in the American sector of Berlin lived in an empty pavilion in the district of Wannsee. It was there in 1942 that the Final Solution to the Jewish problem in Europe, the total destruction of the Jewish people, had been planned.

These tragic ironies only underscored the incredible dilemma of the Jewish DPs. It was as if they were living in one vast Jewish cemetery with no hope of leaving its confines. Entry to Palestine was blocked by British fears of Arab hostility; emigration to the United States and other nations was made almost impossible by

21. Quoted in ibid., p. 43.
22. See Judah Nadich, *Eisenhower and the Jews* (New York, 1953).
23. See Leo W. Schwarz, *The Redeemers* (New York, 1953); Ursula Büttner, "Not nach der Befreiung: Die Situation der deutschen Juden in der britischen Besatzungszone, 1945–1948," in: Ursula Büttner, ed., *Das Unrechtsregime: Internationale Forschung über den Nationalsozialismus* (Hamburg, 1986), vol. 2, pp. 373–406; Irving Heymont, *Among the Survivors of the Holocaust, 1945: The Landsberg DP Camp Letters of Major Irving Heymont, U.S. Army* (Cincinnati, 1982).

unyielding quota systems. Few Jews wished to return to their former homes in eastern Europe. Indeed, after a tragic pogrom on July 4, 1946, in the Polish city of Kielce, in which at least forty Jews were killed, thousands of Jews from Poland, and later Hungary, fled to the American zone of Germany.[24]

Yet despair was never an issue in the camps. Instead of allowing themselves to be overwhelmed by blocked immigration, overcrowded housing, and the continuing anti-Semitism surrounding them, the Jewish DPs resolved to create a new beginning. With the support of Jewish and international relief associations, the Jewish camps became centers of Jewish cultural life. From nothing grew secular schools which provided a curriculum based on the highly successful *Tarbut* (culture) schools in prewar Poland. These schools taught Hebrew, Jewish history, the geography of Palestine, the history of Zionism, and other subjects. Dozens of camp newspapers and magazines were published. Camp theaters and musical groups were organized.[25]

Political parties were formed in the camps, mirroring the various Zionist philosophies and groups then active in Palestine and elsewhere. The political slates that ran against each other in camp elections were distinguished not only by varying Zionist philosophies, but also by the geographic backgrounds of the candidates. In one camp Polish Jews predominated, in another Jews from Lithuania. The development and continuity of religious life was supported by American rabbis, who served as sources of spiritual comfort.[26] "No Jewish DP camp is without a synagogue and the other facilities required by religious Jews," wrote one observer. "Every camp has a kosher kitchen today," he continued, "all the larger camps have officiating rabbis."[27] The Jewish DPs modeled their camps on the small Jewish communities of prewar eastern Europe. Judaism and Zionism,

24. See Dinnerstein, *America and the Survivors of the Holocaust*; Yehuda Bauer, *Flight and Rescue: Brichah* (New York, 1970); Michael Checinski, "The Kielce Pogrom: Some Unanswered Questions," *Soviet Jewish Affairs* 5, no. 1 (1975): 57–72.

25. Toby Blum-Dobkin, "The Landsberg Carnival: Purim in a Displaced Persons Center," in: *Purim: The Face and the Mask* (New York, 1980); Tsemah Tsamriyon, *The Press of the Jewish Holocaust Survivors in Germany as an Expression of Their Problems* (Tel Aviv, 1970) (Hebrew).

26. Louis Barish, *Rabbis in Uniform* (New York, 1962); Alex Grobman, "American Jewish Chaplains and the Remnants of European Jewry" (Ph.D. diss., Hebrew University, Jerusalem, 1981).

27. See Israel Efros, *Heimlose Yidn* (Buenos Aires and Sao Paulo, 1947).

one a religious identity, the other a national identity, became the sources of survivor hope and vitality in the DP camps. Other beliefs such as communism and socialism, once popular among prewar Jews, disappeared for the most part after 1945.

Zionists within the Jewish DP camps insisted that European Jews should henceforth greet the future from a position of strength, organization, and attack – and not from a position dependent upon religious trust and faith. As Isaac Ratner, one of the most important Zionist leaders in the DP camps, wrote in October of 1945, greeting the appearance of the leading Jewish newspaper, *Our Way*: "And when *Our Way* appears – created by strength and organization – we, the Zionists, will utter neither a *brachah* [blessing] nor a *shehehianu* [a thanksgiving blessing]. But we declare, 'Mir szeinen doh' ['We are here'].''[28]

"Mir szeinen doh" was the phrase which best expressed the resolution of the Jewish DPs to rebuild their shattered lives. It was the unshakable belief of a group of survivors who felt that they had seen in the Holocaust, as one survivor stated, "the end of creation – not only an indelible memory of horror – but a permanent warning," that what he and others had experienced was a pilot project for the destruction of humanity. "We are here" was expressed in a number of ways. By the end of 1946 the Jewish DP camps had the distinction of having the highest birthrate of any Jewish community in the world. This resolve to say yes to a Jewish future surprised American-Jewish visitors to the camps, who had come there expecting to find a despair-ridden and essentially pessimistic community.[29]

Even more pronounced than the birthrate was the resolve of the She'erit Hapletah to develop a philosophy of survival which would never again allow Jews to experience such a tragedy as the Holocaust. Writing in April 1946 in the Jewish DP newspapers, J. Nemenczyk related a concentration camp fantasy which he had experienced lying on lice-filled straw in hunger and pain. "I had a vision," he wrote, "that if the world could not give us back our dead brothers and sisters then it could give us a moral world."[30] Even earlier, speaking in June 1945 at the first

28. Isaac Ratner, "Mir Szeinen Doh," *Undzer Veg* [Our Way] 2, October 19, 1945, p. 30. See also Koppel S. Pinson, "Jewish Life in Liberated Germany," *Jewish Social Studies* 9, no. 2 (April 1947): 101–26.

29. See Emma Shaver, *Mir Szeinen Doh* (New York, 1948); Efros, *Heimlose Yidn*; Leivick, *Mit der She'erit Hapletah*.

30. J. Nemenczyk, in *Landsberger Lager-Caytung*, April 15, 1946, p. 3.

ceremony marking the liberation from Nazism, Dr. Zalman Grinberg, one of the earliest acknowledged spokespersons of the She'erit Hapletah, stressed the moral aspect of its existence: "Hitler won the war against the European Jews. If we took revenge, we would descend into the lowest depths . . . in which the German nation has fallen during the past ten years. We are not able to slaughter women and children. We are not able to burn millions of people."[31] *The Free Word*, the journal of the Feldafing camp, echoed Grinberg's message in an article entitled "We Jews and the World." It stated that "what we, the She'erit Hapletah, must do is show that we, the victims of Nazism, have always been and will always be the carriers of humanity."[32]

Thus the nucleus of a philosophy of Jewish survival was being formed. But it would not develop on European soil. Despite the expectations of many, the survivors would not, as had previous generations of European Jews struck by the sword of hatred, cast off its tragedy and rebuild on European soil. "Should we help in the rebuilding of Europe," Grinberg asked in early 1946, "so that Europe will in time erect new crematoria for us?"[33] Instead, they would journey back to the Jewish homeland, Eretz Israel, and rebuild their shattered remnants as other nations were doing in the aftermath of Nazism.

There was an anticipation, a nervous level of activity among the survivors in the months following liberation. The need for Palestine was clear, but so was the need for another source of purpose. In Zalman Grinberg's opening remarks at the first Congress of Liberated Jews in the American zone, he echoed this need: "This is a conference of surviving Kaddish sayers who will not satisfy themselves with merely saying Kaddish."[34] A short time later, the journalist Menahem Sztajer grappled with the ultimate role and purpose of the She'erit Hapletah. In October 1946 he challenged the survivors to decide for themselves. "Will the She'erit Hapletah simply be an accidental term for survivors of a destroyed people," he asked, "or will it mean

31. Zalman Grinberg, "We Are Living Corpses," *Aufbau*, August 24, 1945, p. 6.

32. "Mir Yidn un die Velt," *Dos Freiye Vort*, June 20, 1946, p. 5.

33. Quoted in *Undzer Veg* 17, January 25, 1946, p. 2.

34. Quoted in "Die problematische Stellung der Juden in Deutschland," *Der Weg* 1, March 1, 1946, p. 2.

a revolution in Jewish history – a renaissance in Jewish life."[35]

The ideology of the She'erit Hapletah was crystallized in a series of brilliant essays by Samuel Gringauz in the years 1947 and 1948. Gringauz reiterated the need for European Jews to say farewell to the discredited continent. "Our place is no longer in Europe. We carry with us the legacy of our millenial history to Palestine and America so that the secular continuity of our ethical and cultural values may be assured."[36] It was the survivors, he maintained, who were the victims of civilization, and it was they "who have been called upon to discover the positive basis on which we can unite with it. . . . Our tragedy must become the starting point of a new humanism." This ideal for Gringauz was no less than a neo-humanism, the ideal of the moral and social perfection of humanity.[37]

Thus the ideology of the She'erit Hapletah was formulated and the conditions for its implementation were set. Emissaries spoke to gatherings of Jewish organizations in America, expecting to become the vehicle for revolutionary change within the Jewish people and within the world. But the encounter with the world was only now beginning and it was not a positive one. As early as June 1945, Grinberg had expressed the fear that "mankind does not comprehend what we have gone through and what we experienced during this period of time, and it seems to us," he speculated, "neither shall we be understood in the future."[38]

Grinberg's fear was well founded. Even those who were sent to aid the survivors, to assist them in recovering their humanity, did not understand. The administrator of the Landsberg camp, an American Jew in the employ of the United Nations, told a group of visiting Americans that the camp inhabitants did not deserve too much sympathy. "One must not remind them of their frightful yesterdays – they must forget this and work instead. They must realize that work means freedom."[39]

A psychologist writing in *Commentary* in 1948 commented on

35. Menachem Sztajer, "She'erit Hapletah," *DP Express, Fun Jidiszn Lebn* (October 1946): 2ff.
36. Quoted in "Die Zukunft der jüdischen Kultur," *Jüdische Rundschau* (July 1946): 5–7.
37. Quoted in "Über die Aufgabe der europäischen Judenreste," *Jüdische Rundschau* (July 1946): 5–7.
38. Quoted in Grinberg, "We Are Living Corpses," p. 7.
39. Quoted in Efros, *Heimlose Yidn*, p. 44.

the lack of psychiatric understanding of what the survivors had experienced. Indeed, he wrote, "a number of observers who went to Europe in the early days of relief organizations found the DPs, especially those who had come out of the concentration camps, in a state of elation and enthusiasm bordering on euphoria. Uninformed in matters of psychology these observers reported that the state of mind of the people in the DP camps was almost miraculously unaffected by their recent terrible experiences. But one could have anticipated that it would not take long for the first euphoric reaction to vanish and be replaced by a deep depression. This happened."[40]

And even though the activity associated with the survivor ideology was an important source of hope, by 1950 a deep sense of disillusion and disappointment was already evident. In one of the last issues of *Our Way*, Pesach Pekatsch expressed a sense of that disappointment. "We believed that it was time to conquer evil and inhumanity," he wrote, "that it would be a long time before bestiality would again be able to conquer the idea of freedom." Instead, Pekatsch found a different picture, one in which the "specter of hatred" and the forces advocating the call to destruction and murder emerged freely and openly to attack the democracies they so hated.[41]

Pekatsch realized that the She'erit Hapletah's call for change within the human condition and within the Jewish condition was not being heard. Indeed, the period from 1945 to 1950 (during which most Jews left Germany and Austria for Israel or America) was in many respects the beginning of the conspiracy of silence between Holocaust survivors and society, a silence that was to characterize the lives of most survivors outside of Israel. Interestingly, the conspiracy of silence spread beyond the circle of Holocaust survivors. As the liberators of the concentration camps returned home, they tried to discuss their experiences in the camps, which usually ended with their own silence in reaction to the disbelief, the indifference, and the silence of those they confronted.[42]

During the past forty-odd years the voice of the She'erit Hapletah has been largely ignored. Elie Wiesel has written of

---

40. Paul Friedman, "The Road Back for the DPs," *Commentary* 6 (1948): 502.
41. Pesach Pekatsch, quoted in *Undzer Veg*, September 28, 1950, p. 2.
42. See Abzug, *Inside the Vicious Heart*, chap. 7, "Telling the Story."

this bitter experience: "After liberation, as the survivors re-entered the world, they found themselves in another kind of exile, another kind of prison. People welcomed them with tears and sobs, then turned away." What the survivors wanted, according to Wiesel, was to "transmit a message to you, a message of which they were the sole bearers. Having gained an insight into man that will remain forever unequaled, they tried to share a knowledge with you, their contemporaries. But you discarded their testimony."[43]

We have not listened to this prophetic voice, a voice that sought to take the course of Jewish and human destiny in its own hands. This voice sought to change those courses, to steer a path toward the moral and social perfection of humanity. We have not understood that the Holocaust and the threat of nuclear destruction – one an event that has already taken place and the other but the push of a button away – are two sides of the same phenomenon. While the one symbolized the end of our civilization's innocence, the other represents the end of our world.[44]

43. Wiesel, *A Jew Today*, pp. 185–208.
44. Abraham J. Peck, "From the Very Depths of Our Pain," in Roger Brooks, ed., *Unanswered Questions: Theological Views of Jewish-Catholic Relations* (Notre Dame, Ind., 1988), pp. 176–88.

Glossary and Abbreviations

ADAP	*Akten zur deutschen auswärtigen Politik, 1918–1945*, Series D (1937–45), 11 vols., vols. 1–10 (Baden-Baden, 1950–56; Frankfurt, 1961–64); vol. 11 (Bonn, 1965).
Altreich	the German Reich in its 1937 borders
Anschluß	annexation of Austria in 1938
BA	Bundesarchiv (National Archives), Koblenz
BDM	Bund Deutscher Mädel (League of German Girls), the principal NSDAP-affiliated female youth organization (for girls ages fourteen to eighteen)
Berufsbeamtengesetz	Civil Service Law, proclaimed in April 1933 as the legal basis for the expulsion of Jewish civil servants, academics, and other categories of professionals in state employment
DNB	Deutsches Nachrichtenbüro (German News Bureau), the official news agency in the Third Reich
DP	Displaced Person
Einsatzgruppe	action group, "mobile killing unit"; a special SS/SD murder squad responsible for the liquidation (by mass shooting) of political commissars, Jews, and others behind the lines as the German armies advanced into the Soviet Union; formed in June 1941 and active in Eastern Europe until May 1943

Entjudung	policy of removal, the ousting of Jews from the economy and society
Gauleiter	district chief, the top NSDAP party official in a party district (*Gau*); there were a total of forty-two *Gaue* in the party structure within the Reich
Gauwirtschaftsberater	district economic adviser for the *Gauleiter*; the leading NSDAP official in anti-Jewish economic measures
Gemeinde	autonomous, incorporated Jewish local community to which every Jew who did not officially declare his withdrawal automatically belonged and paid taxes (*Gemeindesteuer*); there were some 1,600 such communities in Germany in early 1933
Generalgouvernement	Government-General, the largest portion of German-occupied Poland, including Warsaw, Cracow, and Lvov
Gestapo	Geheime Staatspolizei (Secret State Police), a branch of the Security Police (SiPo) and SS headed by Heinrich Müller
Hilfsverein	Relief Society, founded in 1901 to aid Jews abroad and transient Jewish migrants in Germany; after 1933, its main activity was assisting needy emigrants
HJ	Hitlerjugend, the main male youth organization for the National Socialist movement
IfZ	Institut für Zeitgeschichte (Institute for Contemporary History), Munich
IMT	*Der Prozeß gegen die Hauptkriegsverbrecher vor dem Internationalen Militärgerichtshof (International Military Tribunal), Nürnberg, 14. Nov. 1945–1. Okt. 1946*, 42 vols. (Nuremberg, 1947–49)

Judenreferat	Department for Jewish Affairs, the section in the Gestapo dealing with all matters pertaining to Jews
Judenreferent	expert on Jewish affairs employed in the Judenreferat
Kreisleiter	chief NSDAP official in a party sub-district (*Kreis*), who was responsible to the *Gauleiter*
Landrat	district head, the chief authority in a rural administrative district in the Prussian civil administration
Mischling	Jew from a "mixed" marriage in the first or second generation
NS	National Socialist
NSDAP	Nationalsozialistische Deutsche Arbeiterpartei (National Socialist German Workers' Party), official name of the Nazi party
NSV	Nationalsozialistische Volkswohlfahrt (National Socialist People's Aid), the principal relief organization in the Third Reich
Ostjude	Eastern European Jew
Regierungspräsident	senior official in a Prussian administrative district (*Regierungsbezirk*), a kind of district governor or superintendent
Reichsbürgergesetz	Reich Citizenship Law, proclaimed in Nuremberg in September 1935, which defined the inferior civil status of Jews of German nationality; most later anti-Jewish legislation was issued in the form of *Verordnungen* (decrees) to this law
Reichsführer SS	Reich leader of the SS and Chief of the German Police, Heinrich Himmler's official title

Reichskristallnacht	"Reich Crystal Night," popular designation for the November 9–10, 1938, pogrom
Reichsvereinigung	Reichsvereinigung der Juden in Deutschland (Reich Association of Jews in Germany), a compulsory organization of all Jews by race (*Rassejuden*) established in February 1939 as successor to the Reichsvertretung (q.v.), which was supervised by the Gestapo
Reichsvertretung	Reichsvertretung der Juden in Deutschland (Reich Representation of Jews in Germany), set up in the autumn of 1933 to represent the interests of German Jews under the Nazi regime
RGBl	Reichsgesetzblatt (Reich Law Gazette), which contains published texts of laws and decrees
RSHA	Reichssicherheitshauptamt (Reich Security Main Office), SS agency set up in September 1939, which incorporated the SD and Security Police, Gestapo, criminal police, headed first by Reinhard Heydrich, and later by Ernst Kaltenbrunner; the Gestapo was Section IV in the RSHA; the RSHA was officially entrusted with implementing the Final Solution and was the nerve center for state terror in the Third Reich, 1939–45
RV/AR	Reichsvertretung der Juden in Deutschland, *Arbeitsbericht* [Annual Report] (1938)
SD	Sicherheitsdienst (Security Service), the intelligence unit of the SS
StA Dahlem	Staatsarchiv (State Archives), Dahlem
StA Münster, GW	Staatsarchiv Münster, Gauleitung Westfalen Süd (State Archives, Münster, Dis-

trict Headquarters, South Westphalia)

Sühneleistung special "atonement fine" of one billion reichsmarks levied on the German-Jewish community on November 12, 1938, two days after the destruction of the November 1938 pogrom; it was increased by 25 percent in a supplementary decree of October 19, 1939

VfZ Vierteljahrshefte für Zeitgeschichte, quarterly journal of the Institut für Zeitgeschichte (Institute for Contemporary History), Munich

Volksgenosse member of the German *Volk*, part of the German *Volksgemeinschaft*, and thus a citizen in the racial sense

YBLI Yearbook, Leo Baeck Institute

YVA Yad Vashem Archives, Jerusalem

Select Bibliography

Abzug, Robert H. *Inside the Vicious Heart: Americans and the Liberation of Nazi Concentration Camps*. New York, 1985.

Adam, Uwe D. *Judenpolitik im Dritten Reich*. 2d ed. Düsseldorf, 1972.

Adler, H[ans] G[ünther]. *Der verwaltete Mensch: Studien zur Deportation der Juden aus Deutschland*. Tübingen, 1974.

———. *Theresienstadt, 1941–1945: Das Antlitz einer Zwangsgemeinschaft*. Tübingen, ²1960.

Adler-Rudel, S[halom]. *Jüdische Selbsthilfe unter dem Nazi-Regime, 1933–1939, im Spiegel der Berichte der Reichsvertretung der Juden in Deutschland*. Schriftenreihe wissenschaftlicher Abhandlungen des Leo Baeck Instituts, vol. 29. Tübingen, 1974.

Allen, William Sheridan. "Die deutsche Öffentlichkeit und die 'Reichskristallnacht': Konflikt zwischen Werthierarchie und Propaganda im Dritten Reich." In Detlev Peuckert and Jürgen Reulecke, eds., *Die Reihen fast geschlossen: Beiträge zur Geschichte des Alltags unterm Nationalsozialismus*. Wuppertal, 1981.

Andreas-Friedrich, Ruth. *Der Schattenmann: Tagebuchaufzeichnungen, 1938–1945*. Berlin, 1947. New ed. Frankfurt, 1983.

Arad, Yitzchak; Gutman, Yisrael; and Margaliot, Abraham, eds. *Documents on the Holocaust: Selected Sources on the Destruction of the Jews of Germany and Austria, Poland, and the Soviet Union*. Jerusalem, 1981.

Ball-Kaduri, Kurt Jakob. *Vor der Katastrophe: Juden in Deutschland, 1934–1939*. Tel Aviv, 1967.

Barkai, Avraham. *From Boycott to Annihilation: The Economic Struggle of German Jews, 1933–1943*. Translated by William Templer. Tauber Institute Series, 11. Hanover, N.H., 1990.

Bauer, Yehuda. *A History of the Holocaust*. New York, 1982.

———. *Flight and Rescue: Brichah*. New York, 1970.

Behrendt-Rosenfeld, Else R. *Ich stand nicht allein: Erlebnisse einer Jüdin in Deutschland, 1933–1944*. Mannheim, ²1965.

Bein, Alex. *Die Judenfrage: Biographie eines Weltproblems*. Stuttgart, 1980.

Ben Elissar, Eliahu. *La diplomatie du IIIe Reich et les Juifs*. [Paris], 1969.

Blau, Bruno. *Das Ausnahmerecht gegen die Juden in den europäischen Ländern*. vol. 1, *Deutschland*. Düsseldorf, ³1965.

———, comp. *Das Ausnahmerecht für die Juden in Deutschland, 1933–1945*. 2d ed. Düsseldorf, 1954.

Boberach, Heinz, ed. *Meldungen aus dem Reich: Die geheimen Lageberichte des Sicherheitsdienstes der SS, 1938–1945*. Vol. 1. Herrsching, 1984.

Botz, Gerhard. *Wohnungspolitik und Judendeportation in Wien, 1938–1945.* Vienna, 1975.

Bracher, Karl Dietrich. *Die deutsche Diktatur: Entstehung, Struktur, Folgen des Nationalsozialismus.* Cologne, 1969.

Broszat, Martin. "Hitler und die Genesis der 'Endlösung': Aus Anlaß der Thesen von David Irving." *VfZ* 25 (1977): 739–55.

———, comp. and ed. *Kommandant in Auschwitz: Autobiographische Aufzeichnungen von Rudolf Höß.* 2d ed. Stuttgart, 1958.

Broszat, Martin; Fröhlich, Elke; and Wiesemann, Falk, eds. *Bayern in der NS-Zeit: Soziale Lage und politisches Verhalten der Bevölkerung im Spiegel vertraulicher Berichte.* Munich, 1977.

Browning, Christopher. *The Final Solution and the German Foreign Office.* New York, 1978.

Bruss, Regina. *Die Bremer Juden unter dem Nationalsozialismus.* Veröffentlichungen aus dem Staatsarchiv der Freien Hansestadt Bremen, vol. 49. Bremen, 1983.

Buchheim, Hans et al. *Anatomie des SS-Staates.* 2 vols. Olten, 1965.

Büttner, Ursula, ed. *Das Unrechtsregime: Internationale Forschung über den Nationalsozialismus.* 2 vols. Hamburg, 1986.

Dawidowicz, Lucy S. *The Holocaust and the Historians.* Cambridge, Mass., 1981.

Deutschkron, Inge. *Ich trug den gelben Stern.* Cologne, 1983.

Diner, Dan, ed. *Ist der Nationalsozialismus Geschichte? Zu Historisierung und Historikerstreit.* Frankfurt, 1987.

Dinnerstein, Leonard. *America and the Survivors of the Holocaust.* New York, 1982.

Dipper, Christof. "Der deutsche Widerstand und die Juden." *Geschichte und Gesellschaft* 9 (1983): 359f.

Dokumentationsarchiv des österreichischen Widerstandes, ed. *Widerstand und Verfolgung in Wien, 1934–1945.* Vol. 3. Vienna, 1984.

Döscher, Hans-Jürgen. *Das Auswärtige Amt im Dritten Reich: Diplomatie im Schatten der "Endlösung."* Berlin, 1987.

Drobisch, Klaus et al. *Juden unterm Hakenkreuz: Verfolgung und Ausrottung der deutschen Juden, 1933–1945.* Frankfurt, 1973.

Eschelbacher, Max. "Der Pogrom vom 10. November 1938 in Düsseldorf." Manuscript, July 1939, Wiener Library, Coll. P II d, No. 151, Tel Aviv University.

Eschwege, Helmut. "Resistance of German Jews against the Nazi Regime." *YLBI,* 15 (1970): 143–80.

———, ed. *Kennzeichen 'J': Bilder, Dokumente, Berichte zur Geschichte der Verbrechen des Hitlerfaschismus an den deutschen Juden, 1933–1945.* Frankfurt, 1979.

Esh, Shaul. "Between Discrimination and Extermination: The Fateful Year 1938." *Yad Vashem Studies* 2 (1958).

Faust, Anselm. *Die Kristallnacht im Rheinland: Dokumente zum Judenpogrom im November 1938*. Düsseldorf, 1987.

Feilchenfeld, W.; Michaelis, D.; and Pinner, L. *Haavara-Transfer nach Palästina und Einwanderung deutscher Juden, 1933–1939*. Tübingen, 1972.

Fleming, Gerald. *Hitler und die Endlösung*. Wiesbaden and Munich, 1982.

Fliedner, Hans-Joachim. *Die Judenverfolgung in Mannheim, 1933–1945. Dokumente*. Veröffentlichungen des Stadtarchivs Mannheim, vol. 2. Mannheim, 1971.

Focke, Harald, ed. *Alltag der Entrechteten: Wie die Nazis mit ihren Gegnern umgingen*. Reinbek, 1980.

Förster, Jürgen. "Das Unternehmen 'Barbarossa' als Eroberungs- und Vernichtungskrieg." In *Das Deutsche Reich und der Zweite Weltkrieg*. vol. 4, *Der Angriff auf die Sowjetunion*, ed. Militärgeschichtliches Forschungsamt. Stuttgart, 1983, pp. 413–50.

Franke, Manfred. *Mordverläufe, 9./10. XI. 1938* [documentary novel on the Reichskristallnacht]. Neuwied, 1973.

Freimark, Peter, and Kopitzsch, Wolfgang. *Der 9./10. November 1938 in Deutschland: Dokumente zur "Kristallnacht."* Hamburg, 1978.

Genschel, Helmut. *Die Verdrängung der Juden aus der Wirtschaft im Dritten Reich*. Göttingen, 1966.

Gibbons, Robert. "Allgemeine Richtlinien für die politische und wirtschaftliche Verwaltung der besetzten Ostgebiete." *VfZ* 25 (1977): 252–61.

Gilbert, Martin. *Auschwitz and the Allies*. New York, 1981. German ed. *Auschwitz und die Allierten*. Munich, 1981.

———. *The Holocaust: The Jewish Tragedy*. London, 1986.

Ginzel, Günther B. *Jüdischer Alltag in Deutschland, 1933–1945*. Düsseldorf, 1984.

Glaser, Hermann, and Straube, Harald, eds. *Wohnungen des Todes, Jüdisches Schicksal im Dritten Reich: Dokumente und Texte*. Bamberg, 1961.

Goldhagen, Erich. "Weltanschauung und Endlösung: Zum Antisemitismus der nationalsozialistischen Führungsschicht." *VfZ* 24 (1976): 379–405.

Goodman, Eric [Erich Guttmann]. "Die Tage nach dem 9. November: Ein Bericht." London, Spring 1941. Wiener Library, P II d, No. 528, Tel Aviv University. Microfilm, Archives IfZ, MZS 1/1.

Gordon, Sarah. *Hitler, the Germans, and the "Jewish Question."* Princeton, 1984.

Graml, Hermann. *Der 9. November 1938: "Reichskristallnacht."* Bonn, 1956.

Greive, Hermann. *Die Juden: Grundzüge ihrer Geschichte im mittelalterlichen und neuzeitlichen Europa*. Darmstadt, 1980.

Gross, Leonhard. *The Last Jews in Berlin*. New York, 1982.

Grossmann, Kurt R. *Die unbesungenen Helden: Menschen in Deutschlands dunklen Tagen*. Berlin,² 1961.

Gruchmann, Lothar. "'Blutschutzgesetz' und Justiz: Zur Entstehung und Auswirkung des Nürnberger Gesetzes vom 15. September 1935." *VfZ* 31 (1983): 418–42.

Hanke, Peter. *Zur Geschichte der Juden in München zwischen 1933 and 1945*. Schriftenreihe des Stadtarchivs München, Heft 3. Munich, 1967.

Heiber, [Helmut]. "Die Ausweisung von Juden polnischer Staatsangehörigkeit im Oktober 1938." *Gutachten des Instituts für Zeitgeschichte* 1 (Munich, 1958): 90–93.

——. "Der Fall Grünspan." *VfZ* 5 (1957): 134–72.

Heller, Celia S[topnicka]. *On the Edge of Destruction: Jews of Poland between the Two World Wars*. New York, 1977.

Hilberg, Raul. *The Destruction of the European Jews*. 2d ed. Chicago, 1967. German ed. *Die Vernichtung der europäischen Juden: Die Gesamtgeschichte des Holocaust*. Berlin, 1982; rev. and enlarged, 3 vols., Frankfurt 1990.

——. *Sonderzüge nach Auschwitz*. Mainz, 1981.

Hirsch, Martin; Majer, Diemut; and Meinck, Jürgen, eds. *Recht, Verwaltung und Justiz des Nationalsozialismus: Ausgewählte Schriften, Gesetze und Gerichtsentscheidungen von 1933 bis 1945*. Cologne, 1984.

Hirschfeld, Gerhard, ed. *The Politics of the Genocide: Jews and Soviet Prisoners of War in Nazi Germany*. London, 1986.

Irving, David. *Hitler's War*. London, 1977.

Jäckel, Eberhard, and Rohwer, Jürgen, eds. *Der Mord an den Juden im Zweiten Weltkrieg: Entschlußbildung und Verwirklichung*. Stuttgart, 1985.

Jacobmeyer, Wolfgang. *Vom Zwangsarbeiter zum heimatlosen Ausländer*. Göttingen, 1985.

Jacobsen, Hans-Adolf, and Jochmann, Werner, eds. *Ausgewählte Dokumente zur Geschichte des Nationalsozialismus, 1933–1945*. Vol. 2. Bielefeld, 1961.

Jochmann, Werner. "Struktur und Funktionen des deutschen Antisemitismus." In Werner E. Mosse and Arnold Paucker, eds., *Juden im Wilhelminischen Deutschland, 1890–1914*. Tübingen, 1976, pp. 389–477.

Kaul, Friedrich Karl. *Der Fall des Herschel Grünspan*. Berlin (East), 1965.

Kershaw, Ian. "German Popular Opinion and the 'Jewish Question,' 1939–1943: Some Further Reflections." In Arnold Paucker, ed., *Die Juden im nationalsozialistischen Deutschland/The Jews in Germany, 1933–1943*. Tübingen, 1986, pp. 365–408.

——. "The Persecution of Jews and German Popular Opinion in the Third Reich." *YLBI* 26 (1981): 261–89.

——. *Popular Opinion and Political Dissent in the Third Reich: Bavaria, 1933–1945*. Oxford, 1983.

Kochan, Lionel. *Pogrom: 10. November 1938*. London, 1957.

Kogon, Eugen. *Der SS-Staat: Das System der deutschen Konzentrationslager*. 2d ed. Frankfurt, 1965.

Kogon, Eugen; Langbein, Hermann; Rückerl, Adalbert et al., eds., *Nationalsozialistische Massentötungen durch Giftgas*. Frankfurt, 1983.

Krausnick, Helmut. "Kommissarbefehl und 'Gerichtsbarkeitserlaß Barbarossa' in neuer Sicht." *VfZ* 25 (1977): 682–738.

Krausnick, Helmut, and Wilhelm, Hans-Heinrich. *Die Truppen des Weltanschauungskrieges: Die Einsatzgruppen der Sicherheitspolizei und des SD, 1938–1942*. Stuttgart, 1981.

Kulka, Otto Dov. "The 'Jewish Question' in the Third Reich: Its Significance in National Socialist Ideology and Policy and Its Role in Determining the Status and Activities of the Jews." Vol. 2, Documents. Ph.D. diss., Hebrew University, Jerusalem, 1975.

——. "Popular Christian Attitudes in the Third Reich to National-Socialist Policies toward the Jews." In *Judaism and Christianity under the Impact of National Socialism (1919–1945)*. The Historical Society of Jerusalem, June 1982.

——. "Public Opinion in Nazi Germany and the 'Jewish Question.'" *Zionist Quarterly for Research in Jewish History* 40 (1975): 186–290. Revised version also published in *The Jerusalem Quarterly* 25/26 (1982): 121–44, 34–45.

Kwiet, Konrad. "Zur historiographischen Behandlung der Judenverfolgung im Dritten Reich." *Militärgeschichtliche Mitteilungen* 27 (1980): 171f.

——. "Die Integration deutsch-jüdischer Emigranten in Australien." In Büttner, *Das Unrechtsregime*, vol. 2, pp. 309–12.

——. "The Ultimate Refuge: Suicide in the Jewish Community under the Nazis." *YLBI* 29 (1984): 135–67.

Kwiet, Konrad, and Eschwege, Helmut. *Selbstbehauptung und Widerstand: Deutsche Juden im Kampf um Existenz und Menschenwürde, 1933–1945*. Hamburg, 1986.

Laqueur, Walter. *The Terrible Secret: Suppression of the Truth about Hilter's "Final Solution."* Boston, 1980.

Laqueur, Walter, and Breitman, Richard. *Der Mann, der das Schweigen brach: Wie die Welt vom Auschwitz erfuhr*. Frankfurt and Berlin, 1986.

Lauber, Heinz. *Judenpogrom, "Reichskristallnacht" November 1938 in Großdeutschland: Daten, Fakten, Dokumente, Quellentexte, Thesen und Bewertungen*. Gerlingen, 1981.

Lewy, Guenter. *The Catholic Church and Nazi Germany*. New York 1964.

Majer, Diemut. *"Fremdvölkische" im Dritten Reich: Ein Beitrag zur nationalsozialistischen Rechtssetzung und Rechtspraxis in Verwaltung und Justiz unter besonderer Berücksichtigung der eingegliederten Ostgebiete und des Generalgouvernements*. Boppard, 1981.

Matzerath, Horst, ed. " . . . *vergessen kann man die Zeit nicht, das ist nicht möglich . . ."*: *Kölner erinnern sich an die Jahre 1929–1945*. Cologne, 1985.

Maurer, Trude. "Ausländische Juden in Deutschland, 1933–1939." In Arnold Paucker et al., eds., *Die Juden im nationalsozialistischen Deutschland, 1933–1943*. Schriftenreihe wissenschaftlicher Abhandlungen des Leo Baeck Instituts, vol. 45. Tübingen, 1986, pp. 189–210.

——. "Medizinalpolizei und Antisemitismus: Die deutsche Politik der Grenzsperre gegen Ostjuden im Ersten Weltkrieg." *Jahrbücher für Geschichte Osteuropas* 33 (1985): 205–30.

——. *Ostjuden in Deutschland, 1918–1933*. Hamburger Beiträge zur Geschichte der deutschen Juden. vol. 12. Hamburg, 1986.

Mayer, Milton. *They Thought They Were Free: The Germans, 1933–1945*. Chicago, ³1966.

Melzer, Emanuel. "Relations between Poland and Germany and Their Impact on the Jewish Problem in Poland (1935–1938)." *Yad Vashem Studies* 12 (1977): 193–229.

Mendelsohn, Ezra. *The Jews of East Central Europe between the World Wars*. Bloomington, 1983.

Mendelsohn, John, ed. *The Holocaust*, vol. 3: *The Crystal Night Pogrom*. New York and London, 1982.

Milton, Sybil. "The Expulsion of Polish Jews from Germany, October 1938 to July 1939: A Documentation." *YLBI* 29 (1984): 169–99.

Mommsen, Hans. "Der nationalsozialistische Polizeistaat und die Judenverfolgung vor 1938." *VfZ* 10 (1962): 68–87.

——. "Die Realisierung des Utopischen: Die 'Endlösung der Judenfrage' im Dritten Reich." *Geschichte und Gesellschaft* 9 (1983): 381–420.

Müller-Claudius, Michael. *Der Antisemitismus und das deutsche Verhängnis*. 2d ed. Frankfurt, 1966.

Obenaus, Herbert. "Haben sie wirklich nichts gewußt? Tagebuch vom Alltag, 1933–45," *Journal für Geschichte* 2 (1980): 26–31.

Oppenheimer, Max; Stuckmann, Horst; and Schneider, Rudi, eds. *Als die Synagogen brannten: Zur Funktion des Antisemitismus gestern und heute*. Frankfurt, 1978.

Paucker, Arnold, ed. *Die Juden im nationalsozialistischen Deutschland/The Jews in Germany, 1933–1943*. Tübingen, 1986.

Peck, Abraham J. "The Children of Holocaust Survivors." In Allon Schoener, ed., *The American Jewish Album, 1654 to the Present*. New York, 1983.

——, ed. *Jews and Christians after the Holocaust*. Philadelphia, 1981.

Philipp, Erna. "Ereignisse in der Pogrom-Nacht 9.–10. November 1938." Wiener Library, P II d, No. 98, Tel Aviv University, Microfilm, Archives IfZ, MZS 1/1.

Poliakov, Léon and Wulf, Josef. *Das Dritte Reich und seine Diener*. Berlin, ² 1956.

Präg, Werner, and Jacobmeyer, Wolfgang, eds. *Das Diensttagebuch des deutschen Generalgouverneurs in Polen, 1939–1945.* Stuttgart, 1975.

Rabinowitz, Dorothy. *New Lives: Survivors of the Holocaust Living in America.* New York, 1976.

"Reichskristallnacht" in Hannover: Eine Ausstellung zur 40. Wiederkehr des 9. November 1938. Hanover, 1978.

Richarz, Monika, ed. *Jüdisches Leben in Deutschland.* 3 vols. Vol. 3, *Selbstzeugnisse zur Sozialgeschichte, 1933–1945.* Stuttgart, 1982.

Roizen, Ron. "Herschel Grynszpan: The Fate of a Forgotten Assassin." *Holocaust and Genocide Studies* 1 (1986): 217–28.

Rosenkranz, Herbert. *"Reichskristallnacht" 9. November 1938 in Österreich.* Vienna, 1968.

Rosenstock, Werner, "Exodus, 1933–1939: A Survey of Jewish Emigration from Germany." *YLBI* 1 (1956): 377.

Rothschild, Ina. "Bericht über die Kristallnacht im israelitischen Waisenhaus 'Wilhelmspflege' in Esslingen." In Paul Sauer, *Die Schicksale der jüdischen Bürger Baden-Württembergs während der nationalsozialistischen Verfolgungszeit, 1933–1945.* Stuttgart, 1969, p. 420.

Rürup, Reinhard. *Emanzipation und Antisemitismus: Studien zur "Judenfrage" der bürgerlichen Gesellschaft.* Göttingen, 1975.

———, ed. "Juden in Deutschland zwischen Assimilation und Verfolgung." *Geschichte und Gesellschaft* 9 (1983): 331–478.

Sauer, Paul, comp. *Dokumente über die Verfolgung jüdischer Bürger in Baden-Württemberg durch das nationalsozialistische Regime, 1933–1935.* 2 vols. Stuttgart, 1966.

Schleunes, Karl A. *The Twisted Road to Auschwitz: Nazi Policy toward German Jews, 1933–1939.* Urbana, Chicago, and London, 1970.

Schoenberner, Gerhard. *Wir haben es gesehen: Augenzeugenberichte über Terror und Judenverfolgung im Dritten Reich.* Wiesbaden, 1981.

———, ed. *Der gelbe Stern: Die Judenverfolgung in Europa, 1933–1945.* Munich, 1978.

Scholl, Inge. *Die Weiße Rose.* Rev. ed. Frankfurt, 1985.

Schultheis, Herbert. *Die Reichskristallnacht in Deutschland: Nach Augenzeugenberichten.* Bad Neustadt, 1985.

Steinbach, Peter. *Nationalsozialistische Gewaltverbrechen: Die Diskussion in der deutschen Öffentlichkeit nach 1945.* Berlin, 1981.

Steinert, Marlies. *Hitlers Krieg und die Deutschen: Stimmung und Haltung der deutschen Bevölkerung im Zweiten Weltkrieg.* Vienna, 1978.

Stokes, Lawrence D. "The German People and the Destruction of the European Jews." *Central European History* 6 (1973): 167–91.

Strauss, Herbert. "Jewish Emigration from Germany: Nazi Policies and Jewish Responses, I/II." *YLBI* 25 and 26 (1980 and 1981): 313–58; 343–409.

Streit, Christian. *Keine Kameraden: Die Wehrmacht und die sowjetischen Kriegsgefangenen, 1941–1945.* Stuttgart, 1978.

Thalmann, Rita, and Feinermann, Emanuel. *La nuit de cristal*. Paris 1972. English ed. *Crystal Night: 9–10 November 1938*. London, 1974. German ed. *Die Reichskristallnacht*. Frankfurt, 1987.

Tomaszewski, Jerzy. "Letters from Zbaszyn." *Yad Vashem Studies* 19 (1988): 289–315.

Walk, Joseph, ed. *Das Sonderrecht für die Juden im NS-Staat: Eine Sammlung der gesetzlichen Maßnahmen und Richtlinien – Inhalt und Bedeutung*, Motive-Texte-Materialien. vol. 14. Karlsruhe, 1981.

Weckbecker, Arno. *Die Judenverfolgung in Heidelberg, 1933–1945*. Heidelberg, 1985.

Wertheimer, Jack L. *Unwelcome Strangers: East European Jews in Imperial Germany*. New York and Oxford, 1987.

Wiesemann, Falk. "Judenverfolgung und nichtjüdische Bevölkerung." In: Martin Broszat; Elke Fröhlich; and Falk Wiesemann, eds., *Bayern in der NS-Zeit: Soziale Lage und politische Haltung der Bevölkerung im Spiegel vertraulicher Berichte*. vol. 1. Munich, 1977, pp. 429ff.

Wilhelm, Hans-Heinrich. "Wie geheim war die Endlösung?" In Wolfgang Benz, ed., *Miscellanea: Festschrift für Helmut Krausnick zum 75. Geburtstag*. Stuttgart, 1980.

Wistrich, Robert. *Hitler's Apocalypse: Jews and the Nazi Legacy*. London, 1985.

Wyman, David S. *Das unerwünschte Volk: Amerika und die Vernichtung der europäischen Juden*. Ismaning, 1986.

Notes on Contributors

UWE DIETRICH ADAM, 1940–1987. At his death, Dr. Adam was General Secretary of the German Coordinating Council for the Associations for Christian-Jewish Cooperation in Frankfurt. Selected publications: *Judenpolitik im Dritten Reich* (1972,[2] 1979); *Herrenmenschentum und Rassenvernichtung* (1983); numerous scholarly articles, including "Les chambres à Gaz," in Raymond Aron, ed., *Le National-Sozialisme et les Juifs* (1984); "The Persecution of the Jews: Bureaucracy and Power in Total States," *Leo Baeck Institute Yearbook* 23 (1978).

AVRAHAM BARKAI, born 1921, member of Kibbutz Lehavoth Habashan, Israel, historian and Research Fellow with the Institute for German History, Tel Aviv University. Selected publications: *Das Wirtschaftssystem des Nationalsozialismus: Ideologie, Theorie, Politik, 1933–1945*, rev. ed. (Frankfurt, 1988), English version: *Nazi Economics: Ideology, Theory, and Policy*, trans. R. Hadass-Vashitz (Oxford and New Haven, 1990); *Vom Boykott zur "Entjudung": Der wirtschaftliche Existenzkampf der Juden im Dritten Reich* (Frankfurt, 1988), English edition: *From Boycott to Annihilation: The Economic Struggle of German Jews, 1933–1943*, trans. W. Templer, Tauber Institute Series, 11 (Hanover, N.H., 1990).

WOLFGANG BENZ, born 1941, historian, Technische Universität Berlin. Numerous publications on twentieth-century history, including: *Süddeutschland in der Weimarer Republik* (1970); *Politik in Bayern, 1919–1933* (1971); *Sommer 1939: Die Großmächte und der europäische Krieg* (1979, edited with Hermann Graml); *Bewegt von der Hoffnung aller Deutschen: Zur Geschichte des Grundgesetzes* (1979, ed.); *Die Bundesrepublik Deutschland: Politik, Wirtschaft, Gesellschaft, Kultur* (1989, 4 vols., ed.); *Rechtsextremismus in der Bundesrepublik* (1984, ed.); *Die Gründung der Bundesrepublik* (1984); *Die Vertreibung der Deutschen aus dem Osten: Ursachen, Ereignisse, Folgen* (1985, ed.); *Potsdam, 1945* (1986).

HERMANN GRAML, born 1928, historian on the staff of the Institute for Contemporary History, Munich; chief editor, *Vierteljahrshefte für Zeitgeschichte*. Numerous publications, including: *Der 9. November 1938: "Reichskristallnacht."* (1956); *Europa zwischen den Kriegen* (1969); *Europa* (1972); *Widerstand im Dritten Reich: Probleme, Ereignisse, Gestalten* (1984, ed.); *Die Alliierten und die Teilung Deutschlands* (1985). Together with Wolfgang Benz, he has edited two volumes in the series Weltgeschichte with the Fischer Taschenbuch Verlag in Frankfurt: vol. 35, *Europa nach dem Zweiten Weltkrieg* and vol. 36, *Weltprobleme zwischen den Machtblöcken*.

KONRAD KWIET, born 1941, Associate Professor and Head of the School of German Studies, University of New South Wales, Kensington, Australia. Publications include: *Selbstbehauptung und Widerstand: Deutsche Juden im Kampf um Existenz und Menschenwürde, 1933–1945* (1986, with H. Eschwege); *From the Emancipation to the Holocaust: Essays on Jewish History and Literature in Central Europe* (1987, ed.), as well as a number of essays on the history of anti-Semitism and the persecution of the Jews.

TRUDE MAURER, born 1955, currently on the staff of the Department of Medieval and Modern History, University of Göttingen. Her publications include *Ostjuden in Deutschland, 1918–1933* (1986, awarded the Fritz-Theodor Epstein Prize by the Association for Eastern European History) as well as a number of articles on Jewish history.

HANS MOMMSEN, born 1930, Professor of Modern History, Bochum University. His publications include: *Die Sozialdemokratie und die Nationalitätenfrage im Habsburgischen Vielvölkerstaat* (1963); *Beamtentum im Dritten Reich* (1966); *Industrielles System und politische Entwicklung in der Weimarer Republik* (ed. with D. Petzina, and B. Weisbrod); *Arbeiterbewegung und nationale Frage* (1979) and numerous articles on the workers' movement, social democracy, and National Socialism.

JONNY MOSER, born 1925, interned in concentration camps in Hungary from 1941 to 1944, worked with Raoul Wallenberg. Member of the Executive of the Documentation Archives of the Austrian Resistance since 1964; since 1967, member of the board, Wiener Urania (adult education center). His publications include *Judenverfolgung in Österreich, 1938–1945* (1966), as well as numerous studies of Jewish history in Austria.

ABRAHAM J. PECK, born in 1946 in the DP camp in Landsberg am Lech, Bavaria, Administrative Director of the American Jewish Archives, Cincinnati, Ohio, and Lecturer in Judaic Studies at the University of Cincinnati; Vice-Chairperson of the Committee on Archives, United States Holocaust Memorial Council. His publications include: *Radicals and Reactionaries: The Crisis of Conservatism in Wilhelmine Germany* (1978); *Jews and Christians after the Holocaust* (1981, ed.); *The American Rabbinate: A Century of Continuity and Change, 1883–1983* (1985, ed.); "The Agony of the Lodz Ghetto," *Holocaust Yearbook*, Simon Wiesenthal Center, Los Angeles (1987); *Queen City Refuge: An Oral History of Cincinnati's Jewish Refugees from Nazi Germany* (1989, ed.); *The German-Jewish Legacy in America, 1938–1988: From Bildung to the Bill of Rights* (1989, ed.); *The Papers of the World Jewish Congress, 1933–1950* (2 vols., 1990, ed.).

WALTER H. PEHLE, born 1941, Ph.D. in history, Editor for History and Contemporary History, S. Fischer Verlag, Frankfurt. Collaborator and volume editor of the anthology compiled by Peter Märthesheimer and Ivo Frenzel, *Im Kreuzfeuer, Der Fernsehfilm "Holocaust": Eine Nation ist betroffen* (1979); co-editor of *Der historische Ort des Nationalsozialismus: Annäherungen* (1989).

WOLF ZUELZER, born 1910 in Berlin, died 1987 in Silver Springs, Maryland. M.D., for many years Director of the Child Research Center, Detroit, Michigan, and head of the Department of Hematology and Transfusion Research of NHLBI (National Heart, Lung, and Blood Institute, Washington, D.C.) Numerous medical publications and a biography of the pacifist Georg Friedrich Nicolai, *Der Fall Nicolai* (1981).

Index

Index